IMAGES of America

PLYMOUTH AND WHITEMARSH TOWNSHIPS

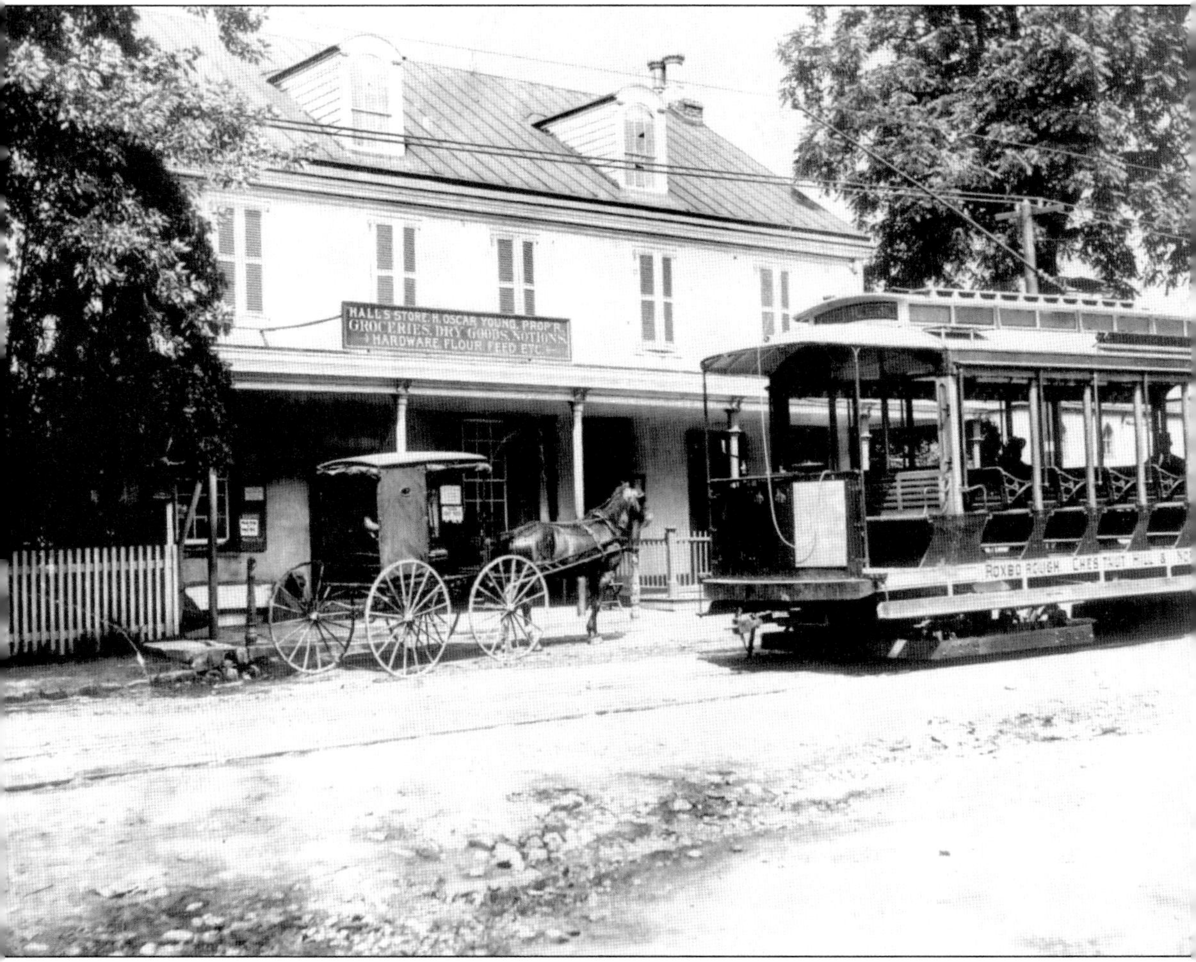

The Roxborough–Chestnut Hill–Norristown trolley and a horse-drawn buggy pause in front of Hall's Store, on Germantown Pike in Plymouth Meeting, *c.* 1900.

IMAGES
of America

PLYMOUTH AND WHITEMARSH TOWNSHIPS

David R. Contosta and Gail C. Momjian
for the Plymouth Meeting Historical Society

ARCADIA
PUBLISHING

ISBN 978-0-7385-1325-6

Published by Arcadia Publishing
Charleston, South Carolina

Printed in the United States of America

Library of Congress Catalog Card Number: 2009934194

For all general information contact Arcadia Publishing at:
Telephone 843-853-2070
Fax 843-853-0044
E-mail sales@arcadiapublishing.com
For customer service and orders:
Toll-Free 1-888-313-2665

Visit us on the Internet at www.arcadiapublishing.com

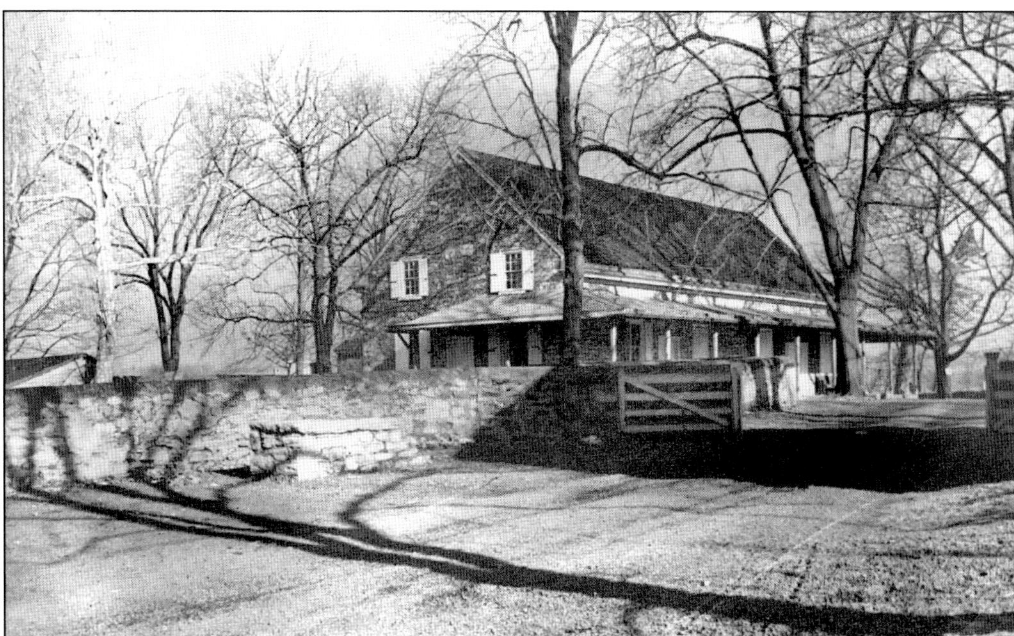

The Plymouth Friends Meeting House has stood at the center of Plymouth Meeting village for 300 years, since the very early 1700s. In the 200th-anniversary program, meeting member A. Conrad Jones stated, "This building has stood for education and enlightenment, for equality of men and women, for peace, and for temperance in all things."

Contents

Acknowledgments 6

Introduction 7

1. The Early Period 9

2. Villages 23

3. Houses, Estates, and Architecture 35

4. Schools and Houses of Worship 55

5. Life in Plymouth and Whitemarsh 75

6. To Serve and Protect 111

7. Postwar Industry and Suburban Development 121

ACKNOWLEDGMENTS

We are grateful to the many volunteers, both past and present, of the Plymouth Meeting Historical Society, whose collections, contributions, and research have made this book possible. We owe many thanks to Suzanne Marinell for her manuscript suggestions and to Edward Addison for his years of research into local history and his careful corrections and additions to the manuscript. We also appreciate the many individuals and organizations who offered assistance, shared memories, and lent photographs: the Historical Society of Fort Washington, the Chestnut Hill Historical Society, the Historical Society of Montgomery County, the Highlands Mansion and Gardens, the Spring Mill Fire Company, the Harmonville Fire Company, St. Philip Neri Catholic Church, Congregation Or Ami, St. Peter's Lutheran Church, St. Thomas Episcopal Church, Plymouth Meeting Evangelical Congregational Church, Fort Washington State Park, the Urban Archives of Temple University, Whitemarsh and Plymouth Townships Parks and Recreation, Mr. and Mrs. F. Eugene Dixon Jr., Bill Lukens, Louise Smith, Virginia E. Ottey, Keith Foster, Romano's School Bus Service, Lownes Family Funeral Home, Foster's General Auto Repairs, the Quaker Chemical Corporation, and most especially Roy Wilson and the Nancy I. Corson Foundation. Special thanks go to Chris Momjian for his technical expertise and support and to Mary Contosta for her encouragement and support.

INTRODUCTION

The history of Plymouth and Whitemarsh Townships stretches back three centuries to the founding of Pennsylvania itself. Over the years, the two townships have been shaped by several major forces, including topography, natural resources, transportation systems, and proximity to Philadelphia.

Plymouth Township, dating from 1686 and named for the Quaker meetinghouse at Plymouth Meeting, is approximately 15 miles northwest of downtown Philadelphia. Whitemarsh Township, established in 1704, was named, according to one tradition, for the white mists that once rose from its broad valleys. Another tradition holds that Whitemarsh is actually a corruption of "Widemarsh," an early description of the area's marshy terrain. Whitemarsh is several miles closer to the center of Philadelphia than Plymouth is, and at its southern boundary, it lies just beyond the modern city limits. Whitemarsh was near enough to Philadelphia to become the scene of several encampments and military actions during the American Revolution, commemorated by the villages of Lafayette Hill and Fort Washington.

The rich soil in both townships supported generations of farmers. With the opening of the Great Plains in the Midwest, local farmers could not compete in grain production and turned mainly to dairy farming by the end of the 1800s. There were also gentlemen farmers, wealthy men who had made fortunes in Philadelphia and who invested part of it in large estates, especially in Whitemarsh Township, which was nearer to the city. For a century and a half, the most famous of these has been Erdenheim Farms, whose hundreds of rolling acres and beautiful stone barns are reminiscent of the English pastoral landscape. Driving through Erdenheim Farms is like wandering into a three-dimensional Constable painting.

Several industries and occupations grew up in the townships to process or handle farm products. Most important were the gristmills that ground grain into flour, recalled in such place names as Spring Mill and Flourtown. Many of these mills stood along the picturesque Wissahickon Creek, which winds its way for three and a half miles through Whitemarsh Township. As early as the 1890s, local residents and civic leaders in Philadelphia urged the creation of a large park along the banks of this creek that would extend Philadelphia's Fairmount Park from Chestnut Hill to Fort Washington. More than a century later, only part of this dream has been realized through the establishment of Fort Washington State Park along with several sections of county parkland, while other properties along the creek have been developed or are threatened by development.

Another early activity in the townships was quarrying, made possible by the thick deposits of almost pure limestone in a belt stretching from Sandy Run at Fort Washington to the Schuylkill River. The first quarry and limekilns were opened at Plymouth Meeting in 1685, to be followed by a number of others, including the G. & W.H. Corson Company, which became the oldest lime quarry in the United States in continuous operation.

There were many uses for lime, from sweetening the soil to making cement, mortar, and whitewash, to providing stone for construction. At a time before synthetic building materials and when it was prohibitively expensive to haul materials from the outside, people used mainly local materials, giving their buildings a distinct look. In Plymouth and Whitemarsh, the local stone gave a creamy grayish-brown cast to houses, barns, churches, and schools. Marble, which comes from naturally compressed limestone, was also quarried in the area.

The discovery of iron ore between Conshohocken and Harmanville (later spelled Harmonville) led to small iron furnaces and forges, one of which grew into Alan Wood Steel, a major 20th-century employer. Once the local iron deposits were depleted, ore was brought in on the Schuylkill Canal, which ran through Conshohocken, and later by railroad.

All these enterprises depended on access to transportation. The earliest roads, such as the Ridge Road and the Germantown Road, were originally American Indian trails that the European settlers widened into pack trails and later into wagon roads. In the early 1800s, private turnpike companies obtained the right from the state to improve these thoroughfares, keep them in repair, and charge tolls for expenses, including dividends to their stockholders. Railroads, which first came to the area in the 1830s, eventually ruined the turnpike companies, which were unable to compete with this faster and cheaper way of moving people and goods.

Although roads and railroads were sufficient to sustain the local economy, Plymouth and Whitemarsh were too far from Philadelphia to become densely populated or to support substantial cities or towns. Instead, there were small villages that clustered around the major crossroads.

In an age before electricity and with Philadelphia's theaters and concert halls too far away for easy access, residents of Plymouth and Whitemarsh had to make their own entertainment. Going to a religious service or attending a church social were common ways to break down isolation and escape from the daily grind. Families played cards and read and, if they had the talent, performed on their own musical instruments. Residents swam in local millponds and flooded quarries during the summer, and much later at swim clubs. By the 1890s, more prosperous families played tennis and rode bicycles. During the first half of the 20th century, several golf and country clubs took advantage of the rolling terrain and cheap land to locate in the townships.

The completion of the Pennsylvania Turnpike through the lower part of Plymouth Township in the 1950s ended the area's relative isolation and accelerated a suburban boom that had begun in the early post–World War II period. Shopping centers and malls replaced the old village stores, while burgeoning school populations led to the construction of large new buildings, to which many students had to be bused in contrast to walking to the old village schoolhouses.

Today, residents of Plymouth and Whitemarsh enjoy their superhighways but not the accompanying suburban sprawl, disappearance of open space, and destruction of historic buildings and landscapes. The authors hope to give readers a better understanding of how these communities have evolved, along with a stronger sense of belonging and a renewed commitment to saving the area's rich and unique heritage.

One

The Early Period

Life in the townships before 1900 was so very different from today that it is hard to imagine what it was like. At first, only draft animals such as horses and mules, along with water-powered mills, relieved the backbreaking labor of everyday existence. The townships were overwhelmingly rural, dotted with farms of various sizes and sparsely populated, especially compared to the present, with its dozens of suburban communities, acres of office buildings, and large shopping malls.

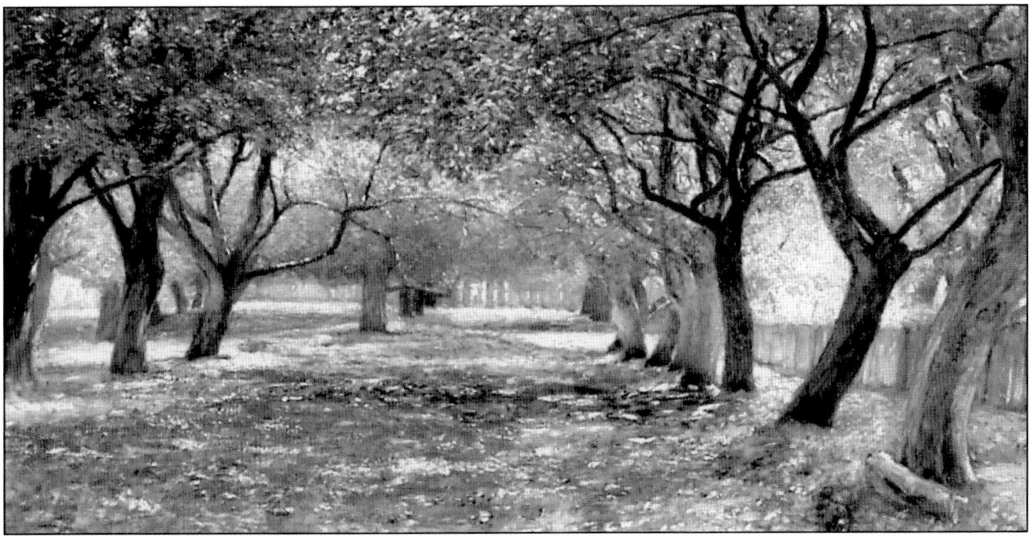

View in Pennsylvania Woods (1886), Thomas Hovenden.

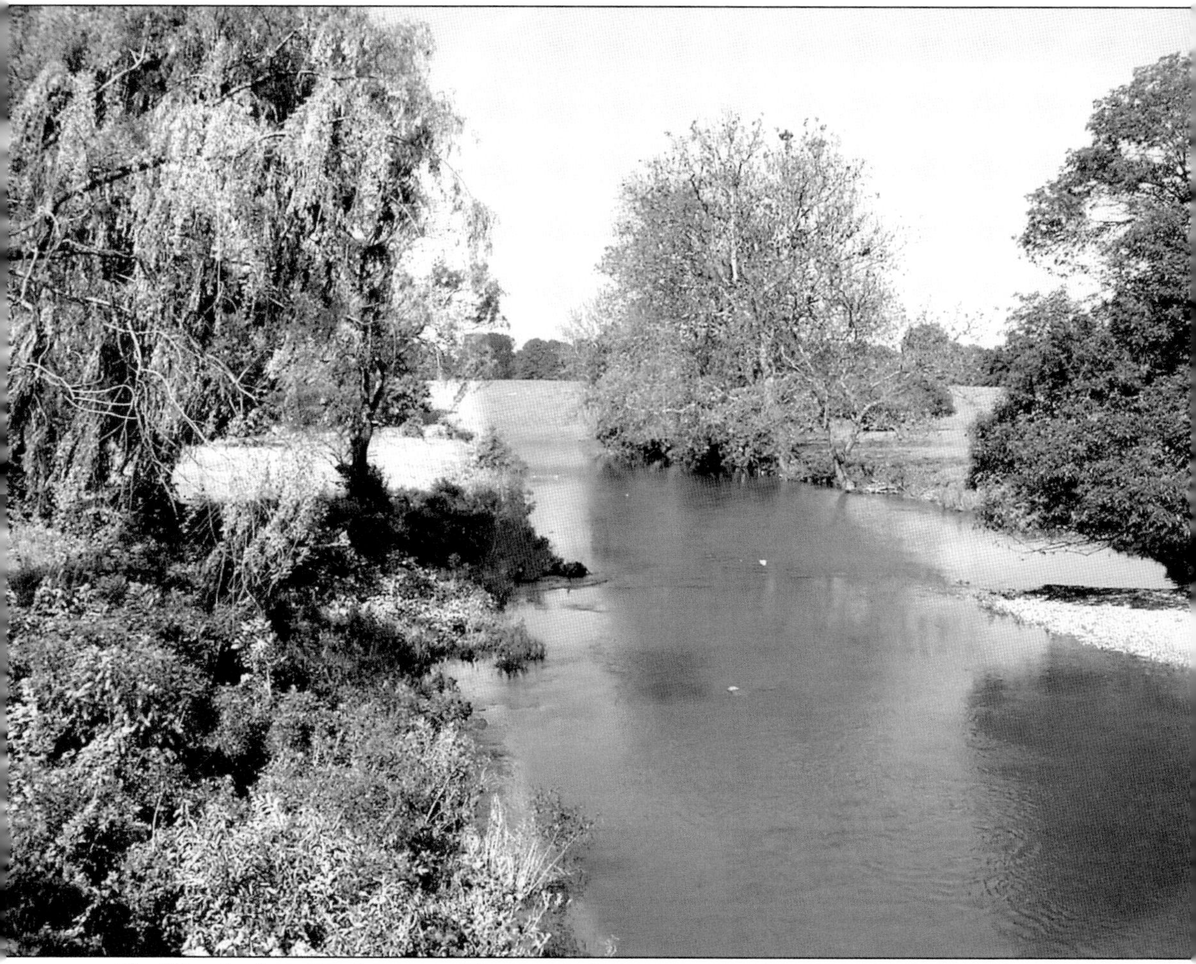

The Wissahickon Creek, a central feature in the picturesque character of Whitemarsh Township, winds through three and a half miles of rolling hills and once provided the waterpower for more than a dozen mills during the 18th and 19th centuries. These mills ground grain, sawed wood, and provided power for simple manufacturing processes. This historic waterway, which now contributes so much to the quality of life in local communities, is under siege by development and other environmental threats. (Courtesy of Gail C. Momjian.)

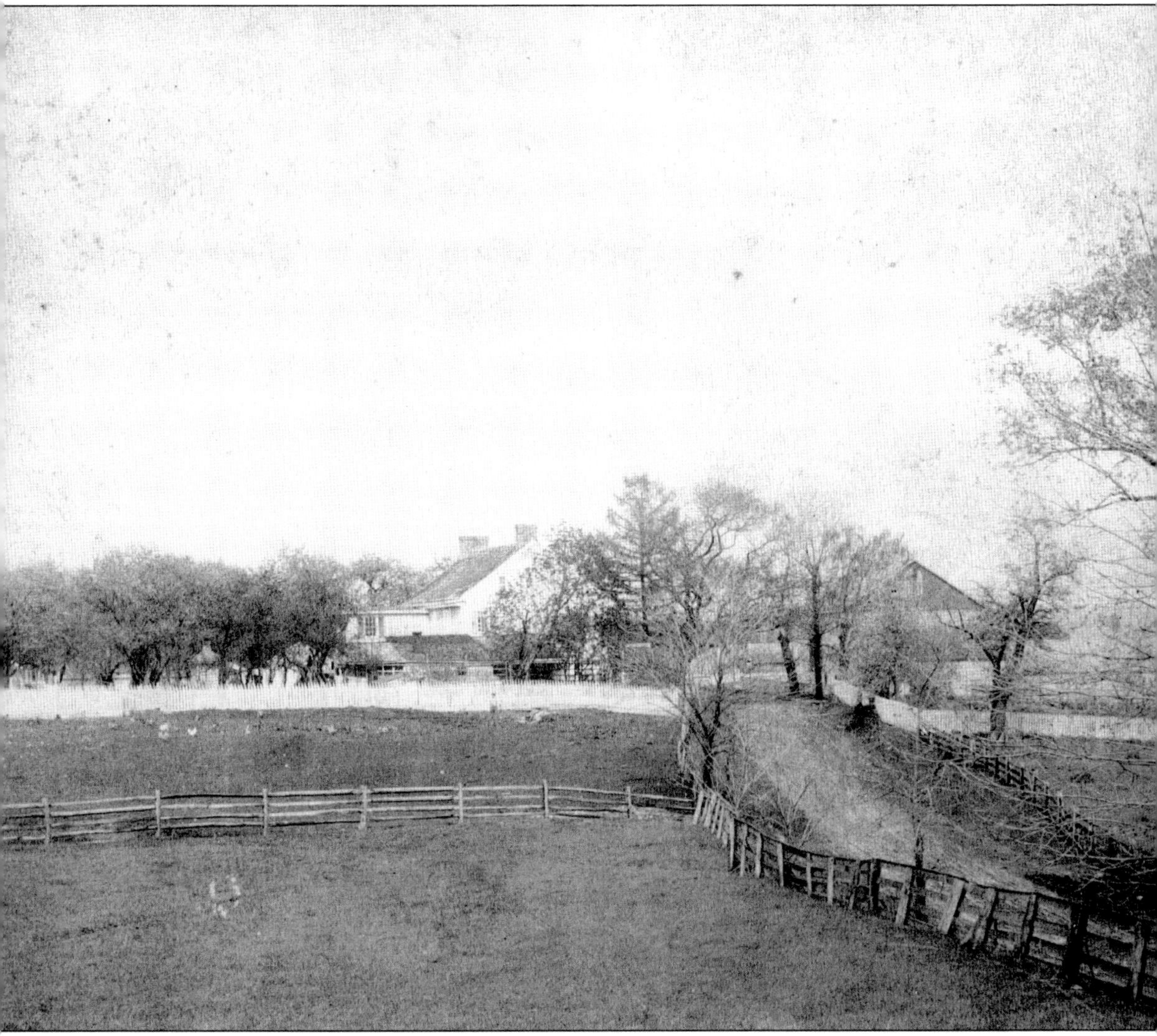

Pictured is a typical farm in Plymouth and Whitemarsh. The view features a long, unpaved road leading past acres of fields and fences. A barn sits at the end of the lane. Farming was the mainstay of most residents during the very early years of the two townships. Rolling pastures and hedgerows dotted the sprawling landscape. Averaging 20 to 40 acres, most farms were self-sufficient, growing hay to feed a small herd of cows. Many farmers raised chickens as well.

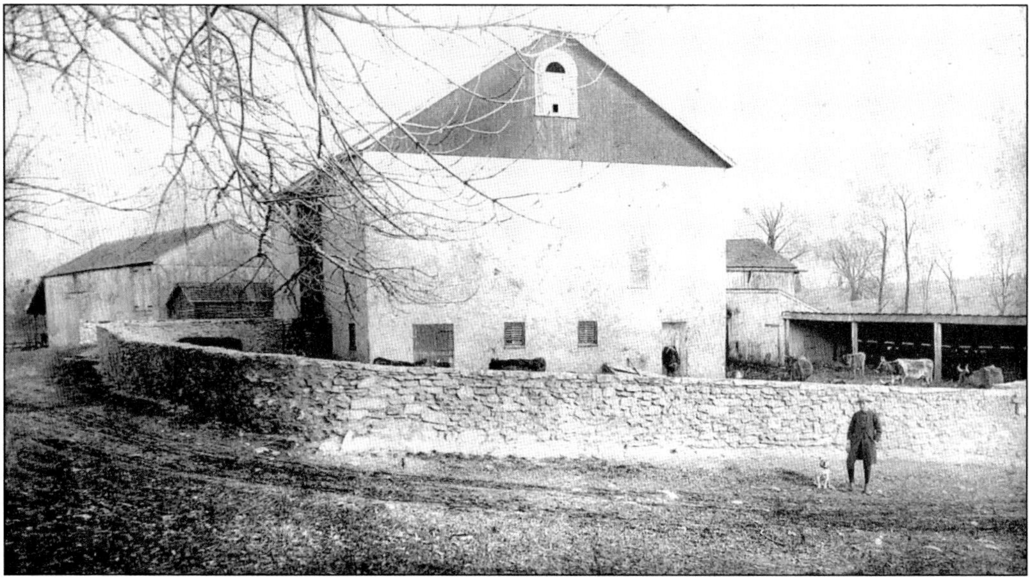

The Jonathon A. Jones Farm, located on what is now Alan Wood Road, was one of Plymouth Township's largest and most prosperous farms. Taking advantage of the local natural resources, Jones (1800–1876) was both a farmer and a lumber trader.

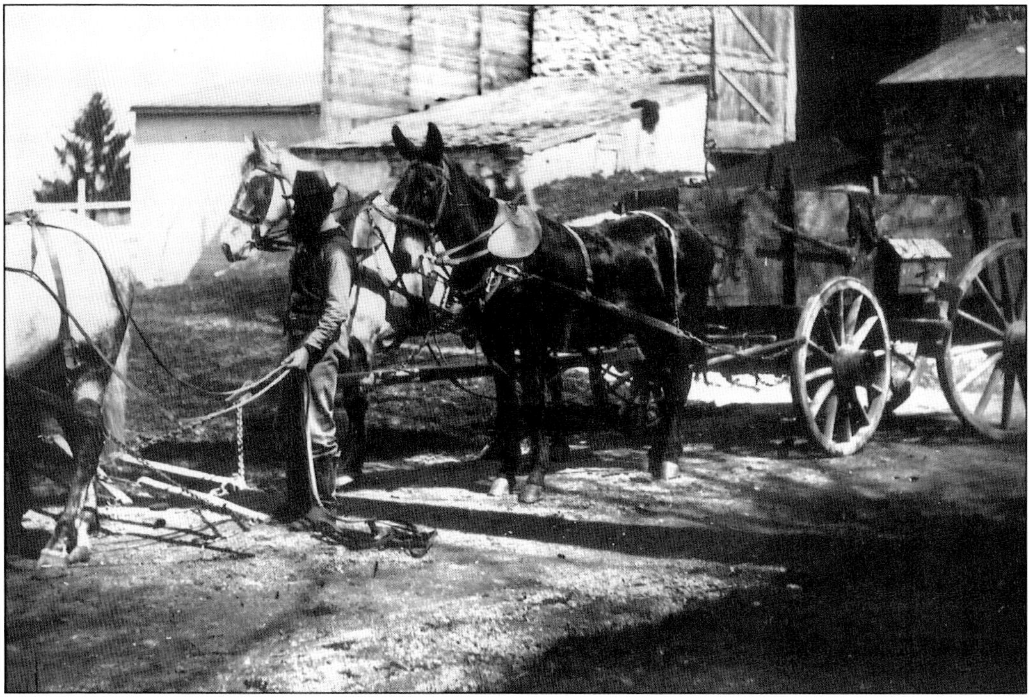

Mules were used regularly in Plymouth and Whitemarsh to make the drudgery of farming a bit easier. Stone-bank barns like this one near Butler Pike in Plymouth Meeting were typical in the area during the 18th and 19th centuries. (Courtesy of the Nancy I. Corson Foundation.)

Rural children play barefoot on a dirt road. (Courtesy of the Nancy I. Corson Foundation.)

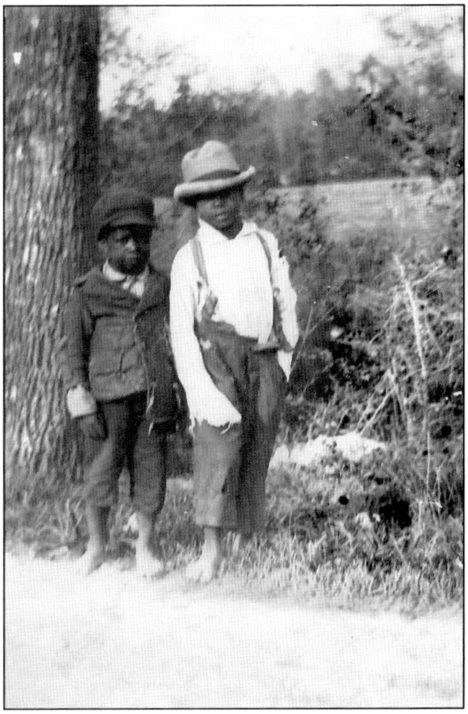

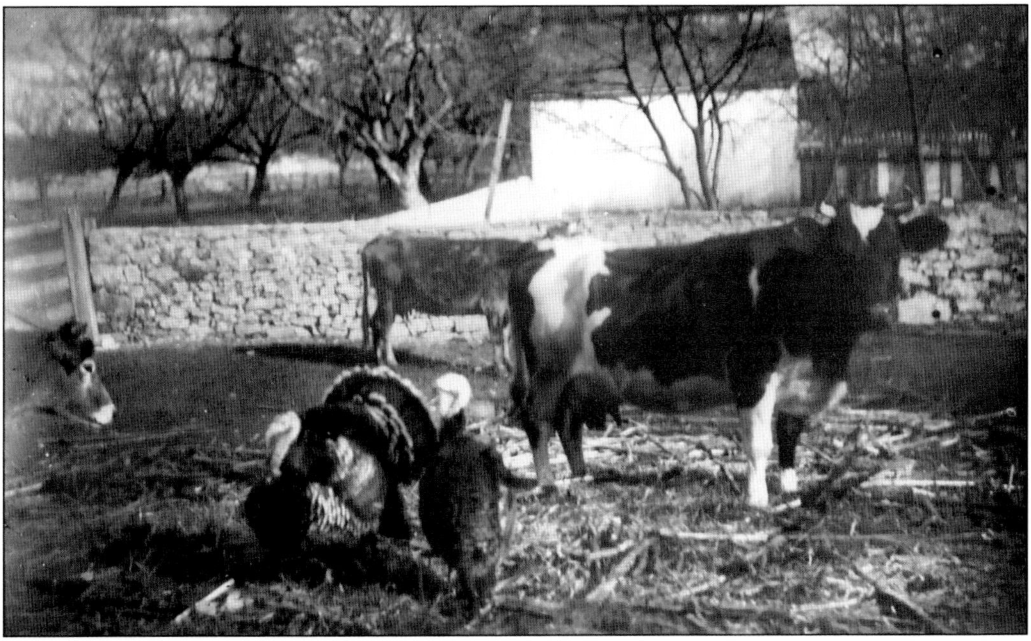

A familiar barnyard included cows, turkeys, and chickens and was surrounded by walls made of limestone. Farmers gathered limestone rubble from their fields and often used it to put up walls and outbuildings. (Courtesy of the Nancy I. Corson Foundation.)

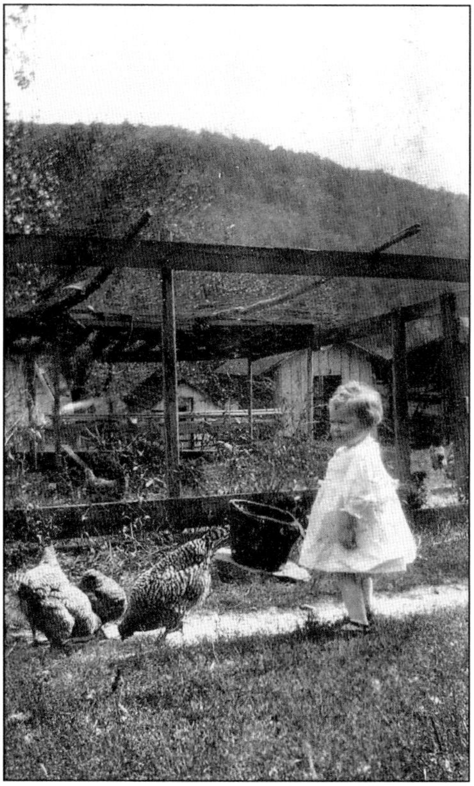

Rural children in the late 19th century enjoyed playing with the farm animals. This child is talking to her family's chickens.

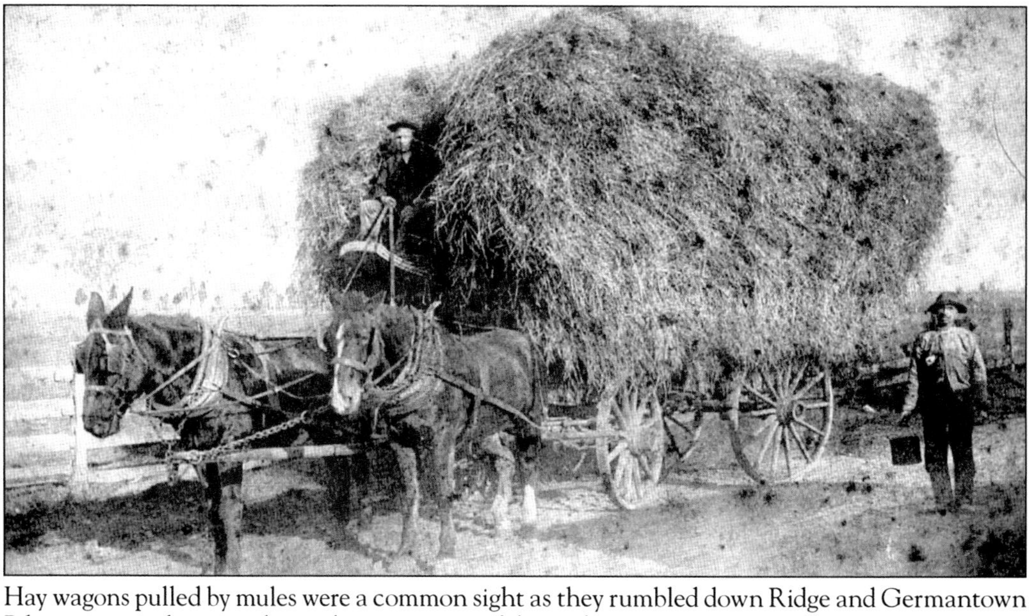

Hay wagons pulled by mules were a common sight as they rumbled down Ridge and Germantown Pikes twice a day—in the early morning and late afternoon—delivering feed for the horses in Philadelphia.

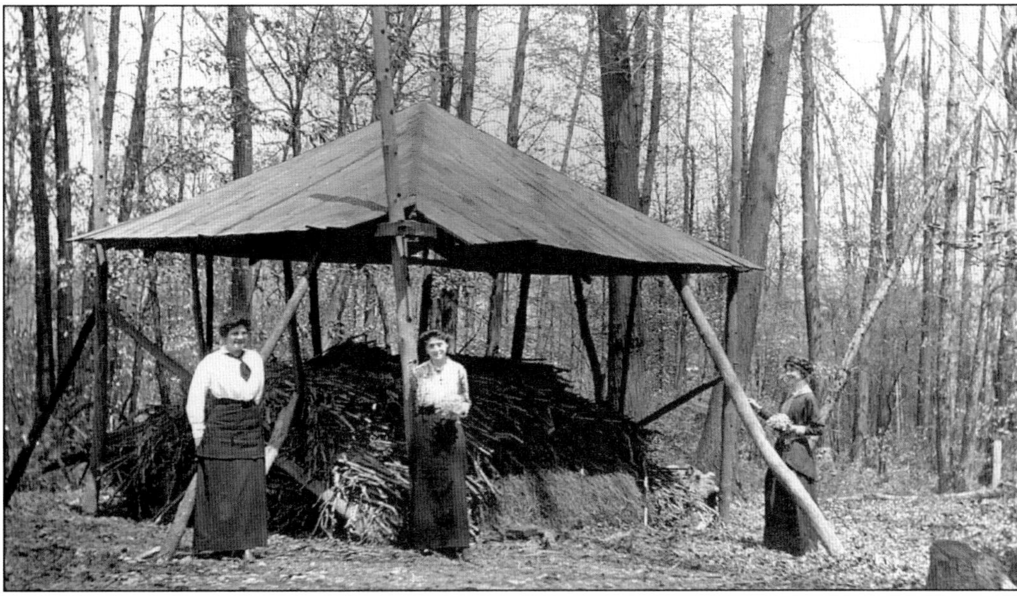

In the 19th century, farming was a family enterprise. Men, women, and children all had to lend a hand during harvest time. Above, women are storing hay beneath a field shelter. Children, especially boys, were kept out of school, often until late fall, to help with the endless work and were usually taken out of class early in the spring for plowing.

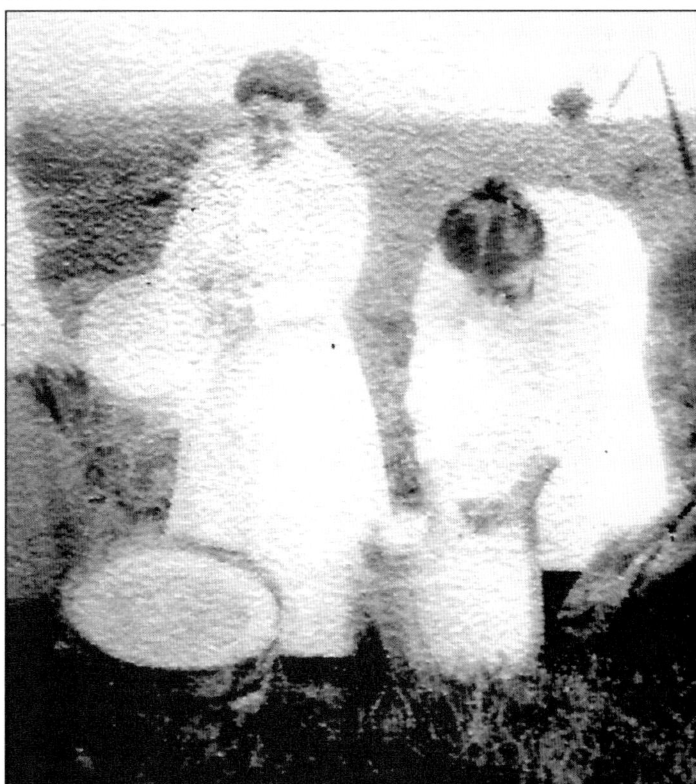

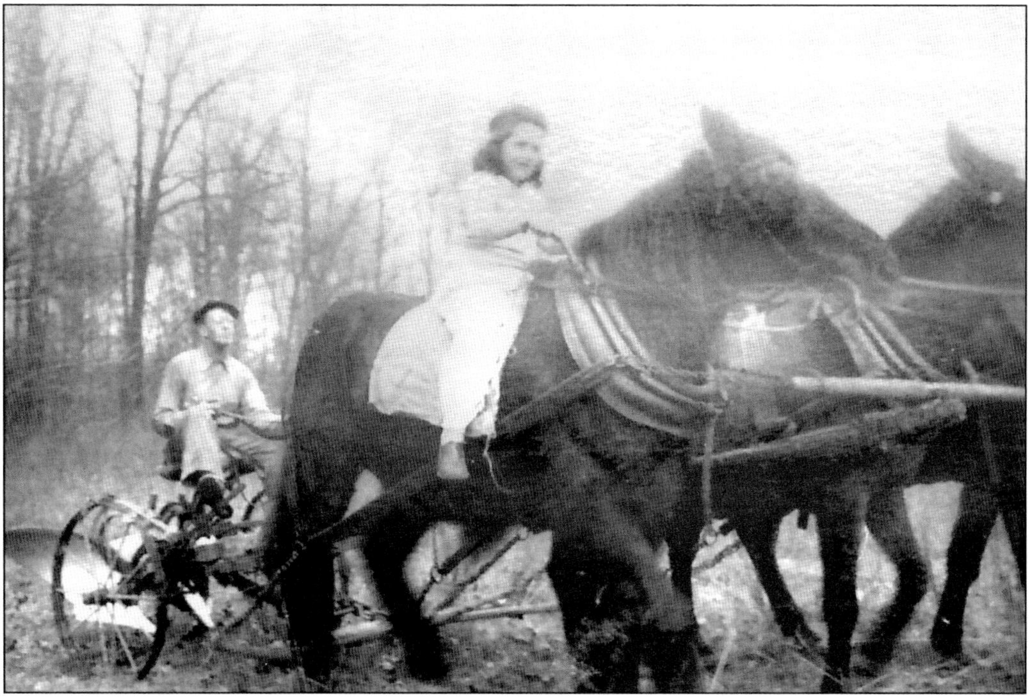

Horse power was used well into the early 20th century to propel agricultural implements and ease the enormous effort required to plow acres of farmland.

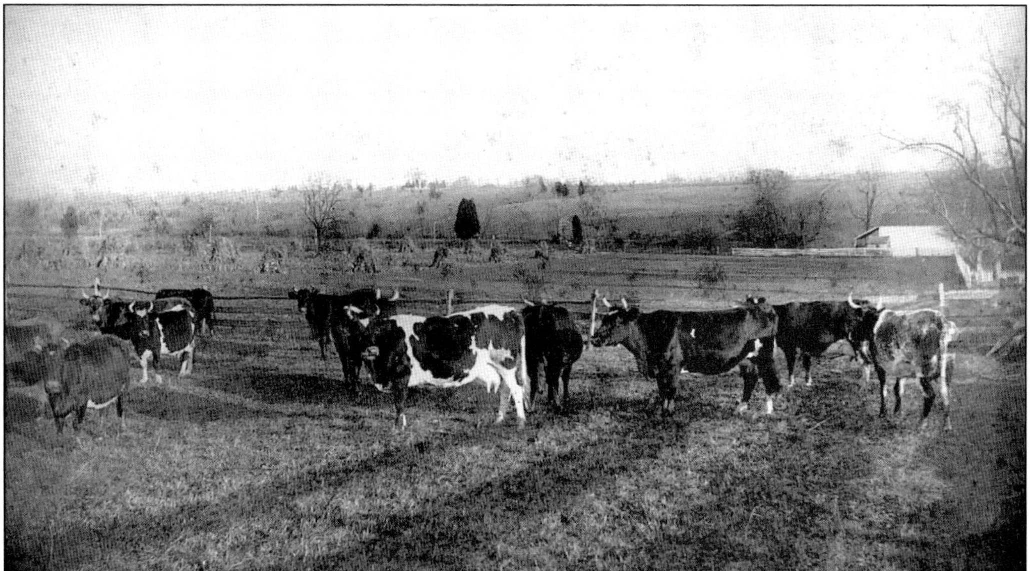

By the end of the 19th century, local grain farmers could no longer compete with huge spreads on the Midwestern plains and often turned to dairy farming. Creameries, or dairies, were businesses that grew out of the extensive dairy farming in the townships and were established to collect and process milk. Local creameries included the Woods Dairy, on Township Line and Narcissa Roads, and the Plymouth Valley Creamery, which belonged to an association of farmers.

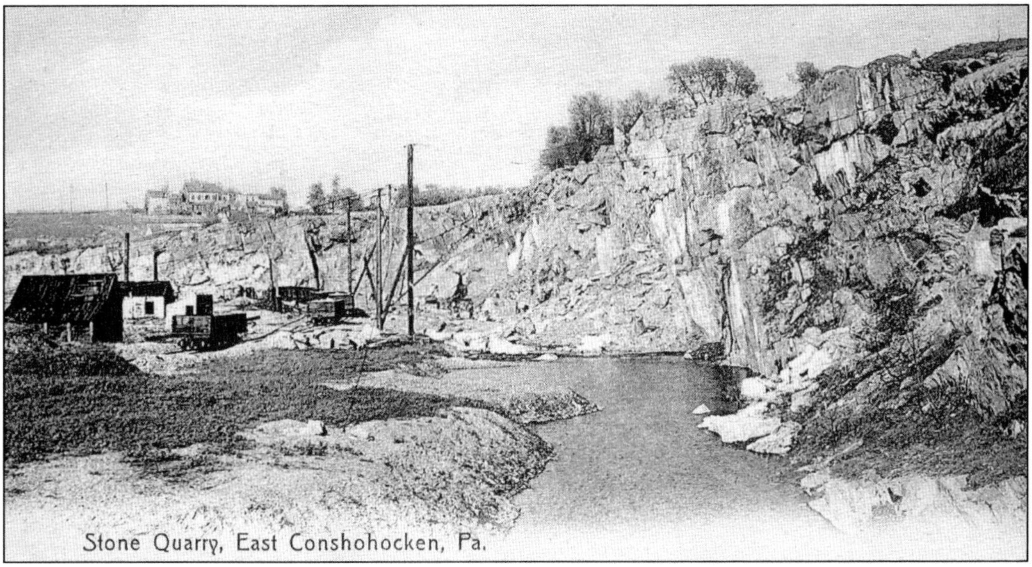

Both Plymouth and Whitemarsh relied on quarrying the abundant local minerals: limestone, marble, and iron ore. Quarrying reached its peak in the mid-1800s and was the principal employer at that time.

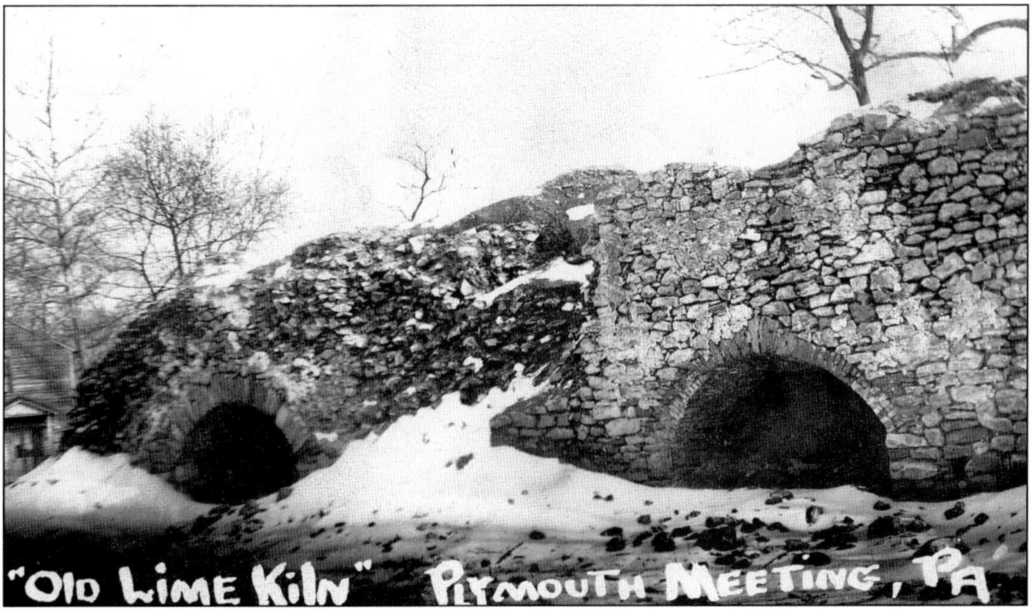

The area's rich limestone was not only important to local farmers to sweeten the soil but was also used for building mortar. Many buildings in Philadelphia, including Independence Hall, were constructed using lime from Plymouth and Whitemarsh. Limestone had to be burned in a kiln prior to use as mortar. These kilns, constructed of local stone (but not limestone), were fired by hardwoods, which were also in abundance.

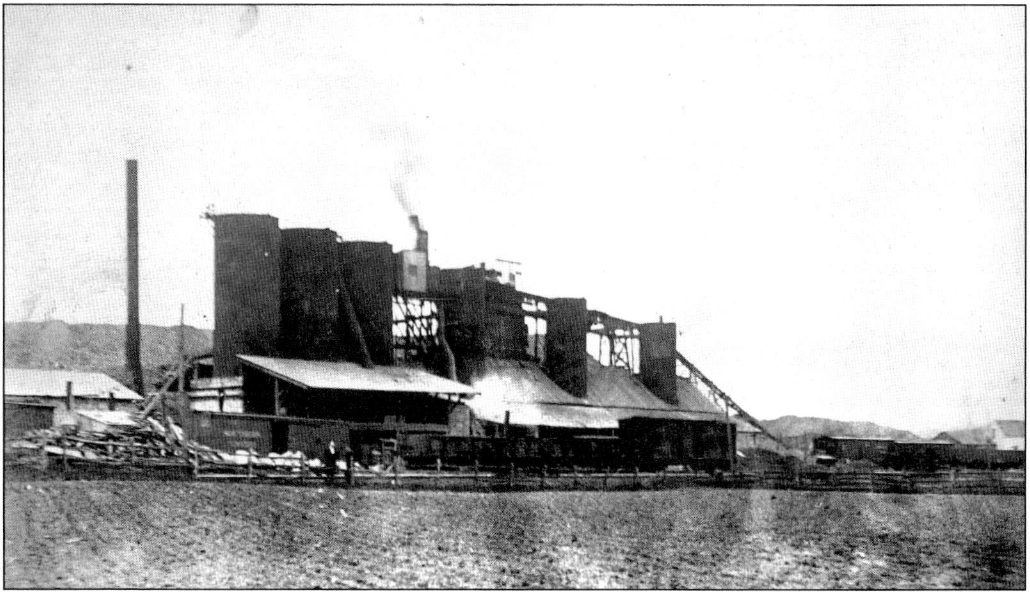

The G. & W.H. Corson Company was the successor to a lime works that had been in operation in Whitemarsh since 1822. Its main operations were moved to the quarries at Stenton Avenue and Joshua Road in 1910. The company was founded by Alan W. Corson for himself and his brother and was one of the nation's oldest lime quarries in continuous operation.

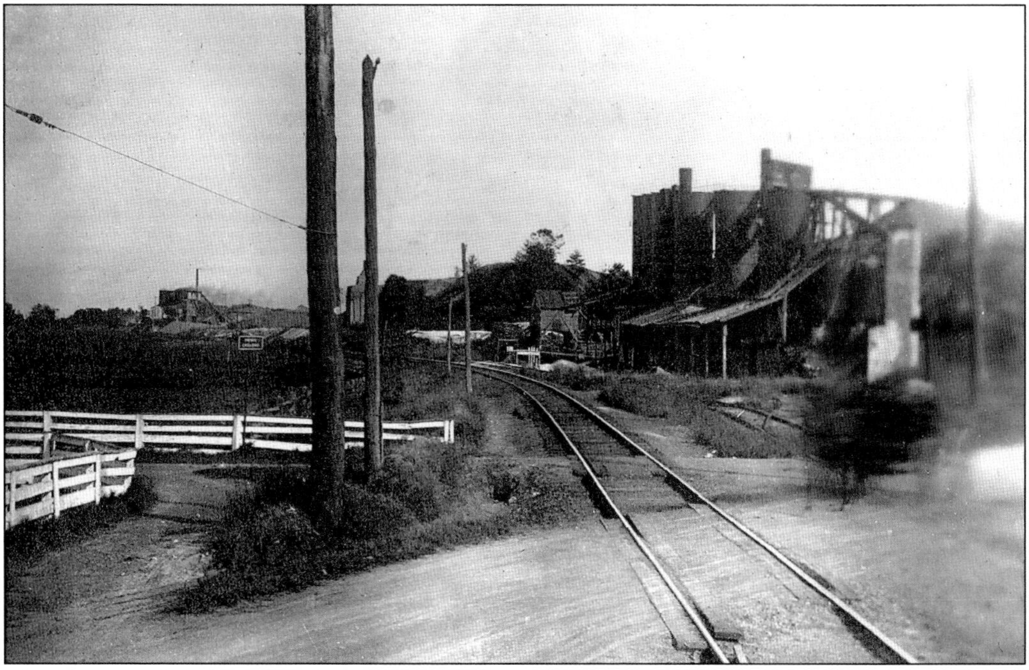

The coming of the railroads helped end the rural isolation of Plymouth and Whitemarsh and led it into the industrial era. Shown here are the tracks for the Pennsylvania Railroad's Trenton Branch, which, along with the Reading Railroad, carried lime from Corson's Quarry twice each day. Limestone was loaded from hoppers over the tracks directly into the cars.

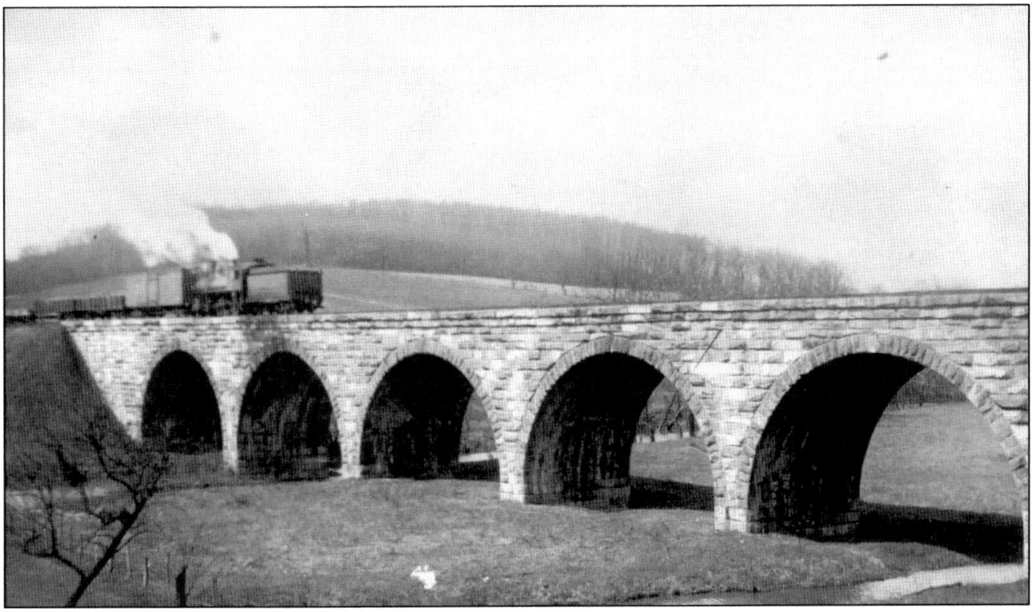

This train chugs along the Trenton Cut-Off Bridge over the Wissahickon Creek in 1905. The bridge is located not far from the intersection of Skippack and Bethlehem Pikes. The Trenton Branch, or Cut-Off route, of the Pennsylvania Railroad allowed trains going to and from New York to travel above Philadelphia, thus avoiding the busy and congested city.

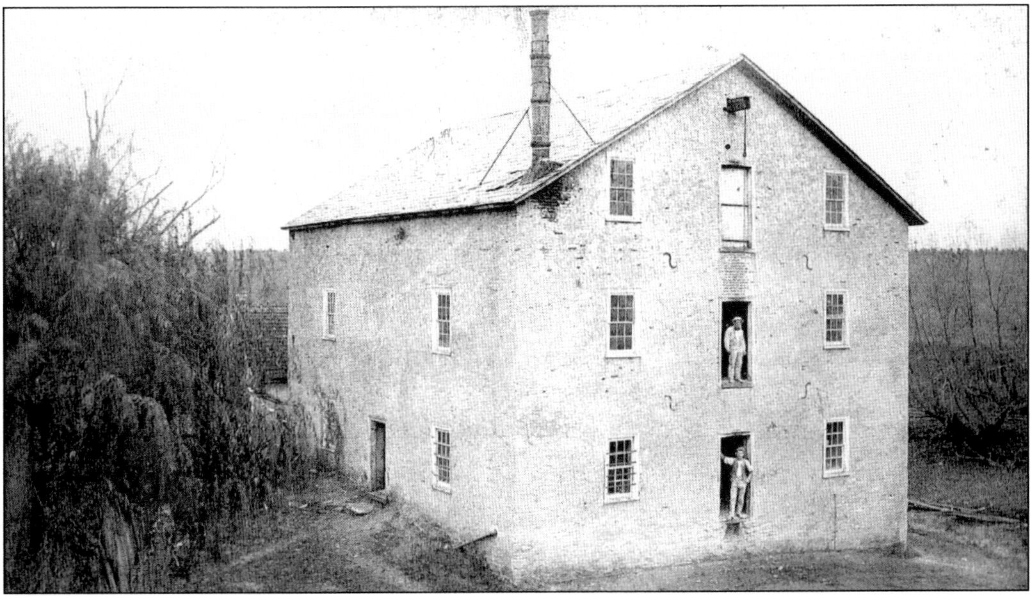

Mills were another business that grew out of the agricultural industry, grinding the local grains—wheat, oats, and barley—into flour and animal feed to be sold at market. The "Old Grist Mill" at Ivy Rock was run by John Davis in the early 1800s and later by John J. Brooks, who is shown standing in the second-floor doorway. The mill was located near what is now Alan Wood Road.

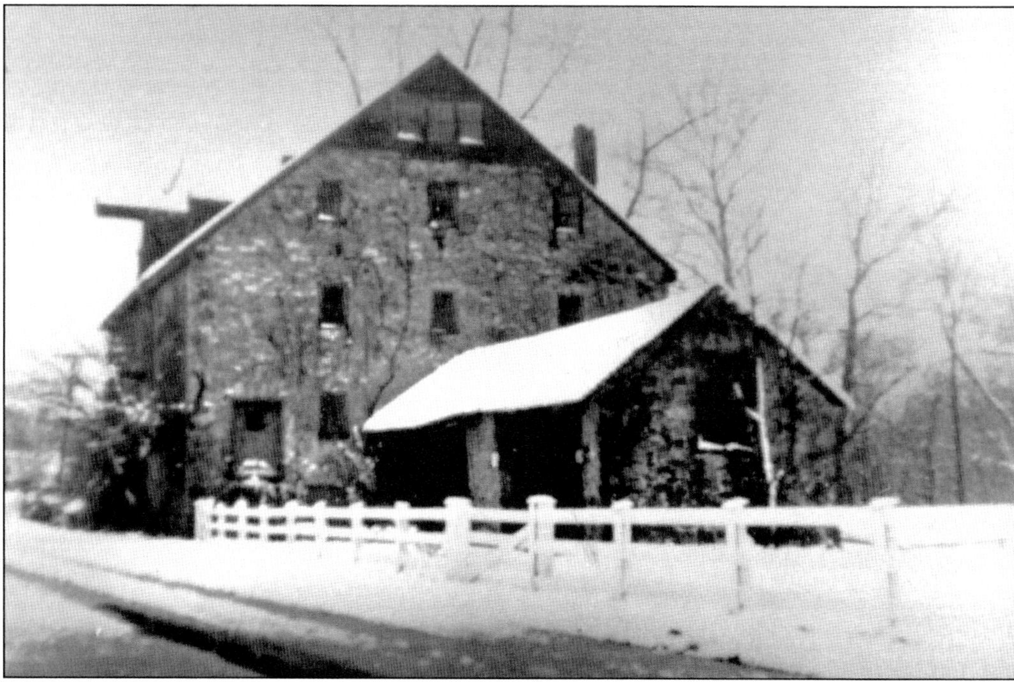

The Farmar-Mather Mill was built by Edward Farmar in the early 1700s near what is now the intersection of Skippack and Bethlehem Pikes. Highly successful, it was operated under a succession of owners until 1896. It has been restored and is listed on the National Register of Historic Places. (Courtesy of the Historical Society of Fort Washington.)

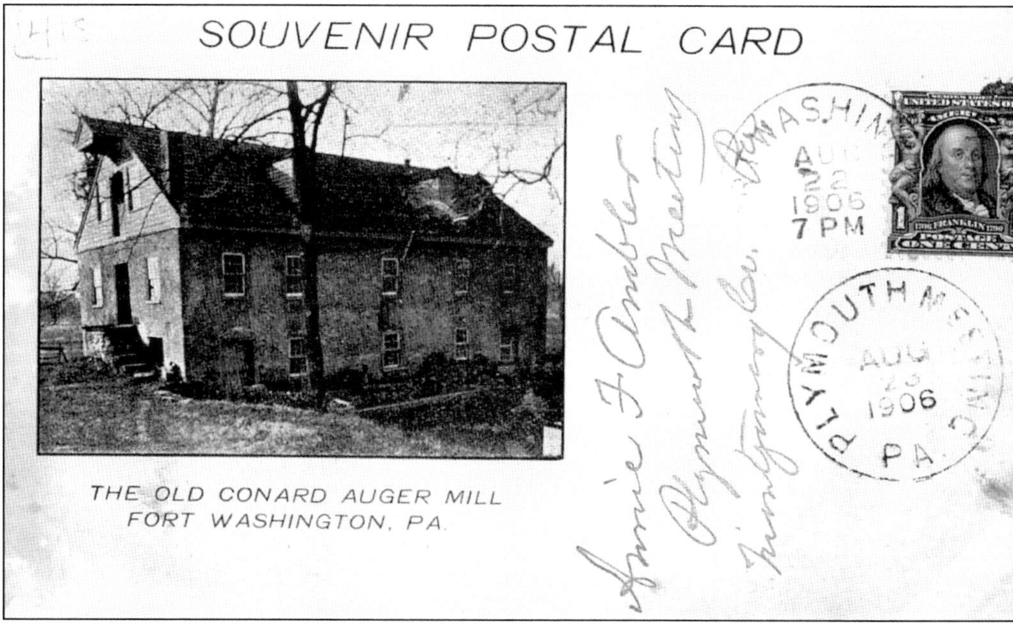

A linseed oil mill was erected by Henry Daub near the Sandy Run Creek c. 1792 and converted to an auger factory in 1846 by Albert Conard. In partnership with his brother Robert, Conard made augers there until 1901. The mill was sold to the Montgomery Electric Light Company in 1905, and the auger-making business was leased to Ralph Werry.

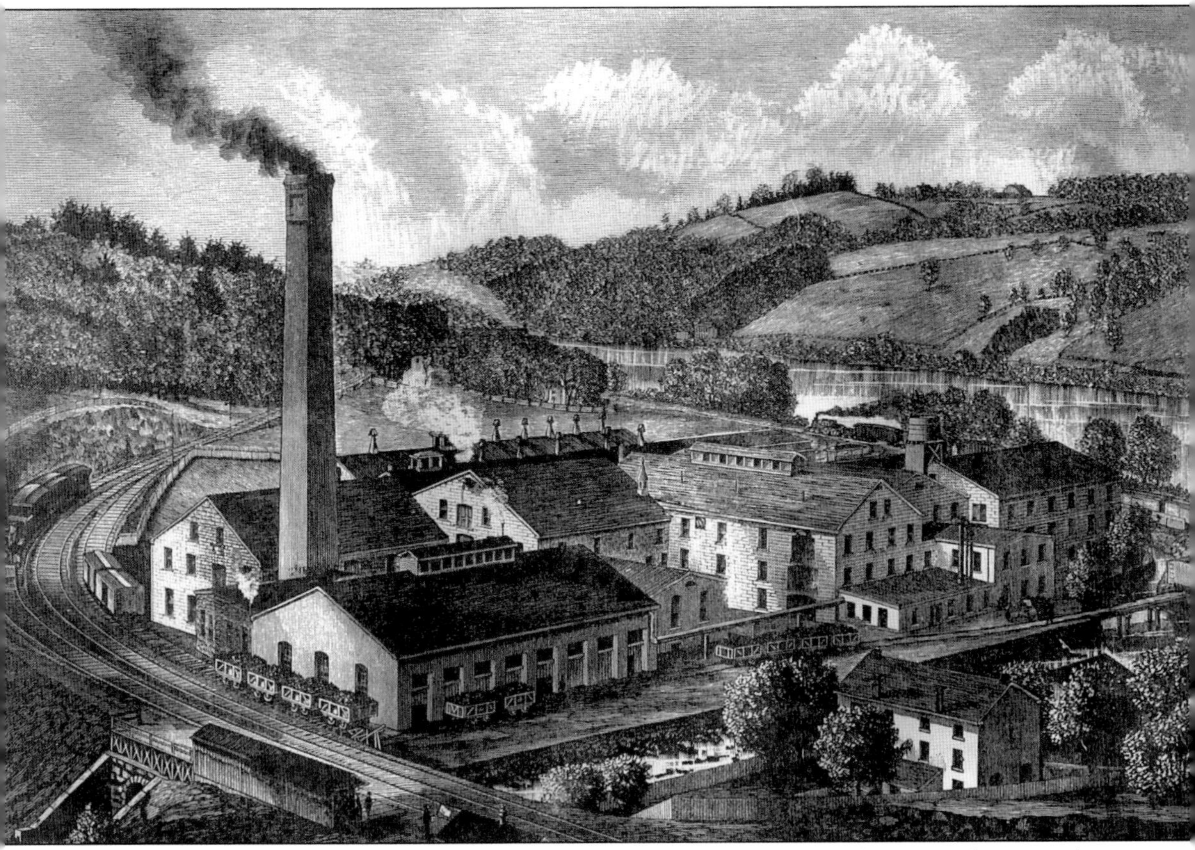

The Riverside Paper Mill was established in what is now Miquon by Anthony Newhouse and was purchased by W.C. Hamilton in 1865. Pure water was secured from the nearby Bubbling Spring through a 21-inch water main, allowing the mill to produce an exceptionally white, high-quality paper. The firm expanded and changed ownership a number of times, and in 1980, it became the Simpson Paper Company.

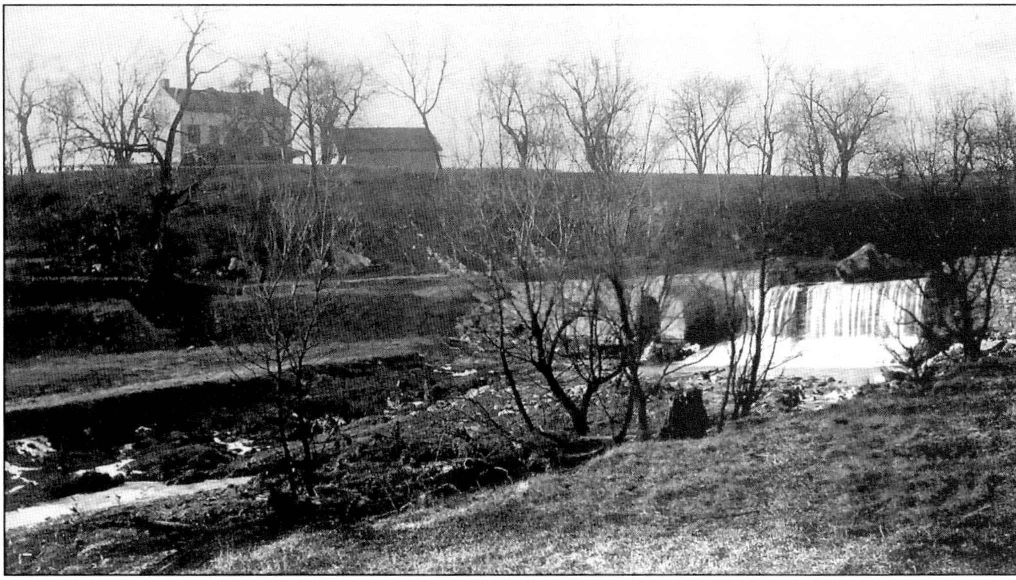

Milldams such as this one impounded water and harnessed the accumulated fall of the creek to provide enough power for the mills. In an age before steam or electricity, these water mills were the only dependable source of power besides draft animals and human muscles.

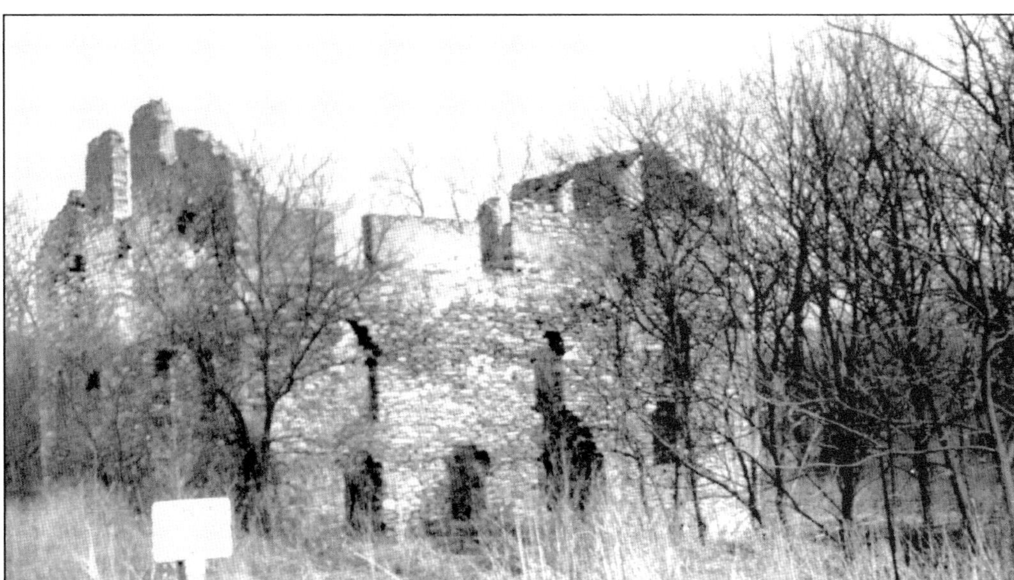

With the coming of steam and electricity, water-powered mills such as Cleaver's Mill, on Valley Green Road, were abandoned, demolished, or left in ruins. (Courtesy of Fort Washington State Park.)

Two

VILLAGES

Clustering around main crossroads in the townships were a number of small villages. Typically, they contained no more than a few dozen houses, a post office and general store, a tavern or small hotel, and perhaps a church and one-room schoolhouse. Today, many of these villages are in danger of disappearing in a flood of development, accompanied by too little regard for historic preservation or for the charm of these old crossroad communities, which add so much to the quality of modern life.

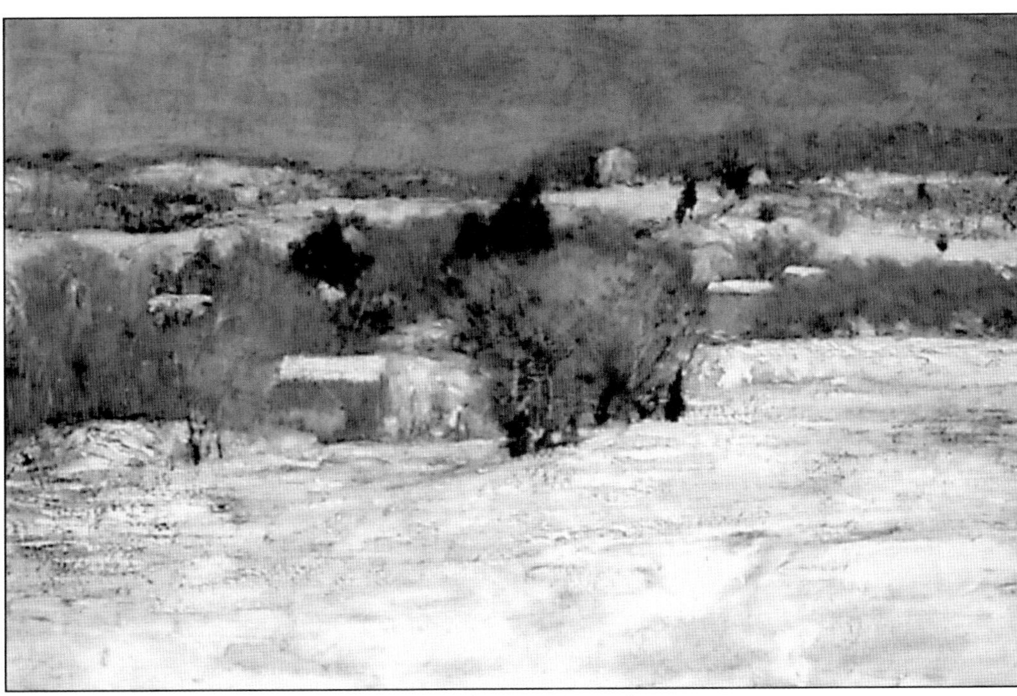

A *Study, Cold Point, Pennsylvania* (1895), Thomas Hovenden.

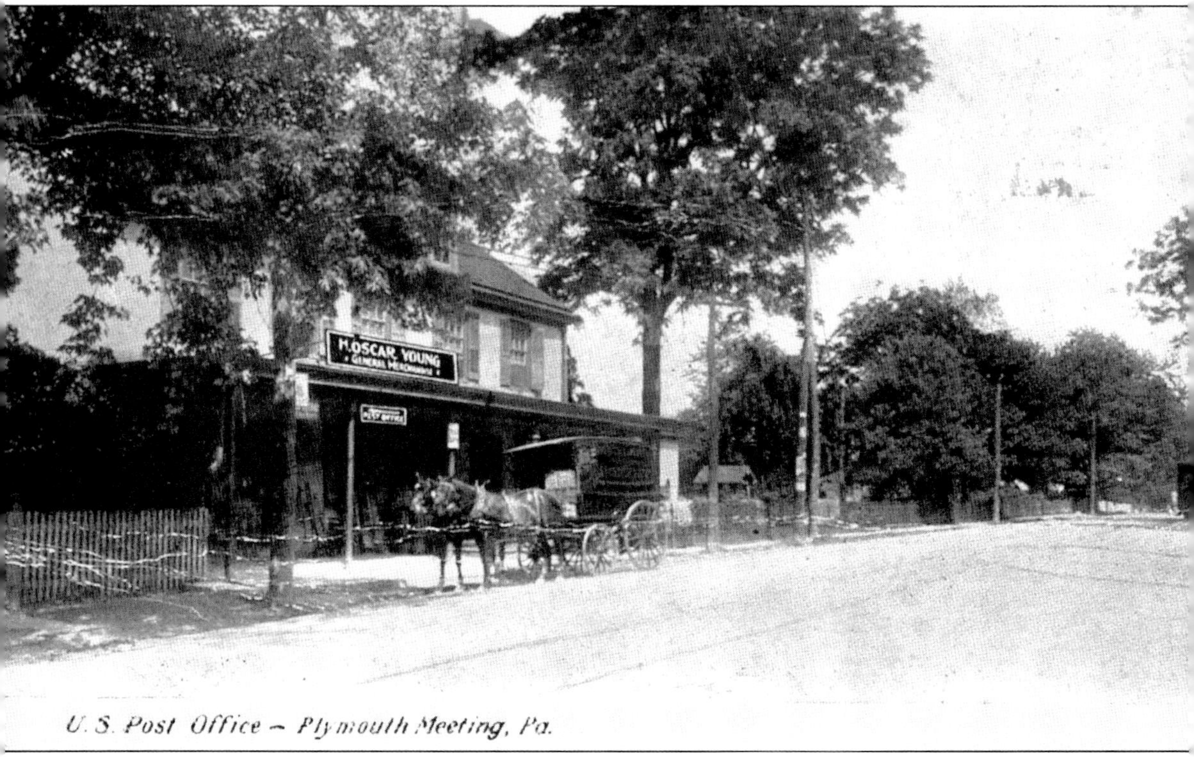

The oldest village, Plymouth Meeting, stands at the crossroads of Germantown and Butler Pikes and was an important hub in the region. Germantown Pike began as an American Indian trail and then became a lime-cart route to Philadelphia. The Oscar Young general store, built in 1827 by Jonathon Maulsby, served customers at 5 East Germantown Pike. On this postcard from the beginning of the 20th century, a horse-drawn wagon waits for a deliveryman who is taking a supply of biscuits inside.

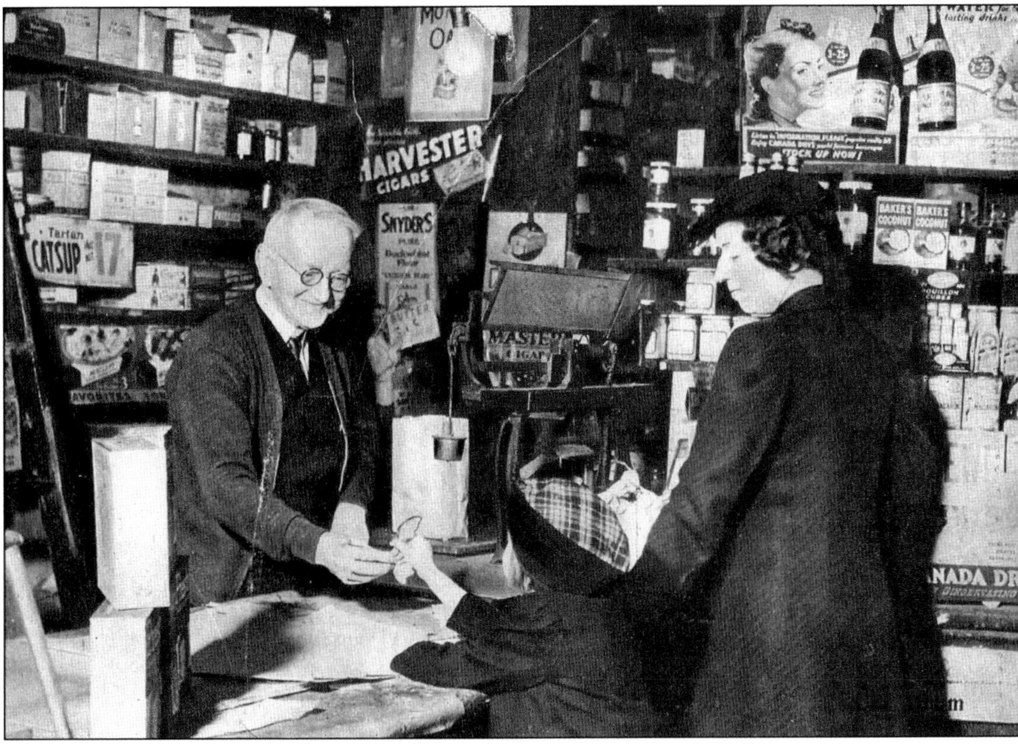

Young ran the store for many years, beginning in the 1890s. He made good use of every possible space in the store. Walls were lined with shelves, and any open surface was plastered with advertisements for some popular product. During the earlier era of Maulsby's ownership, customers could purchase items ranging from a keg of gunpowder to tea, sugar, cloth, and books. Often, customers bartered for items, offering farm produce in exchange for goods.

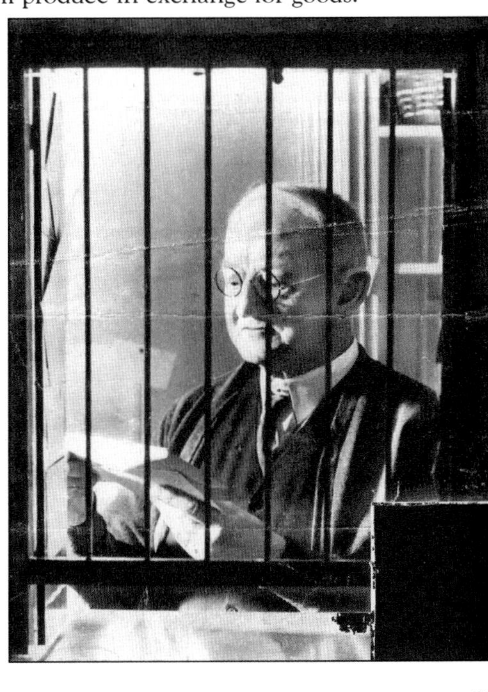

Like many general store proprietors of the time, Young was also the local postmaster, and Plymouth Meeting residents often saw him sorting the daily mail behind the post-office window. The store served, at various intervals, as the post office (1827–1940), with mail delivered to Plymouth Meeting first by horseback and, after 1835, by railroad.

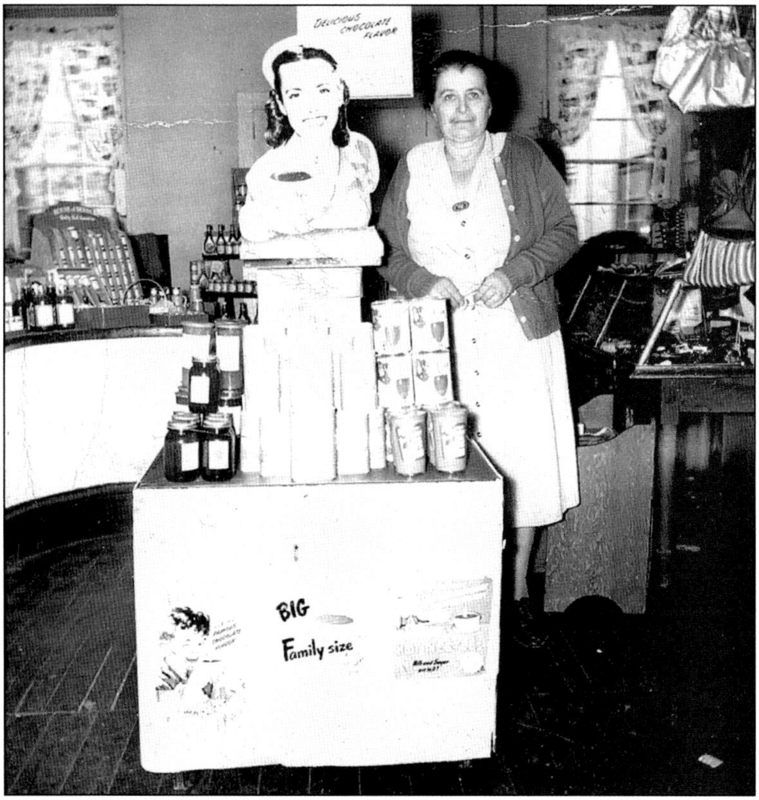

When local grocery and dry goods stores closed, many became country gift shops. Oscar Young's store became Alice Ambler's Country Store, operating from 1947 to 1955. Much admired by those who knew her, Ambler was an ardent preservationist and a cofounder of the Plymouth Meeting Historical Society.

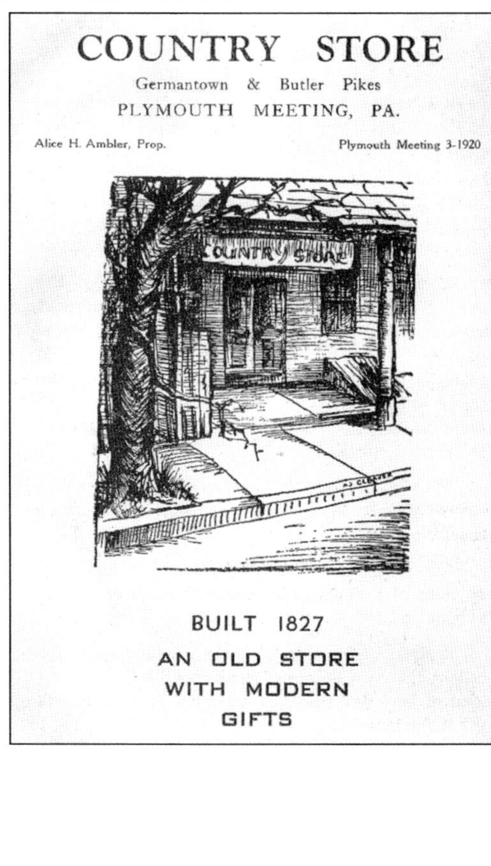

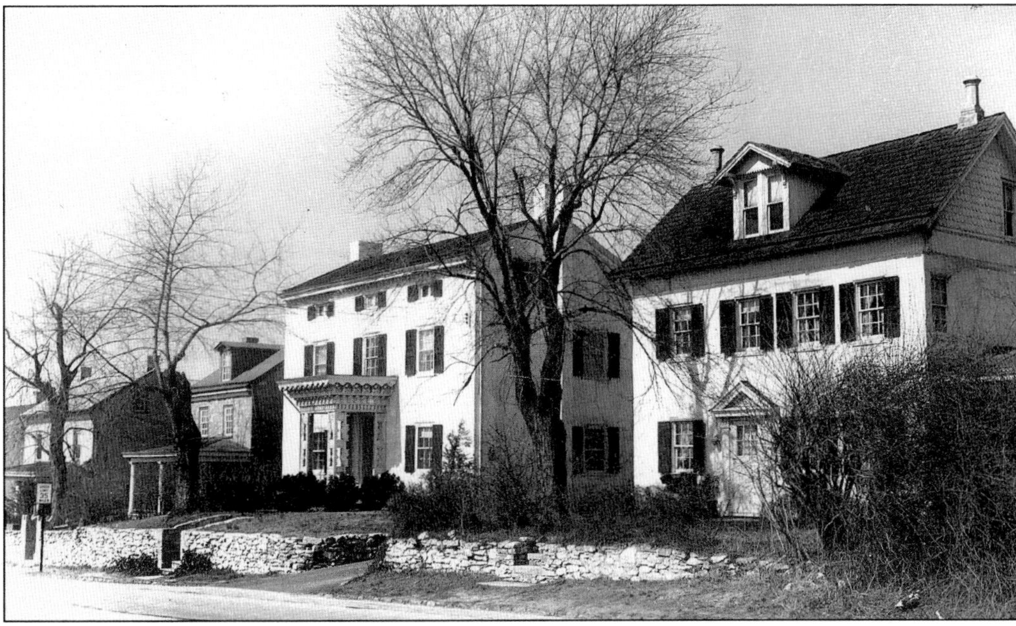

This streetscape along Germantown Pike could date from 1905 or the present day, since very little has changed along the historic corridor. Some of the houses date from as early as the 18th century, with many constructed during the years from 1840 to 1850. Typical features are the small half windows on the upper floor, a feature that was often added to update earlier structures as well as to make more usable space.

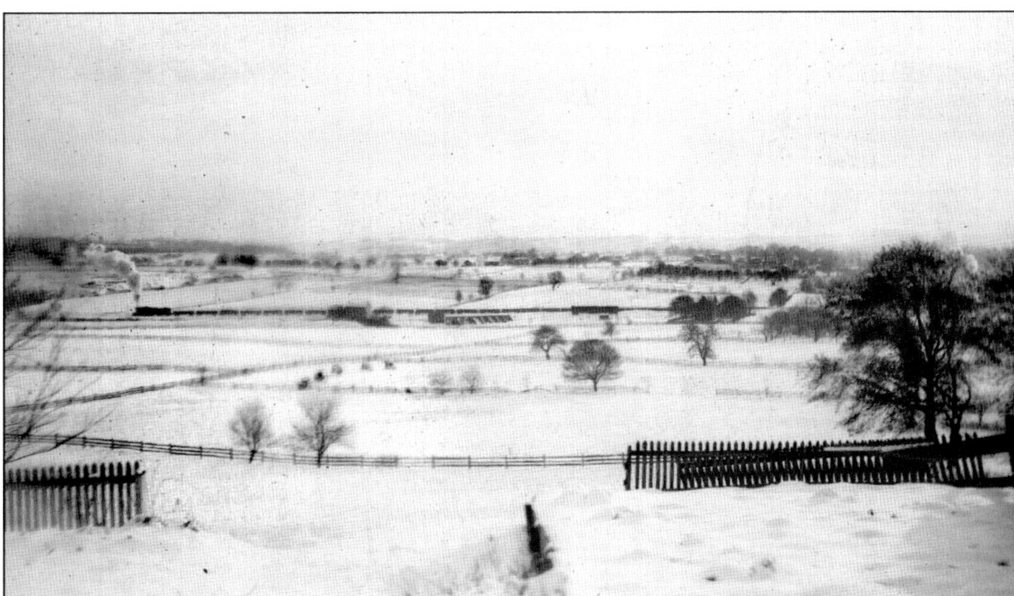

Cold Point is north of Plymouth Meeting along Butler Pike. It is believed to have been named for the high point of ground where the Baptist church is located, which experiences colder temperatures than the surrounding area. The land surrounding the village was used for lime production and farming. Here, a lone steam train puffs through the snow-laden landscape of lower Cold Point.

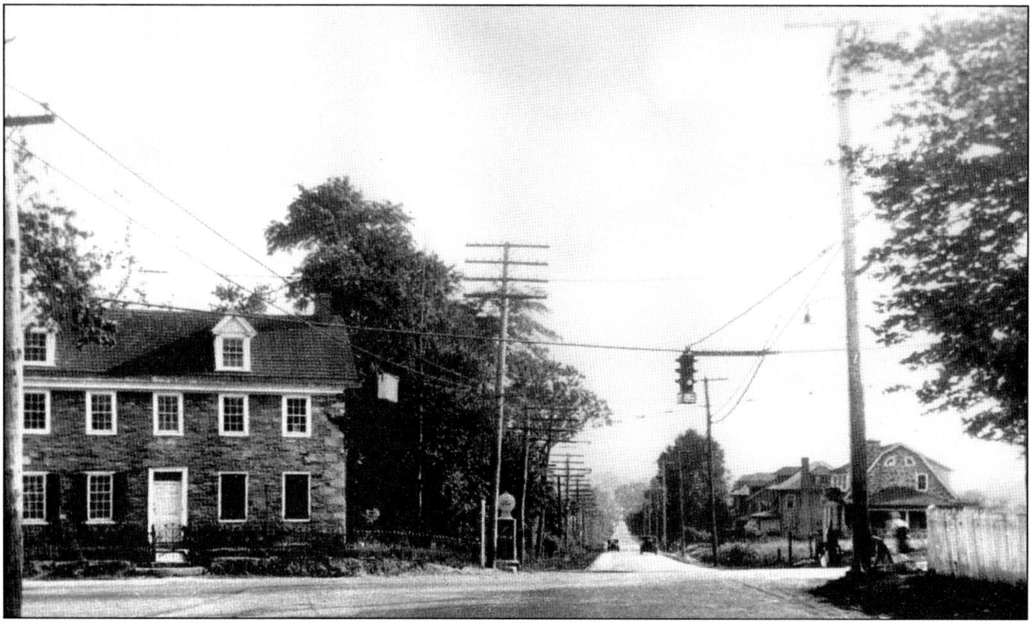

Harmonville, south of Plymouth Meeting at Ridge and Butler Pikes, consisted in the late-1800s of a store, several mechanic shops, and 30 houses. Ore and marble quarrying secured its prosperity. Named for the well-known storekeeper Harman Yerkes, the village changed the spelling of its name from Harmanville to Harmonville sometime after World War II. In this view, looking south toward Conshohocken from the intersection of Ridge and Butler, the old Andorra Inn is on the left with a globe-topped phone booth near the street.

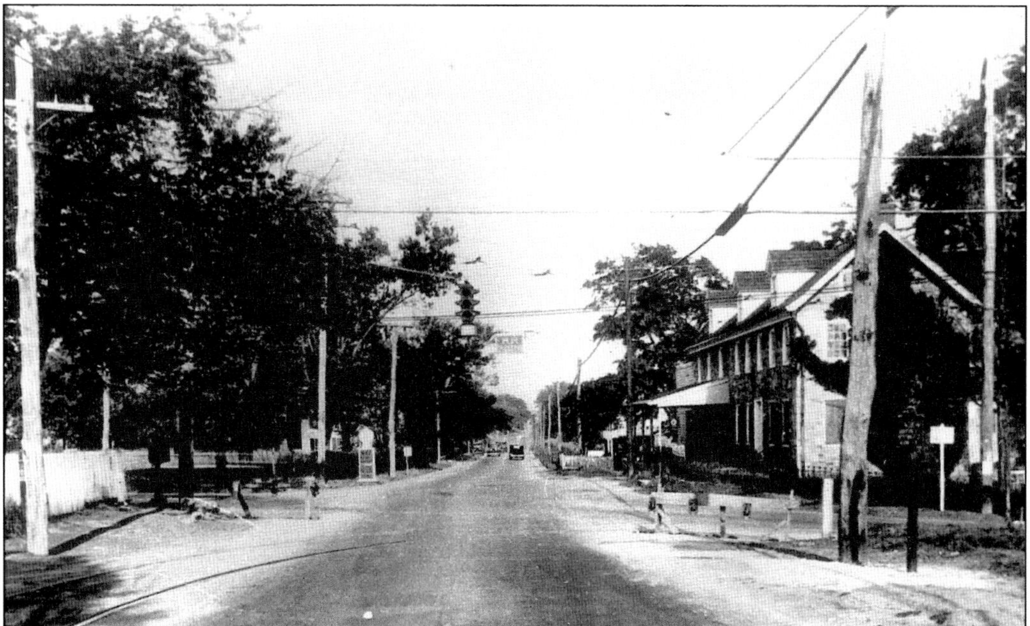

Harmonville focused around the intersection of Ridge and Butler Pikes. This view, looking east toward Philadelphia, shows Ridge Pike. The inn is on the right and is now the site of the Whitemarsh Shopping Center.

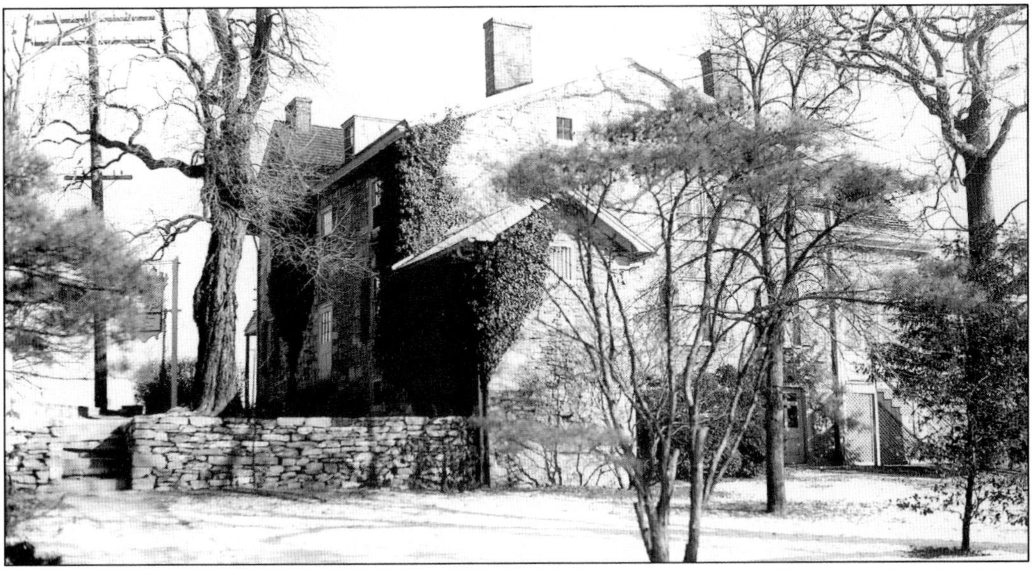

The Andorra Inn stood at the southeast corner of the intersection of Ridge and Butler Pikes until it was demolished in 1956. This is the building where Harman Yerkes kept his general store during the Revolutionary War period. In more recent times, Mabel McCallip operated the Andorra Inn at this location. McCallip later married Arthur Folsom Paul, the head of Andorra Nurseries, who moved the nurseries' headquarters to the building.

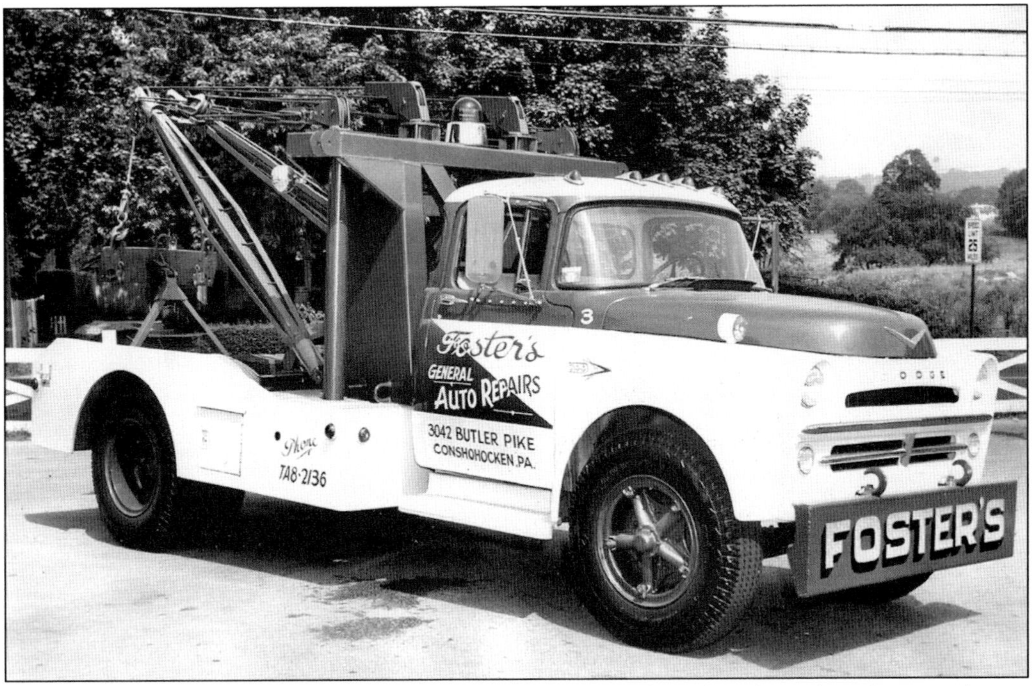

Open fields still came right up to Harmonville along Butler Pike when this photograph was taken in the summer of 1957. A Texaco service station now stands at the edge of the field in the upper right corner of the picture, while the land just beyond it became the housing development along Sierra Road. The occasion of this photograph was a new tow truck for Foster's General Auto Repairs. (Courtesy of Foster's General Auto Repairs.)

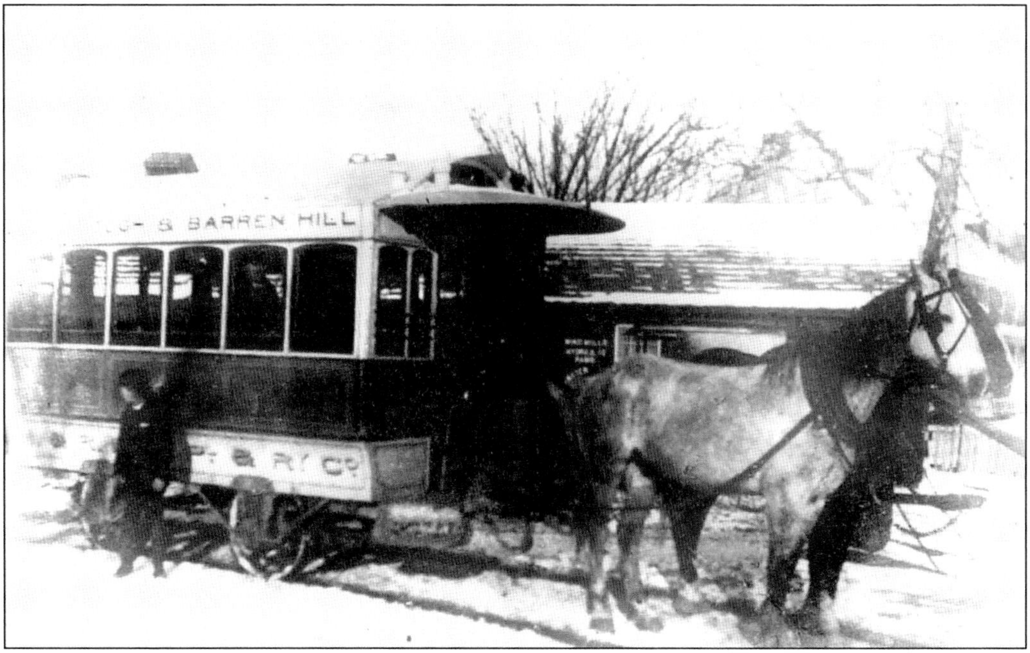

A horsecar waits for passengers in the Whitemarsh Township village of Barren Hill, located east of Plymouth Meeting on Germantown Pike in what is now called Lafayette Hill. Horsecars flourished from the 1850s to the 1890s, when electric trolleys came into service, typically with motors put into the old cars, literally replacing the horses as the means of power.

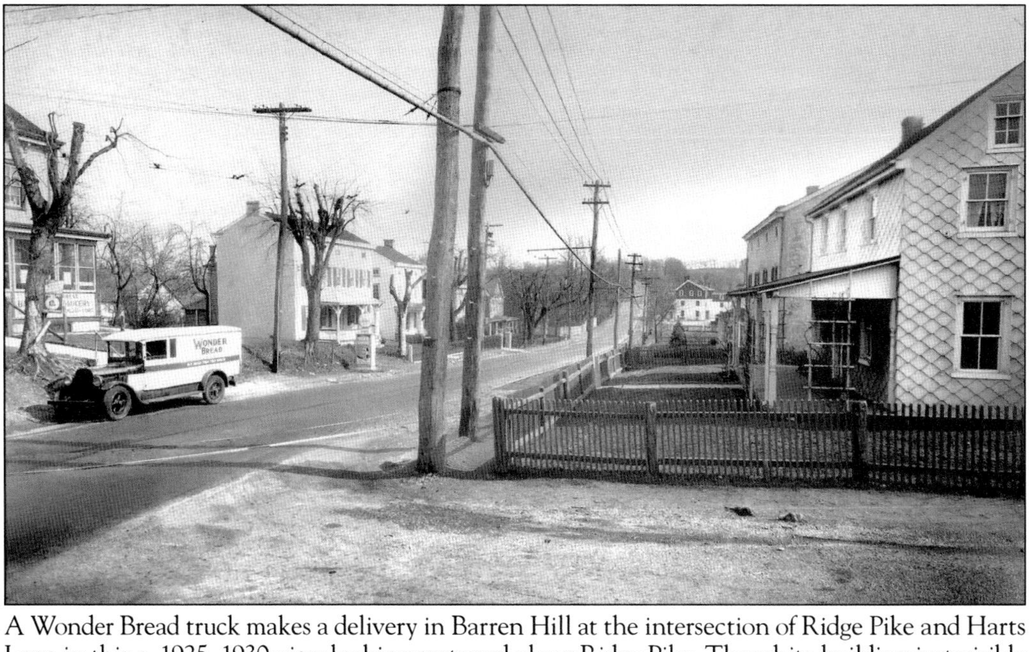

A Wonder Bread truck makes a delivery in Barren Hill at the intersection of Ridge Pike and Harts Lane in this c. 1925–1930 view looking eastward along Ridge Pike. The white building just visible in the distance is the Fountain Inn. (Courtesy of the Lownes Family Funeral Home.)

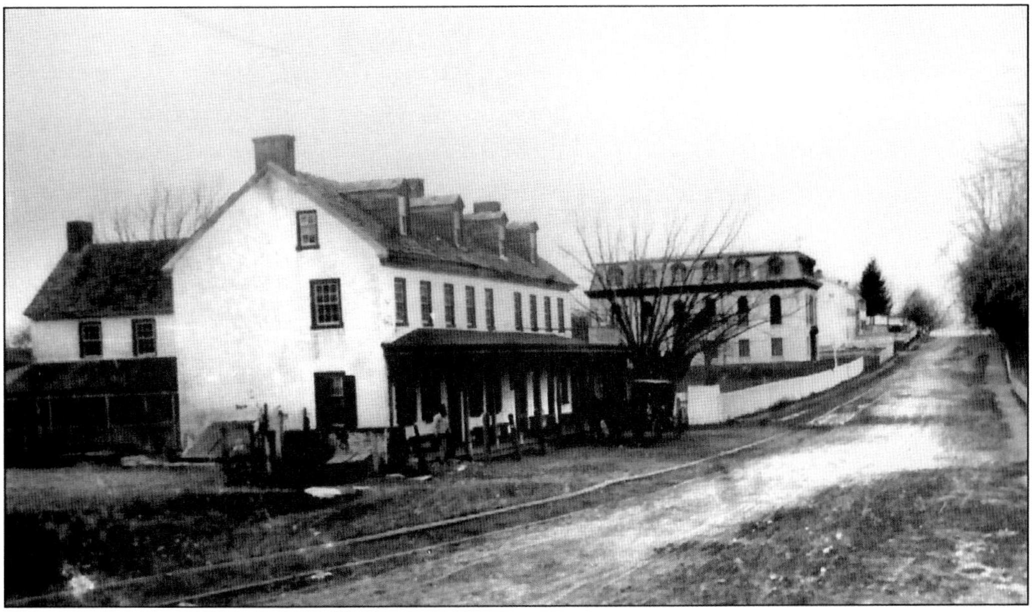

As early as 1806, William Streeper built the Fountain Inn on Ridge Pike adjacent to what is now Holod's True Value Hardware. It is the last local survivor from the stagecoach days of the Ridge Pike. An ever-flowing spring nearby provided both water and a name for the inn. (Courtesy of the Historical Society of Montgomery County.)

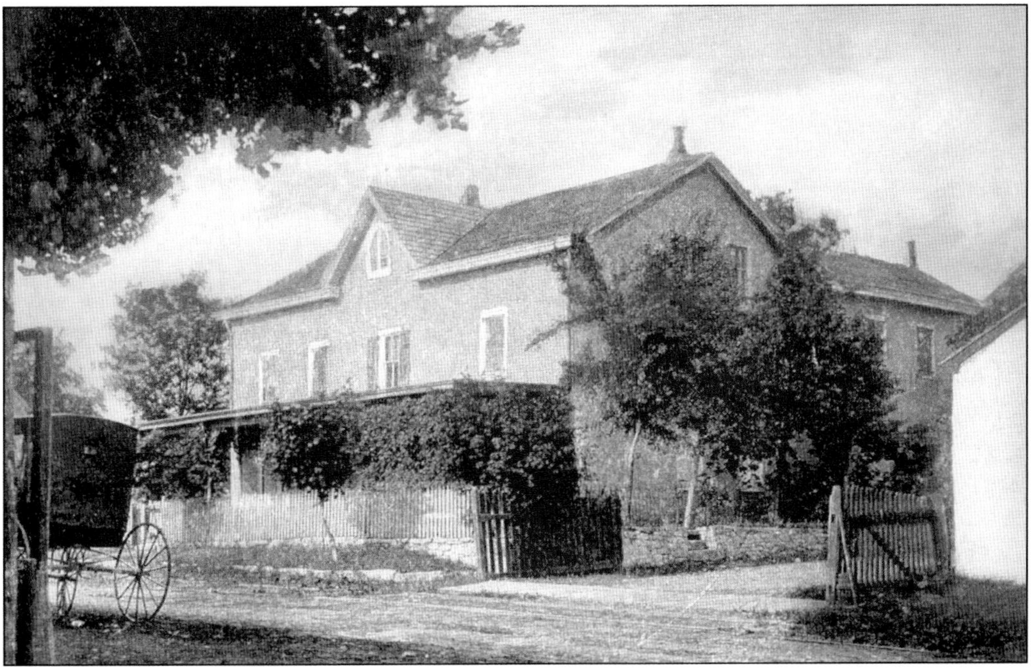

Hickorytown, apparently named because many of its residents cut hickory wood for the numerous limekilns in the region, was located on Germantown Pike, west of Plymouth Meeting. In 1887, the village had the Hickorytown Hotel, a schoolhouse, a blacksmith, a wheelwright shop, and about 30 houses. Joseph Corson and his wife, Hannah, with the help of their children, ran a store in the front part of their Hickorytown home, shown here.

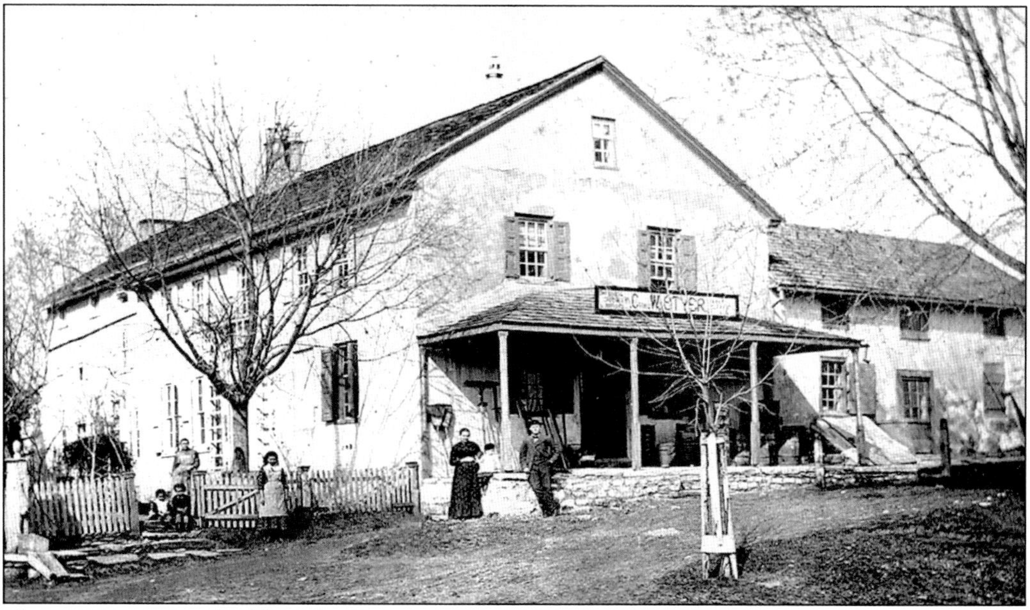

The Livezey store building has stood on the corner of Germantown Pike and Chemical Road since at least 1788. Members of the Livezey family were successful mill owners in the Philadelphia area. The family decided that young Samuel, born in 1760, was too delicate for the mill business and set him up as a merchant. This photograph dates from the late 1800s, when the property was rented to the Styer family.

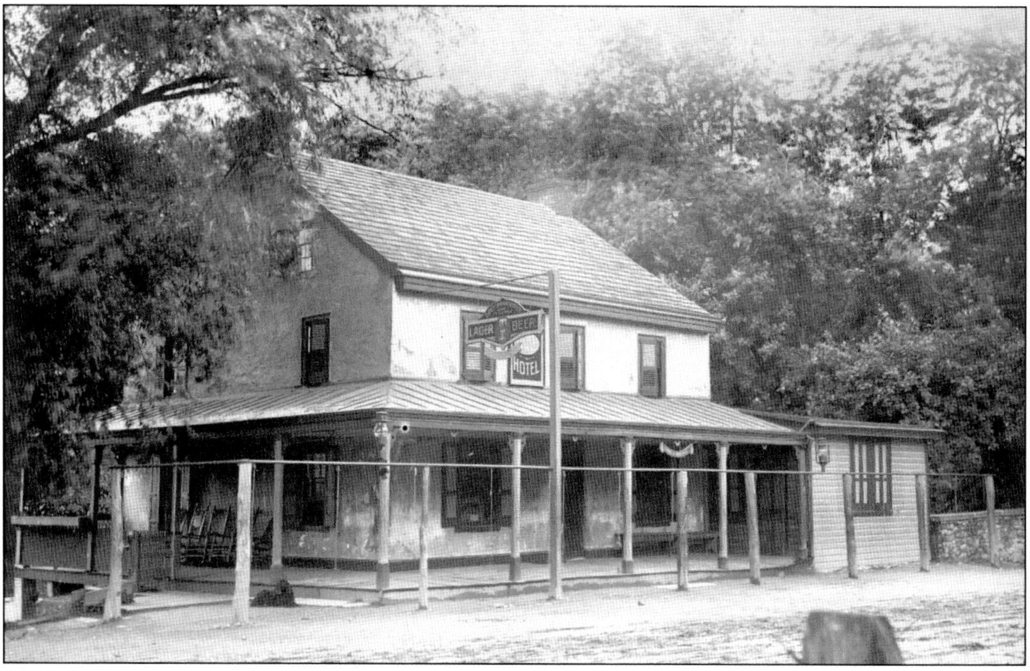

The Seven Stars Inn was typical of the many taverns that stood at an important crossroads in virtually every small village. The Seven Stars stood on Ridge Pike across from what is now Chemical Road. It was demolished for the construction of approach ramps to the Blue Route (Interstate 476). (Courtesy of the Historical Society of Montgomery County.)

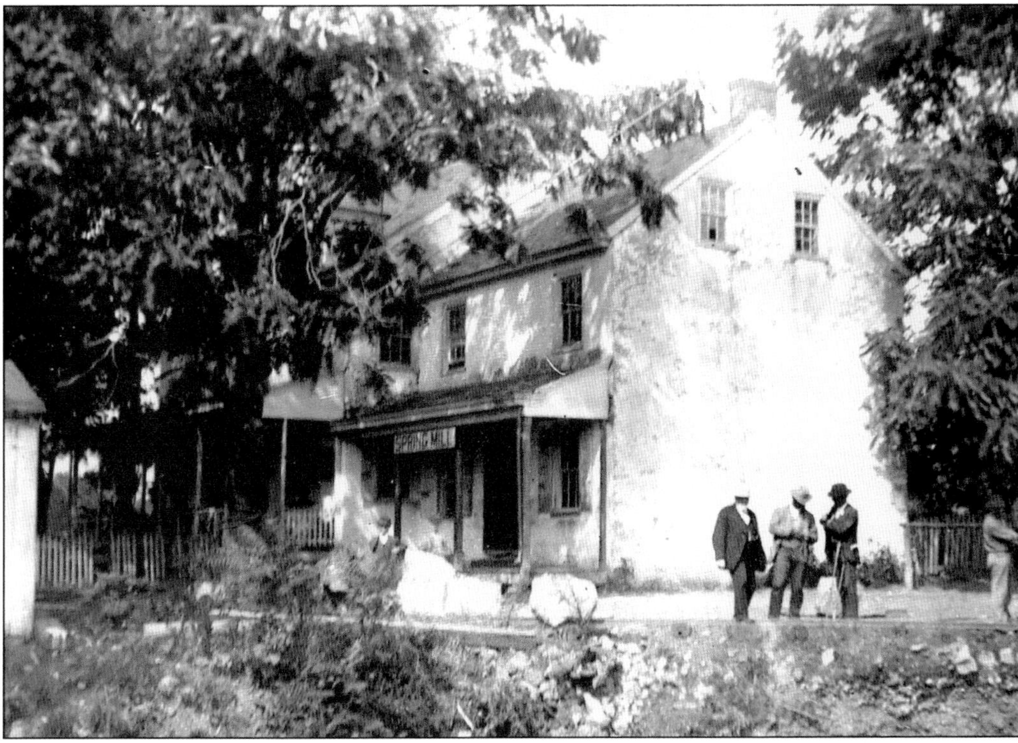

The Bubbling Springs, near the Schuylkill River, gave the village of Spring Mill its name and attracted the papermaking and other industries to the area. The spring was described as having an underground flow of several million gallons of water a day. This enormous overflow fed a creek that powered the village's mills. The railroad made Spring Mill an easily accessible area. The mills and later the highly successful Andorra Nurseries shipped their goods from this location. Below, a horse-drawn wagon is being loaded with newly milled grain.

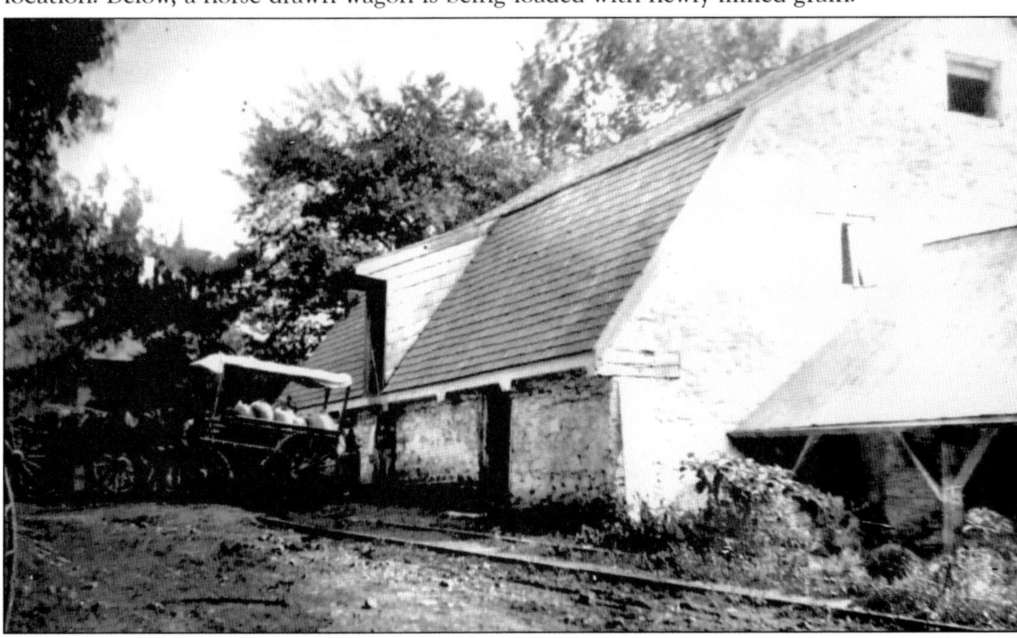

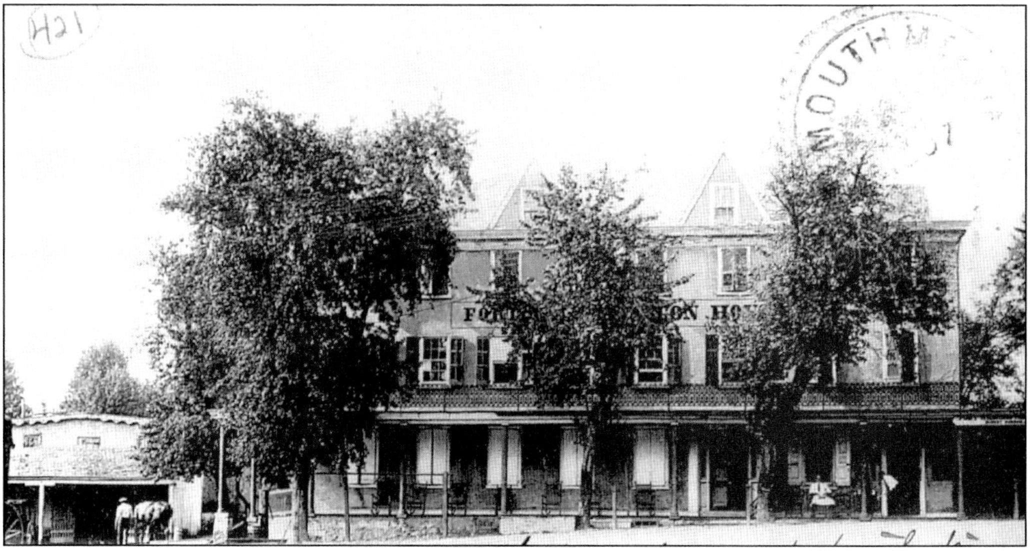

The village of Fort Washington was named for the military encampment in the area during the American Revolution. In 1855, the North Pennsylvania Railroad was extended through Fort Washington into Upper Dublin, bringing growth to the small community. The Fort Washington House (Hotel) was opened in 1855 to accommodate railroad travelers.

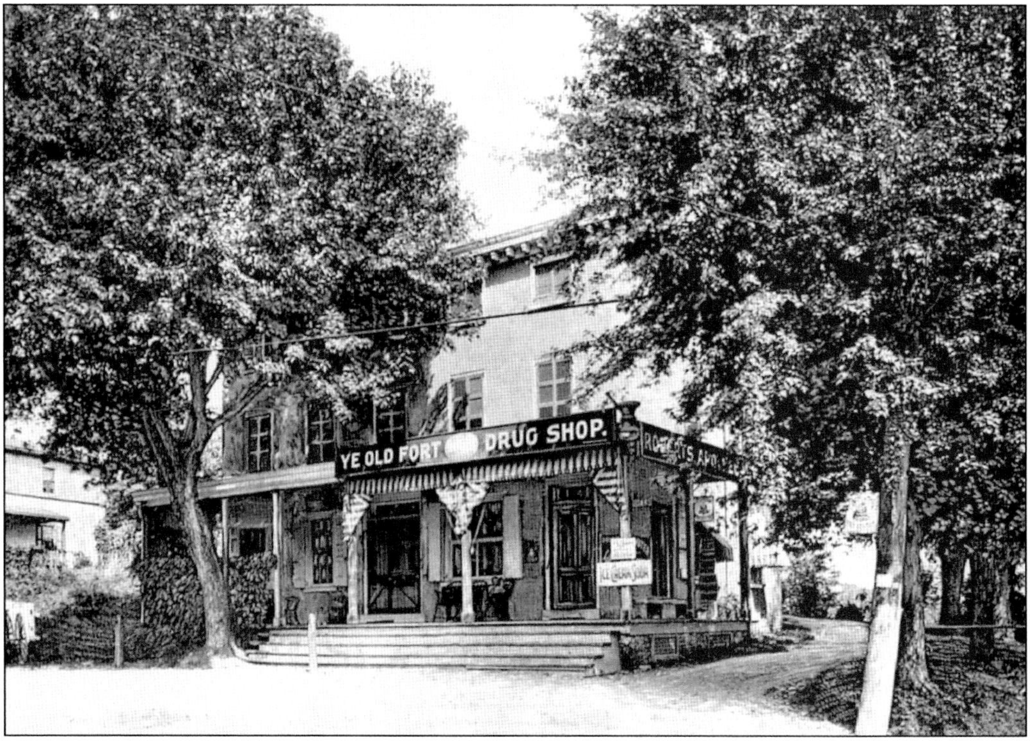

This undated postcard shows "Ye Old Fort Drug Shop," which operated on Bethlehem Pike in Fort Washington just north of the railroad. During the late 1800s, the building was the home of Abram H. Carn.

Three

HOUSES, ESTATES, AND ARCHITECTURE

Plymouth and Whitemarsh Townships have long been known for their historic houses and other buildings. Most of these, despite several spectacular exceptions, fall into the category of vernacular architecture—styles and building techniques that are common to an area, not designed by trained architects, and usually built of local materials. Historic buildings in the townships can reveal much about the habits, tastes, and economic standing of the people who constructed and used them at various periods.

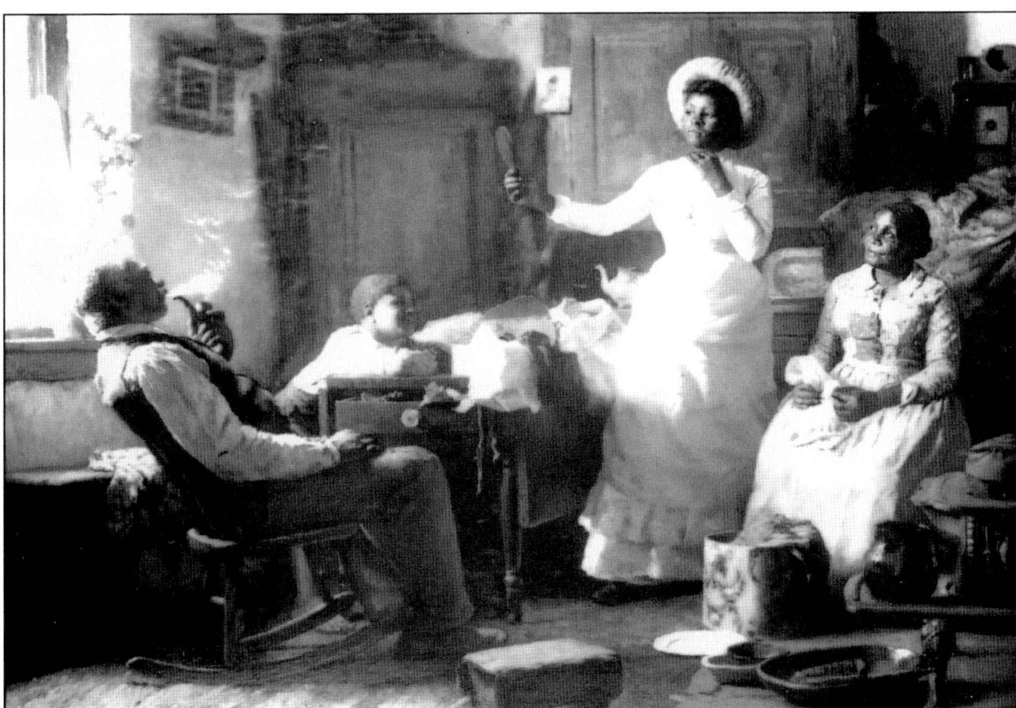

Their Pride (1888), Thomas Hovenden.

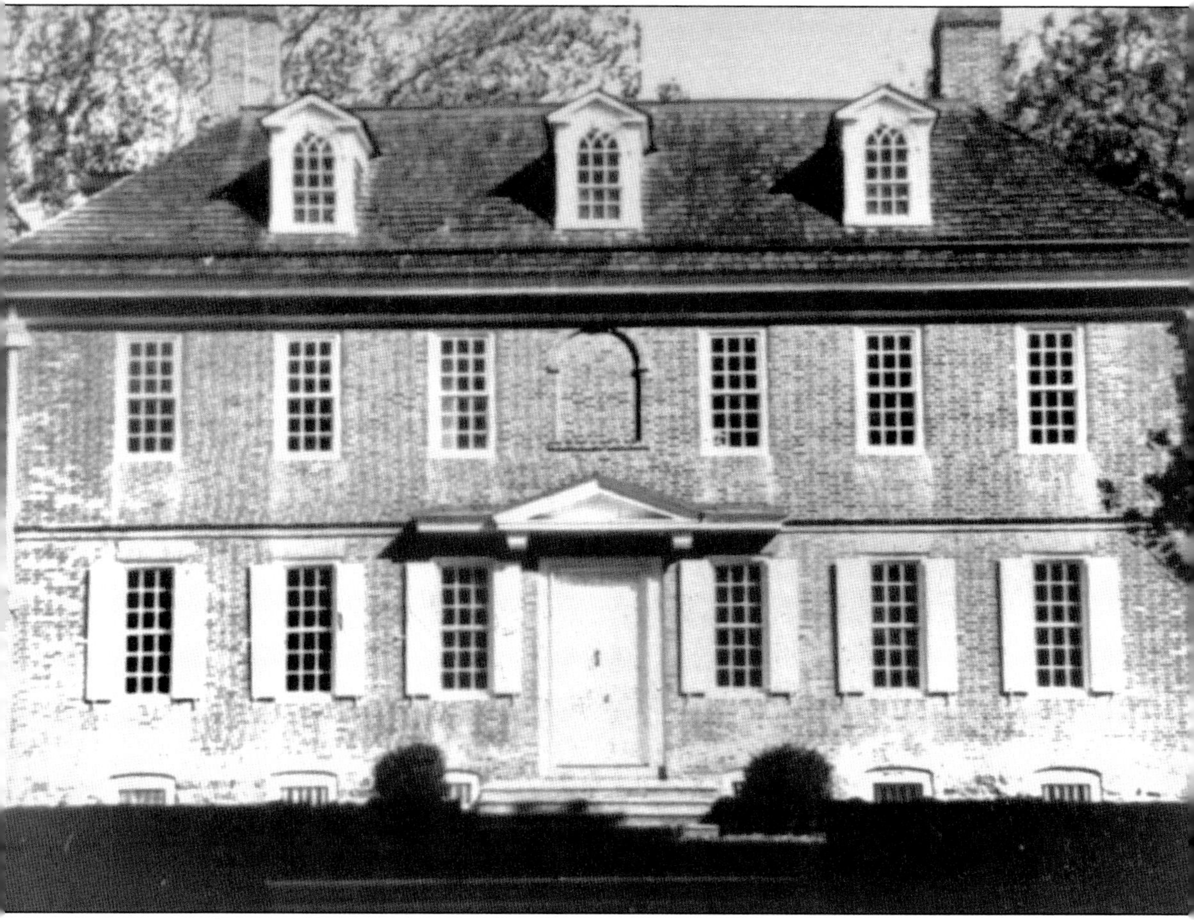

Hope Lodge, built between 1743 and 1748 by Samuel Morris, is considered one of the finest surviving Georgian-style houses. John Cochran, George Washington's surgeon general, used the house as a headquarters for a time during the American Revolution. Ownership of the estate passed through several families, including Henry Hope of Hope Diamond fame. In 1921, the estate was sold to Keasbey and Mattison, two industrialists who intended to demolish the structure in order to enlarge a nearby limestone quarry. To save the house from destruction, early preservationists William and Alice Degn purchased the property in 1922. After their deaths, ownership of the property—which is listed on the National Register of Historic Places—was transferred to the Commonwealth of Pennsylvania. (Courtesy of the Historical Society of Fort Washington.)

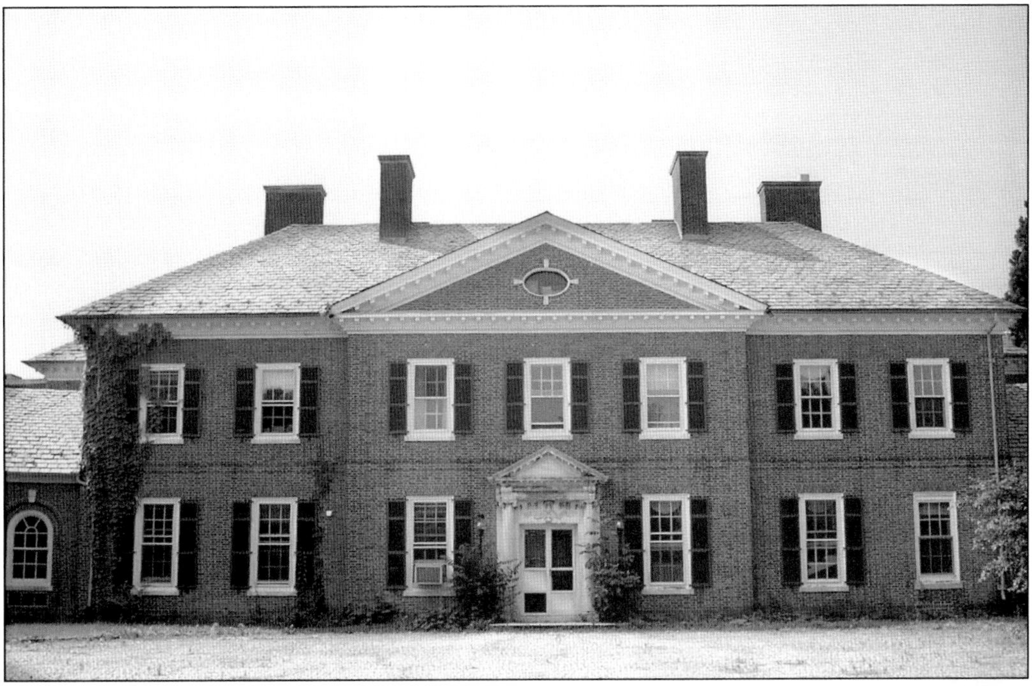

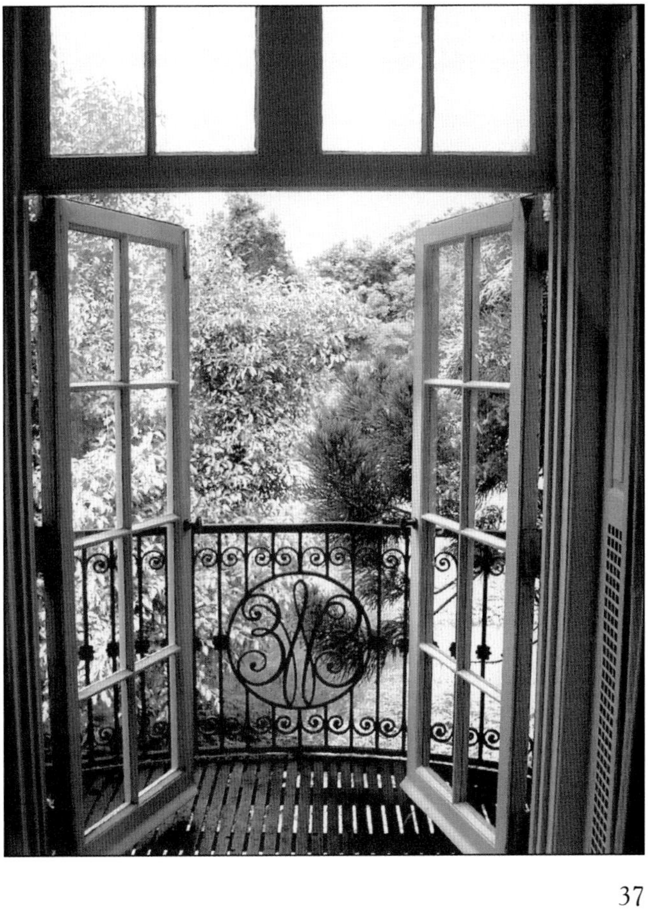

This estate on Thomas Road, designed by the famous Philadelphia architect Horace Trumbauer, was built in the 1930s for William McIntire Elkins. The brick Georgian Revival mansion features two curving side wings wrapping around a patterned cobblestone courtyard, as well as elaborate marble carvings and wood paneling. In the early 1950s, the estate was converted to house the Eugenia Memorial Hospital, later called the Psychiatric Institute of America and, still later, the Progressions Institute. The fate of this fabulous structure is uncertain, as plans are being made to build a retirement community in and around the site. (Courtesy of Gail C. Momjian.)

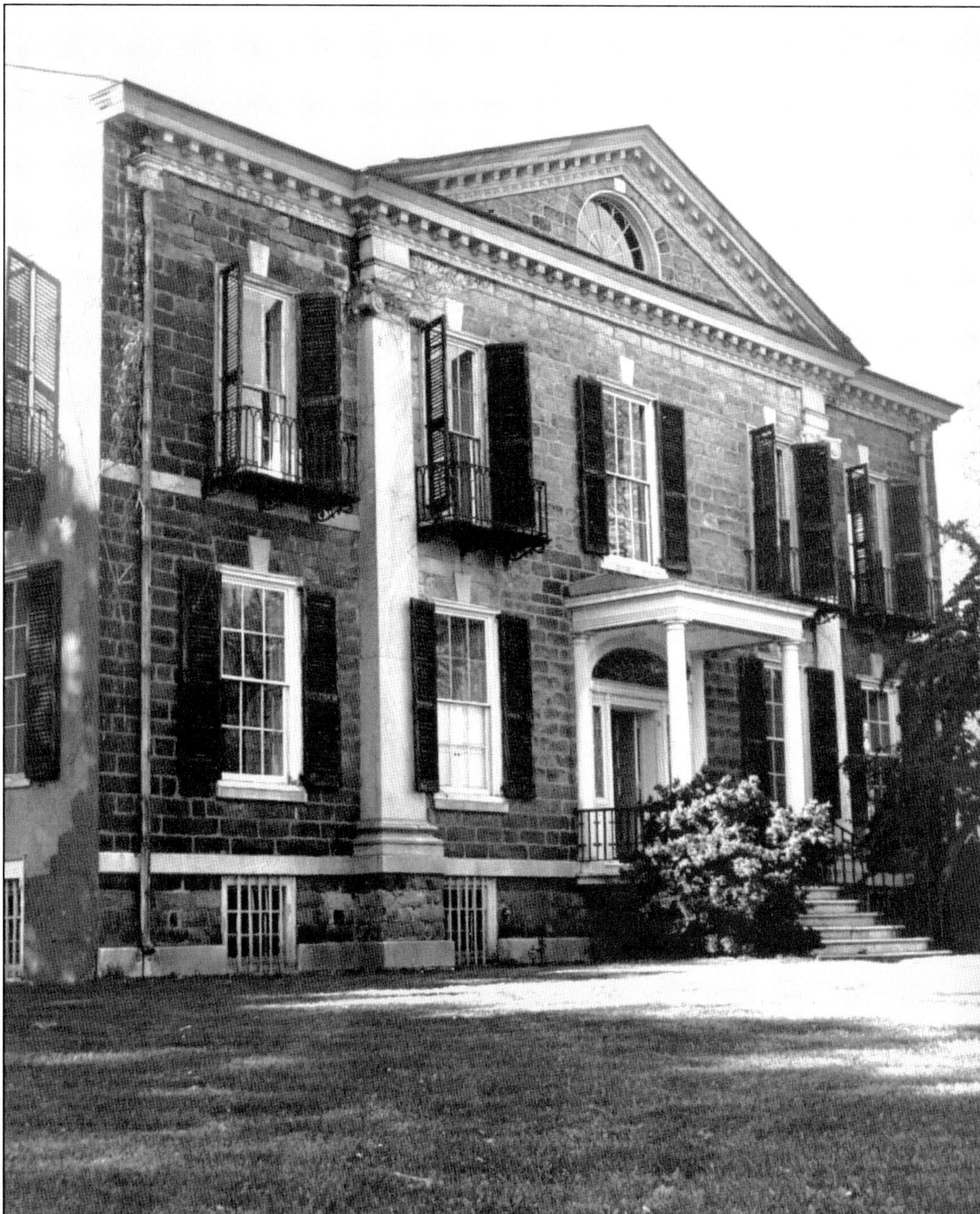

Anthony Morris, son of Samuel Morris, built the Highlands in 1796 on an estate of just over 300 acres in Whitemarsh Township. Morris entertained many prominent political figures in the house, including James Madison and Thomas Jefferson. In 1813, the estate was sold to George Sheaff, at which time it became known as a model working farm, utilizing the latest agricultural methods and theories. (Courtesy of the Highlands Mansion and Gardens.)

George Sheaff planted the formal gardens at the Highlands and added the crenelated walls and Gothic garden houses at each end. By the time Caroline Sinkler purchased the property in 1917, the gardens had suffered from years of neglect. With the assistance of well-known Philadelphia architect Wilson Eyre, Sinkler brought the Highlands back to their former elegance. She added many statues throughout the gardens, including the busts of Shakespeare and Plato shown here. Caroline Sinkler's niece Mary Wickham Bond spent many summer days in the Highland gardens, writing her novels and short stories. (Courtesy of the Highlands Mansion and Gardens.)

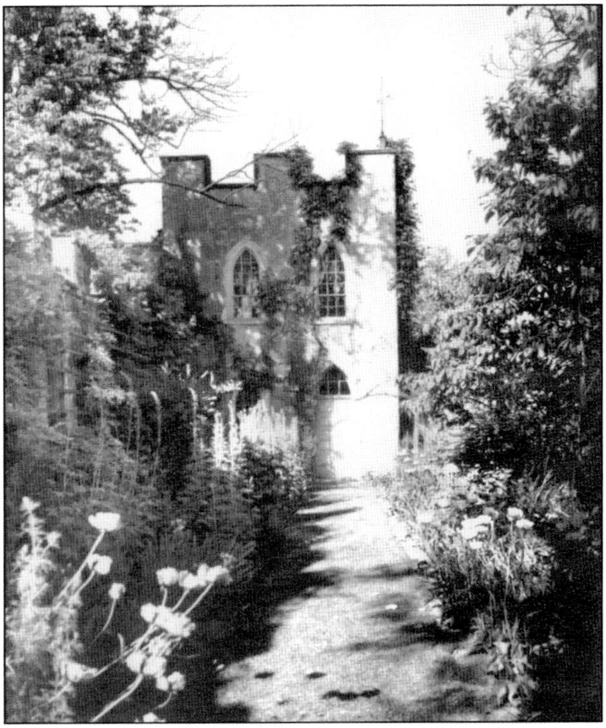

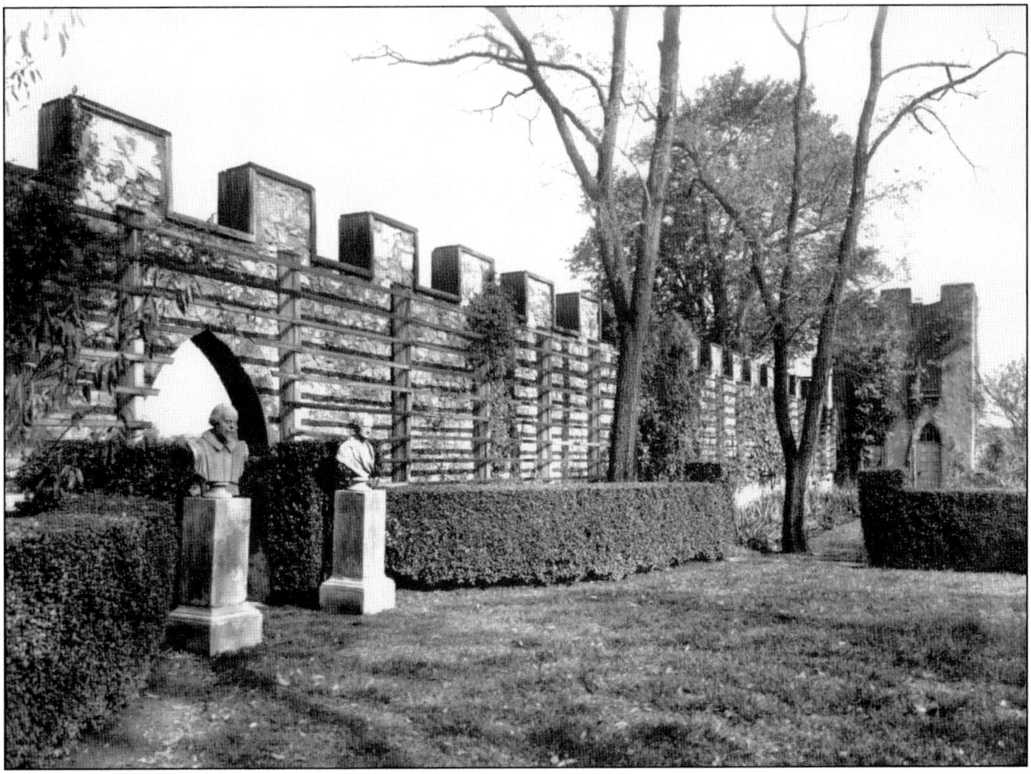

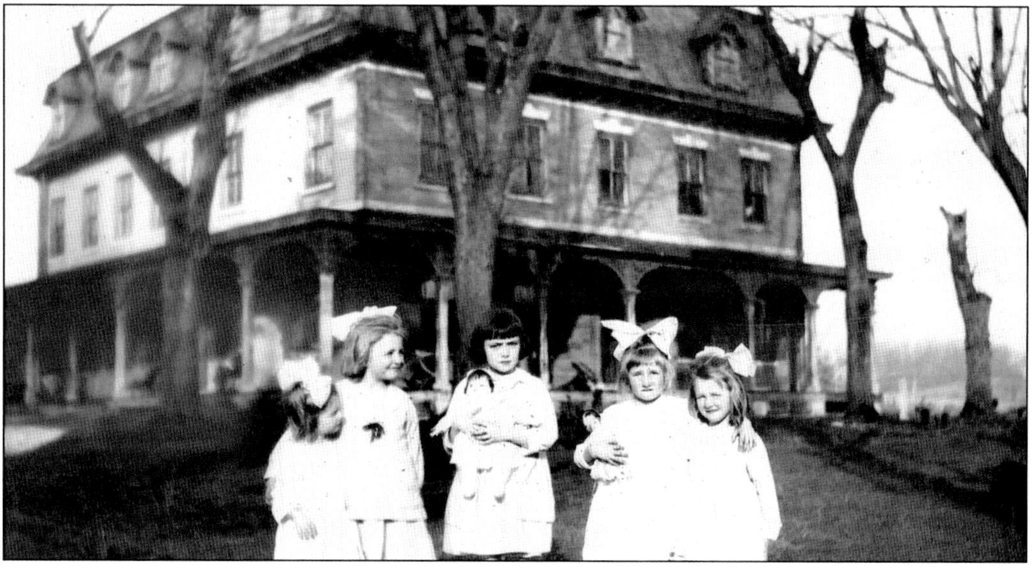

Daniel and Henry Hitner constructed the eight-bedroom Marble Hall Mansion in the 1840s by adding on to a small farmhouse originally owned by their father, Daniel Hitner Sr. Posing in front of Marble Hall in 1921 are, from left to right, Rebecca Boice, Flora Cooke, Verna Hiltner, Jennie Boice, and Myrtle Cook. They could not know then that the huge house would one day be torn down and the land used for a playground at Miles Park.

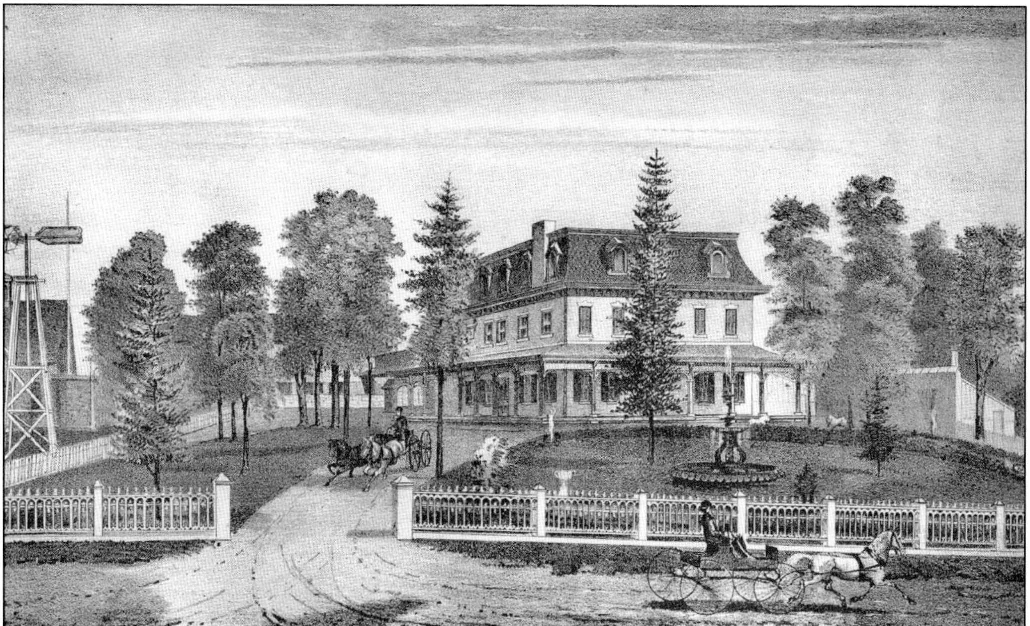

The Henry Hitner House, also known as the Marble Hall Mansion, is shown in the G.M. Hopkins *Atlas of Philadelphia and Its Environs* (1877).

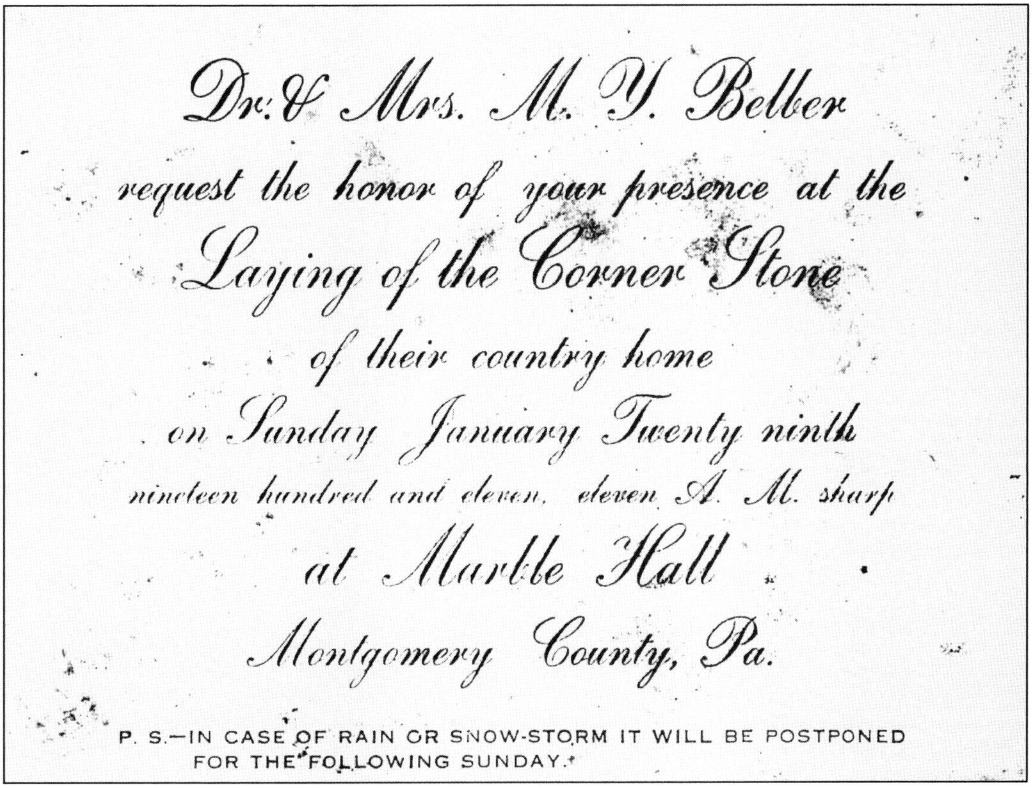

Dr. & Mrs. M. Y. Belber
request the honor of your presence at the
Laying of the Corner Stone
of their country home
on Sunday January Twenty ninth
nineteen hundred and eleven, eleven A. M. sharp
at Marble Hall
Montgomery County, Pa.

P. S.—IN CASE OF RAIN OR SNOW-STORM IT WILL BE POSTPONED
FOR THE FOLLOWING SUNDAY.

The Belbers' country house stood near the southeast corner of Joshua Road and Germantown Pike across from Miles Park. It was demolished in the 1990s for a small housing development. This invitation from 1911 was found under the dated cornerstone.

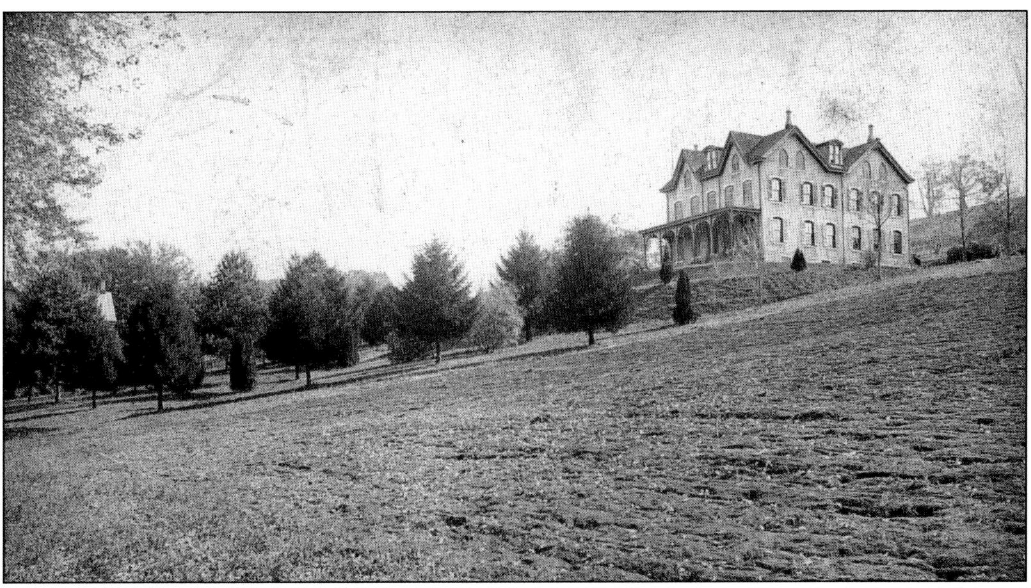

The home of local mill owner Will Ely represents a rural version of the late Gothic Revival style. Built *c.* 1900 on Barren Hill Road in Spring Mill, Whitemarsh Township, the structure features mansard dormers and a multigabled roof.

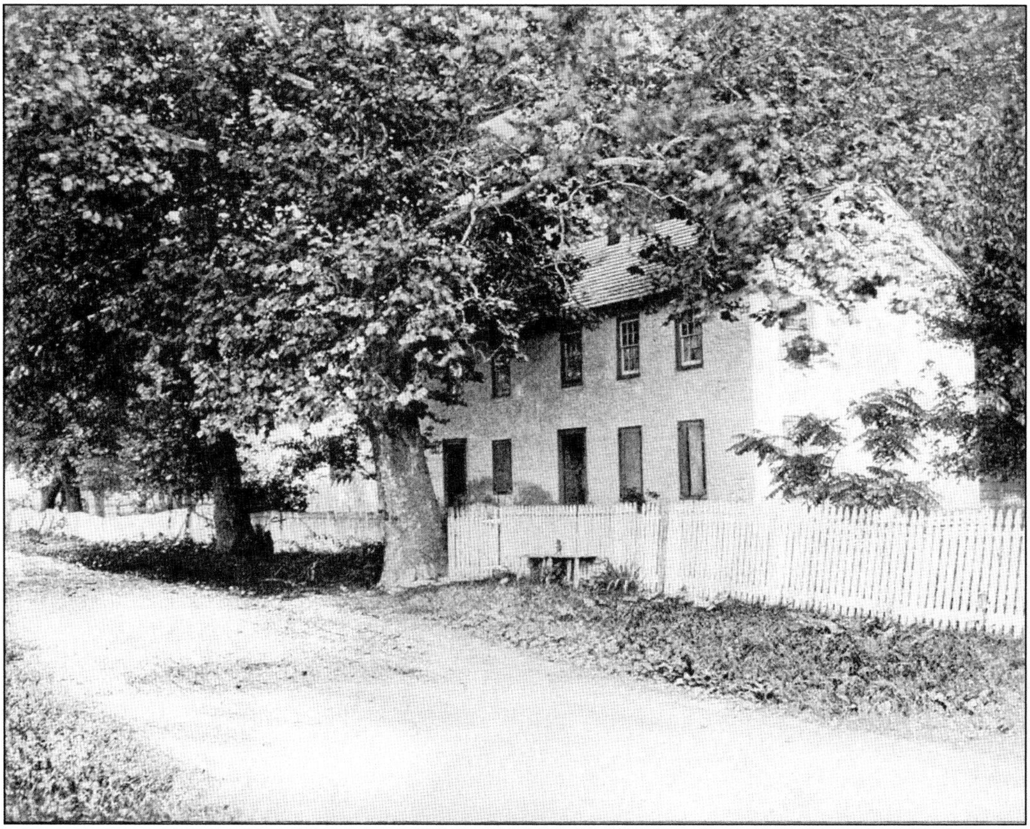

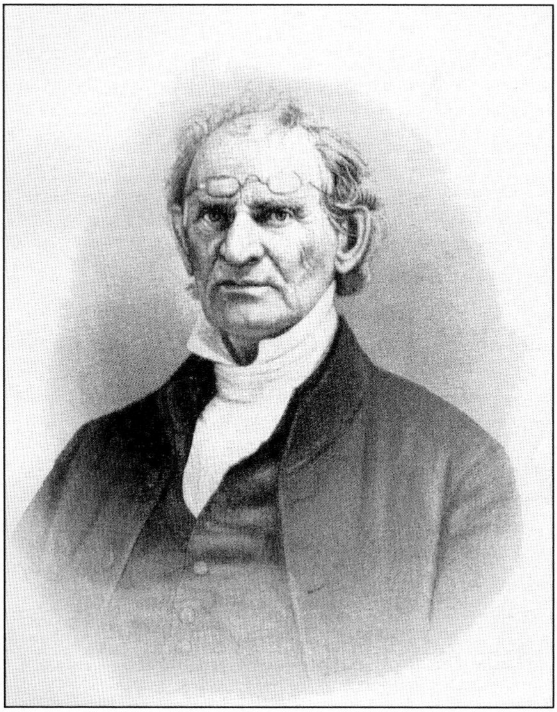

Listed on the National Register of Historic Places, the Alan Corson House, on Butler Pike in Cold Point, featured Corson's famed nursery of unusual trees and shrubs. For a time, Corson ran a private boarding school here, his fine teaching reputation drawing pupils from quite a distance. Corson himself was a celebrated scholar, mastering subjects such as botany, astronomy, geology, entomology, and mineralogy.

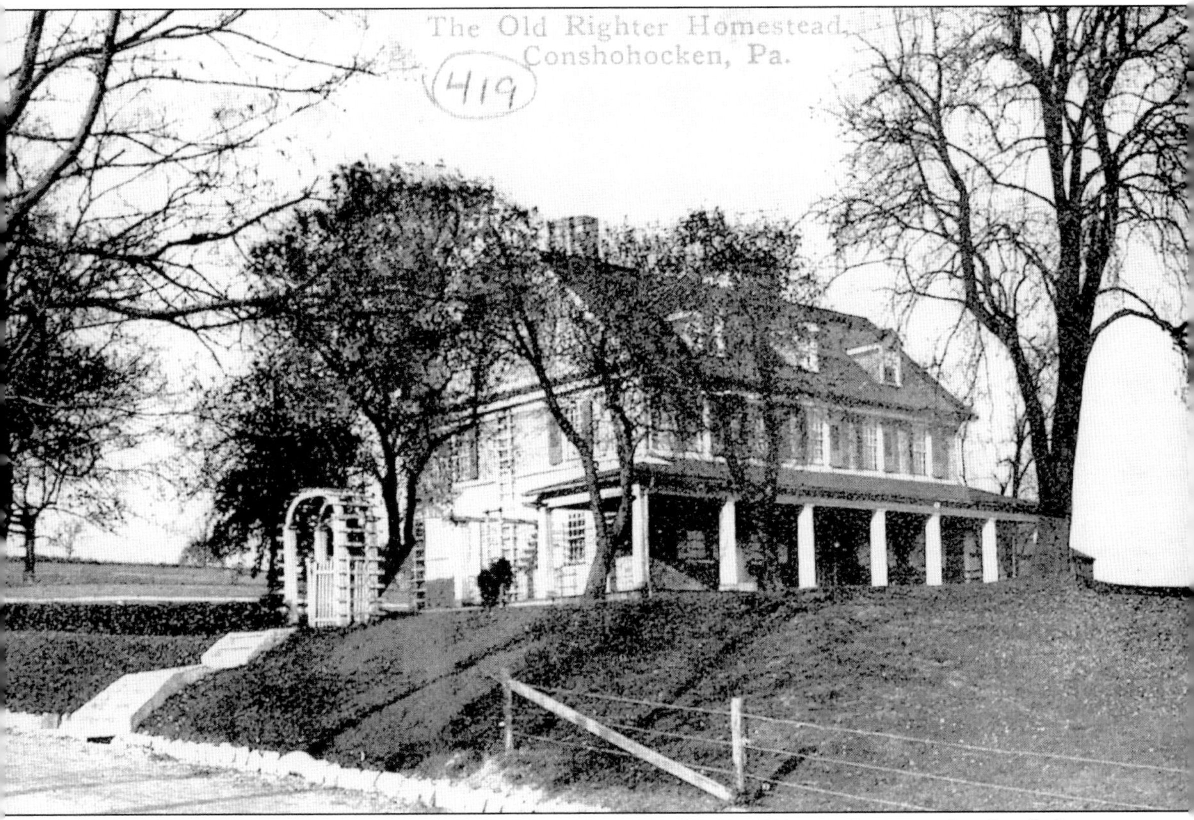

This mansion, originally known as Mount Joy, was built in 1738 on the west bank of the Schuylkill River by Anthony Morris III for his son John. The property was purchased in 1786 by Peter Legaux, who had come from France to settle in America. Legaux laid out gardens and terraces, established a limekiln, and planted a vineyard with a variety of grapes from France. Impressed with Legaux's success, George Washington visited Mount Joy on July 22, 1787. Local legend holds that Mount Joy was actively linked to the Underground Railroad, with hidden spaces on the third floor, which might have been used to hide fugitive slaves.

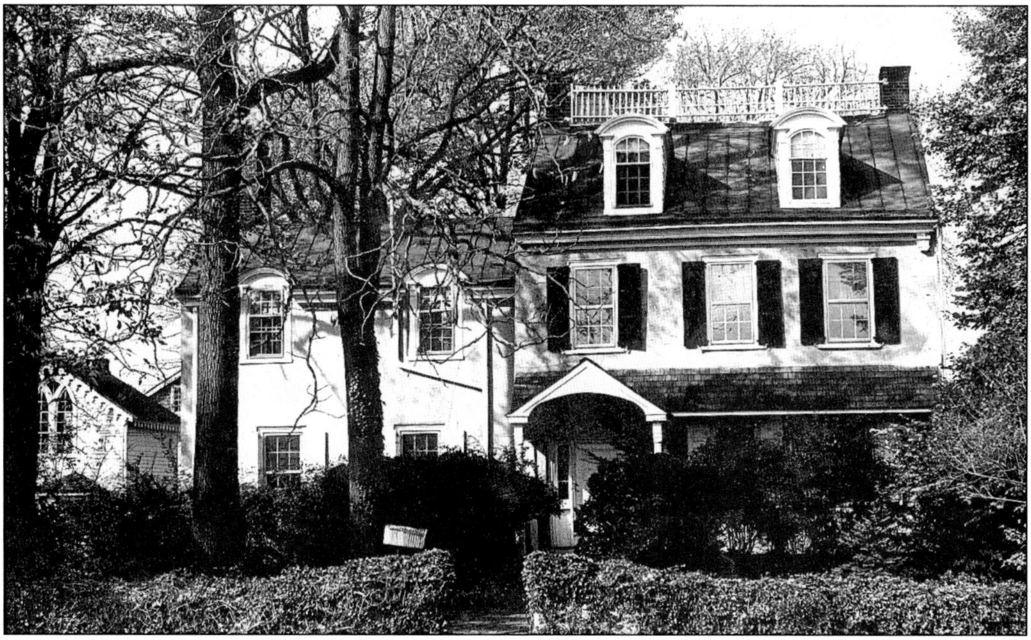

The Spring Mill Road estate of Maple Hill was built in 1833 by Dr. Hiram Corson for his new bride, Ann Foulke, and named for the many maple trees around the lawn. Many of the original outbuildings remain at Maple Hill, including the doctor's office and cookhouse. A barn with a cupola was constructed in 1877, replacing an earlier barn, and a schoolhouse was built at a later date.

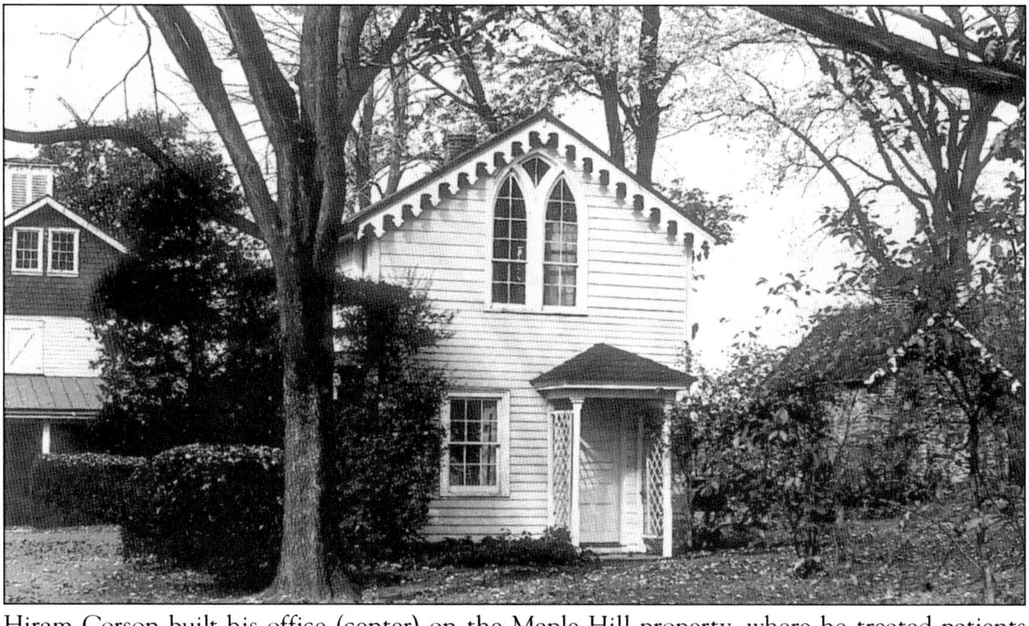

Hiram Corson built his office (center) on the Maple Hill property, where he treated patients for 68 years until his death in 1895 at the age of 91. Corson was one of the founding members of the Plymouth Meeting Abolition Society. Charles Corson, Hiram's son, wrote in his diary on November 9, 1859, "Eleven slaves kept overnight. Three in the second floor of the doctor's office and eight in the hay mow."

Hiram Corson was the first secretary of the Montgomery County Medical Society, contributed literature to the advancement of his profession, and waged a long and successful battle for the recognition of women physicians. In 1883, the Women's Medical College of Pennsylvania honored Corson for his work on behalf of female doctors. (Courtesy of the Nancy I. Corson Foundation.)

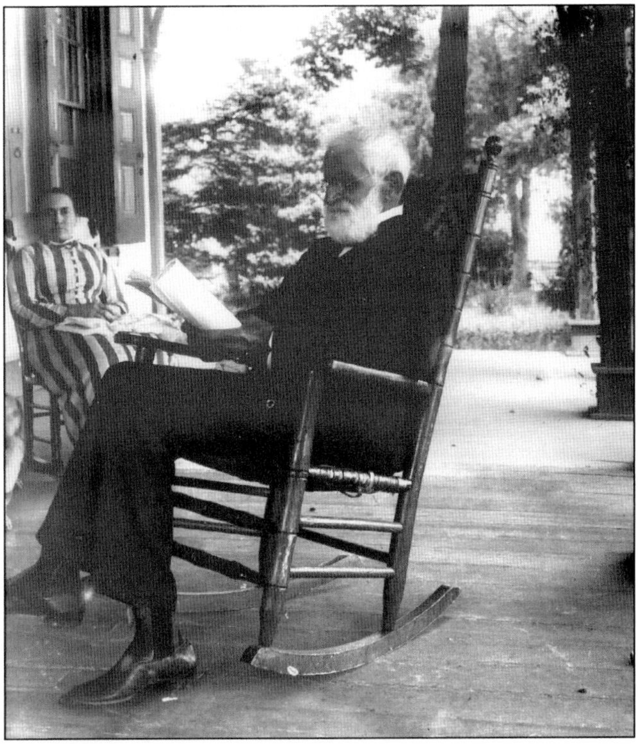

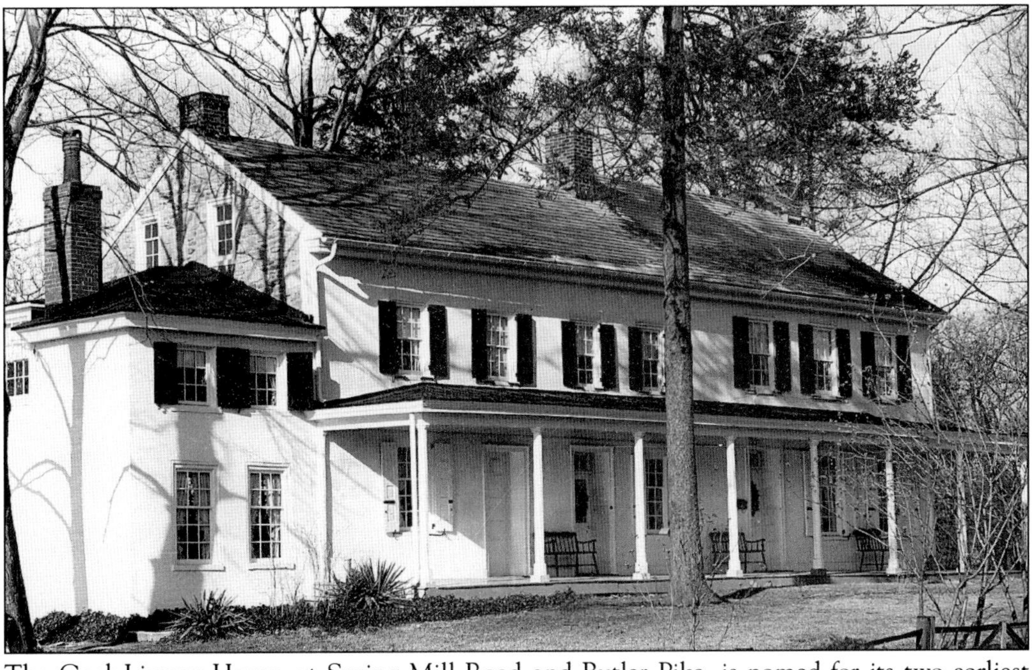

The Cook-Livezey House, at Spring Mill Road and Butler Pike, is named for its two earliest owners, Nathan Cook and Samuel Livezey. Cook built the first part of the house in 1788, and Livezey greatly expanded it *c.* 1820. Part of George Washington's army stayed in the area before the historic encampment at Valley Forge, and early records indicate that some officers were housed here.

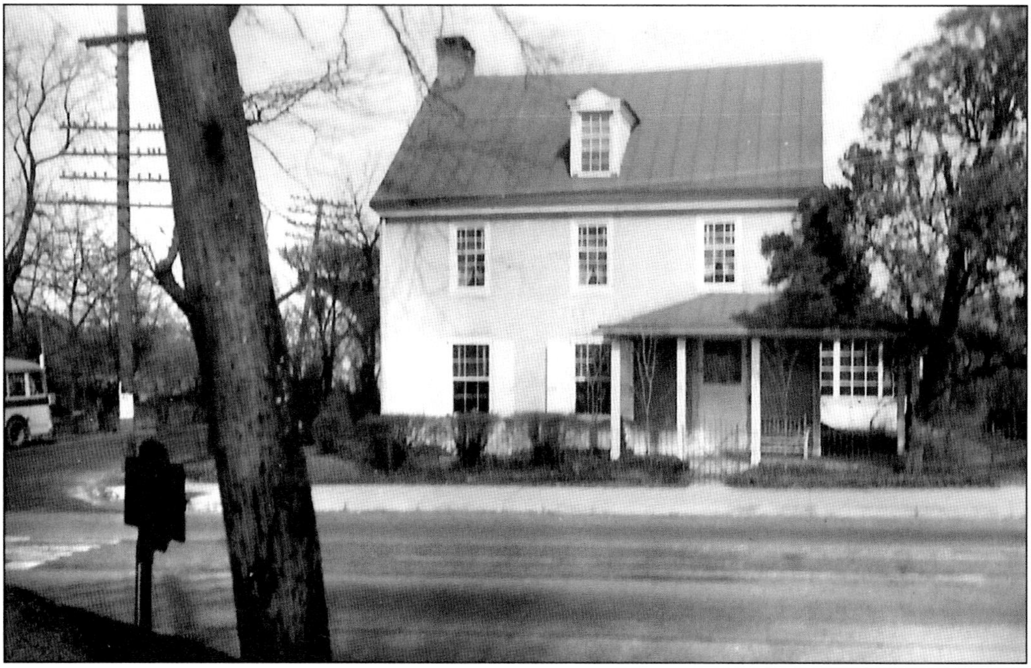

The Hovenden House, at 1 East Germantown Pike, is named for its most notable resident, Thomas Hovenden, a famous 19th-century artist. Hovenden used the interior of the house as a setting for many of his paintings of everyday life. The Corson-Maulsby family has owned the Hovenden House since 1767, when it was built. In the mid-1800s, the property was home to Quaker abolitionist and industrialist George Corson.

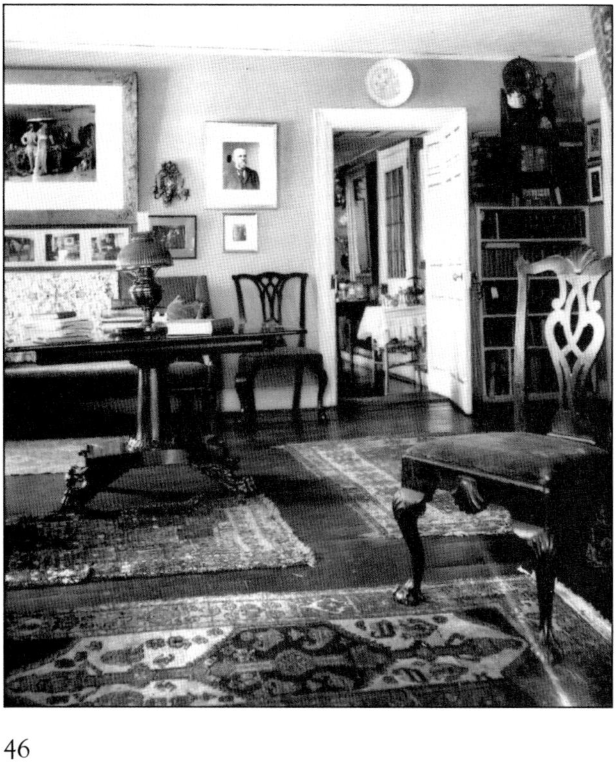

This c. 1890 photograph of the interior of the Hovenden House shows furnishings handed down through the Corson family. On the far wall hangs a photogravure copy of Thomas Hovenden's 1880 painting *In Hoc Signo Vinces* ("in this sign ye shall conquer"), the original now owned by the Detroit Institute of Arts. (Courtesy of the Nancy I. Corson Foundation.)

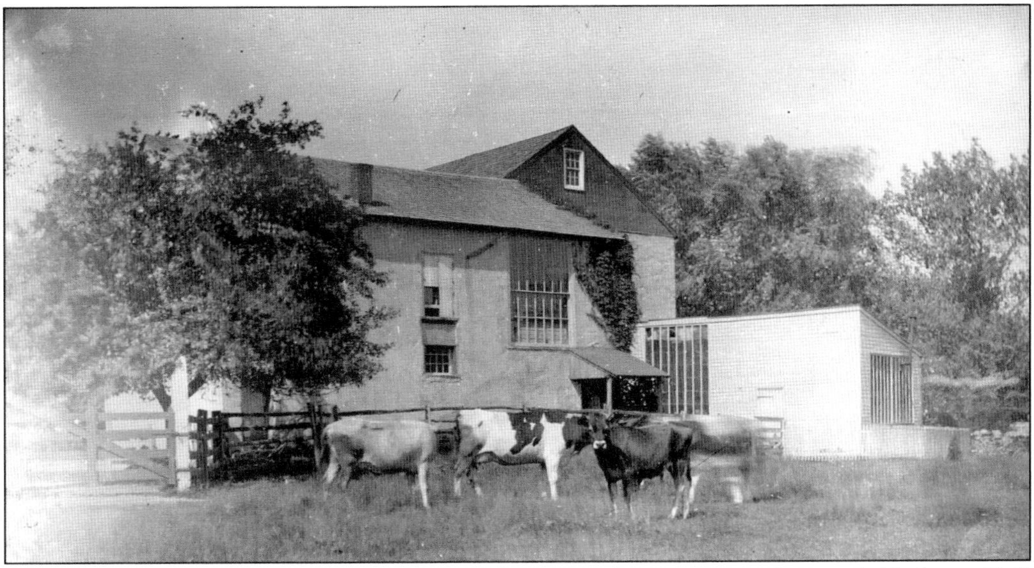

In 1856, George Corson enclosed the carriage house on the property and created Abolition Hall by adding a large second-floor room for use by local abolitionists. Many antislavery meetings took place in Abolition Hall prior to the Civil War, featuring nationally known abolitionist speakers such as Frederick Douglas, Stephen Foster, and Lucretia Mott. From 1881 to 1895, the hall was used as a studio by artists Thomas and Helen Corson Hovenden.

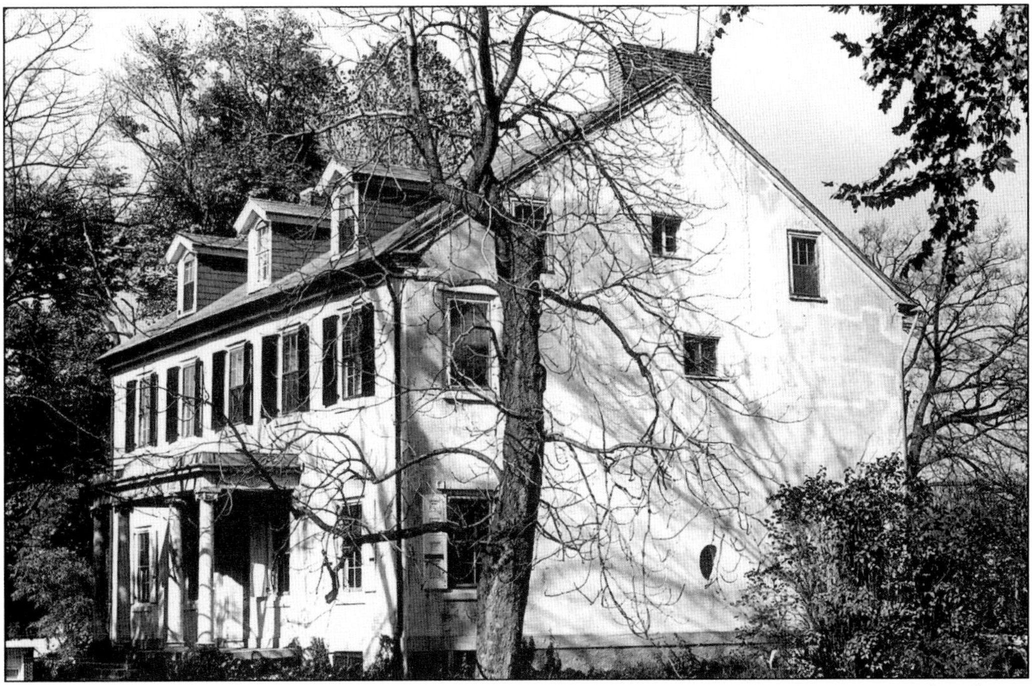

Linden Grove (now known as Bellfield), at Spring Mill Road and Ridge Pike, conveys the classic elegance of proportion and design typical of the Greek Revival style. Peter Dager, owner of the local marble quarry, constructed the house between 1829 and 1832. Marble was used liberally throughout, including the ionic columns at the front entrance, the window lintels and sills, the foundation border and steps, and numerous interior fireplaces.

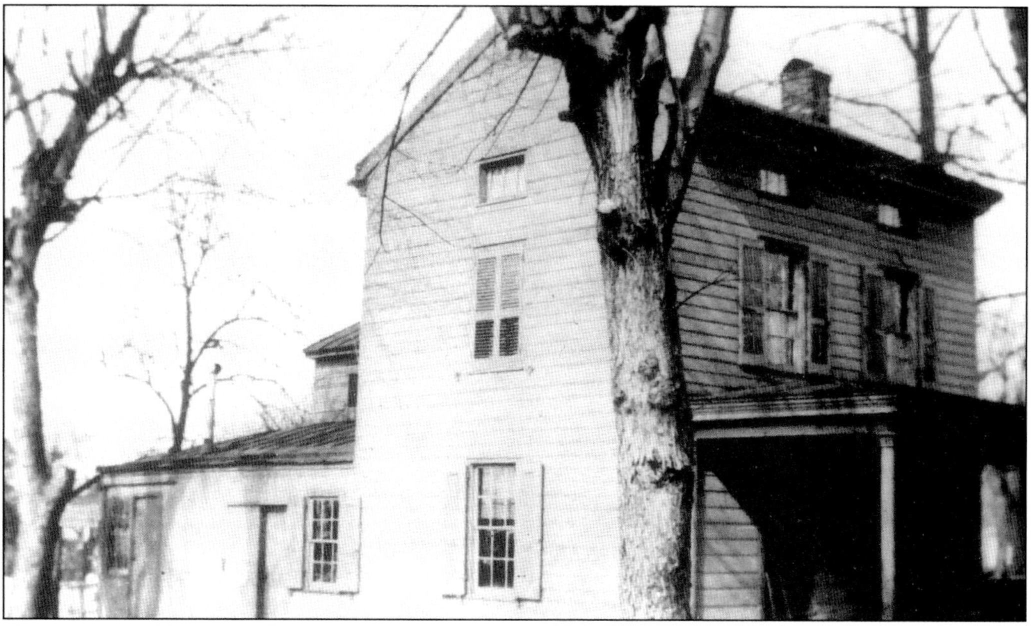

The village of Plymouth Meeting is made up of many small, vernacular-style early-19th-century buildings such as the Mary Baynes House, at 8 East Germantown Pike. Typically, these dwellings were were one room deep and two and a half stories high, with small half windows on the upper floor. Like many area residences, the Mary Baynes House, shown here in 1918, was expanded with a frame addition to the rear.

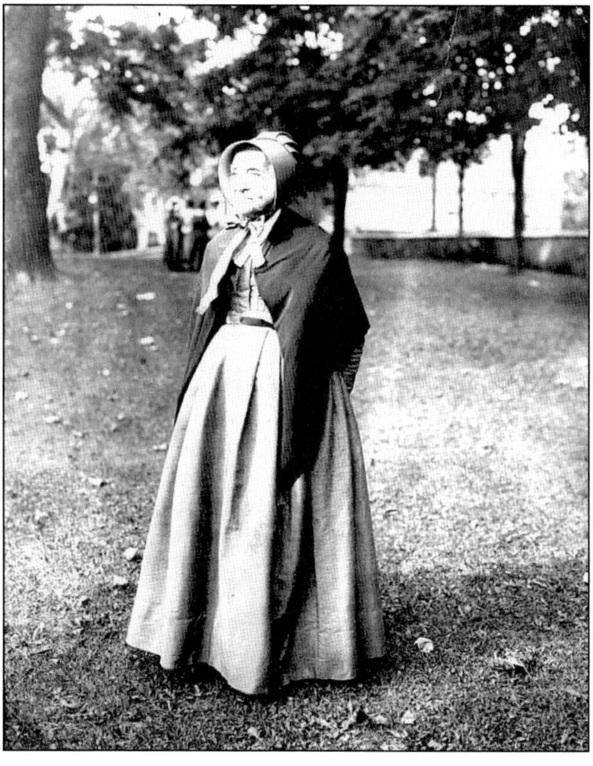

An earnest Quaker, Mary Baynes (1822–1921) lived to be 99 and wore the traditional Quaker garb all her life. She had been known to shovel a path through the snow from her house to the Plymouth Friends Meeting House.

At the rear of the Mary Baynes House stood a stable and carriage house, typical of the 19th century, with a boardwalk leading from the main house. In the automobile age, many such structures were converted into garages.

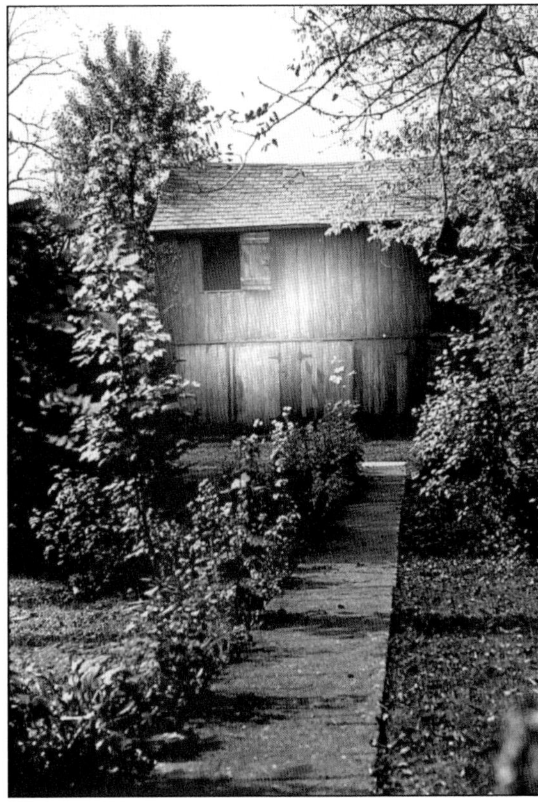

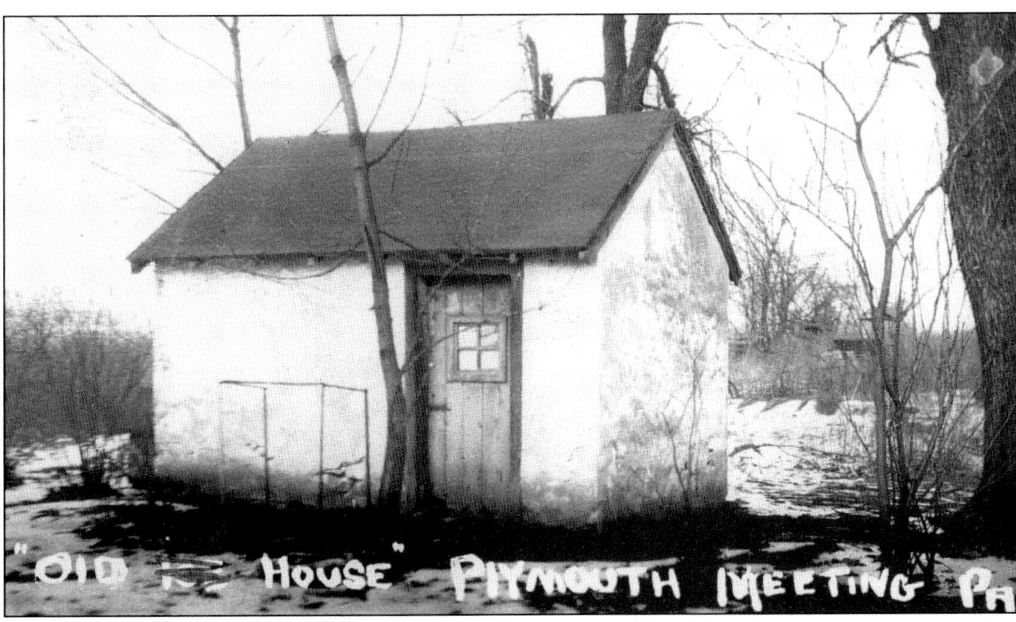

The smokehouse was an important outbuilding in the 1800s. Usually located near a kitchen entrance, the smokehouse was used to cure meats and store nonperishable items and sometimes served as an alternate place for cooking during the heat of the summer.

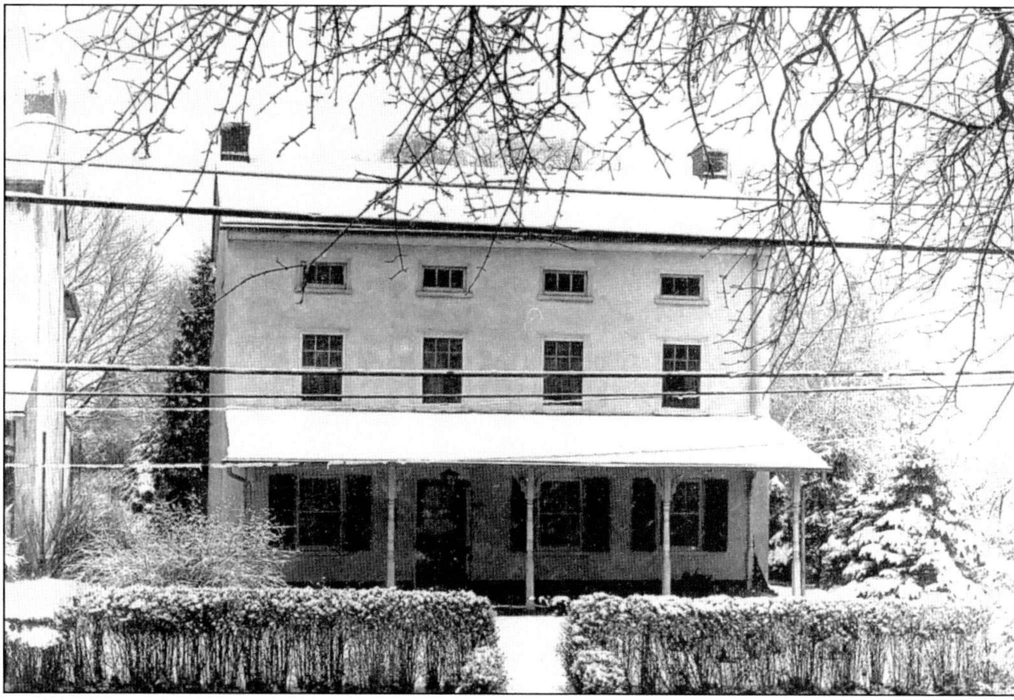

Archbishop Thomas Kennedy was born on March 23, 1858, in this house at 113 West Germantown Pike, which was the home of his parents, Patrick and Maria Burns Kennedy. Kennedy was ordained a priest in 1887 and was consecrated the titular bishop of Adrianople in 1907. He died in Italy on August 28, 1917. In 1966, St. Matthew's High School in Conshohocken, where Kennedy was once the principal, changed its name to the Archbishop Kennedy High School.

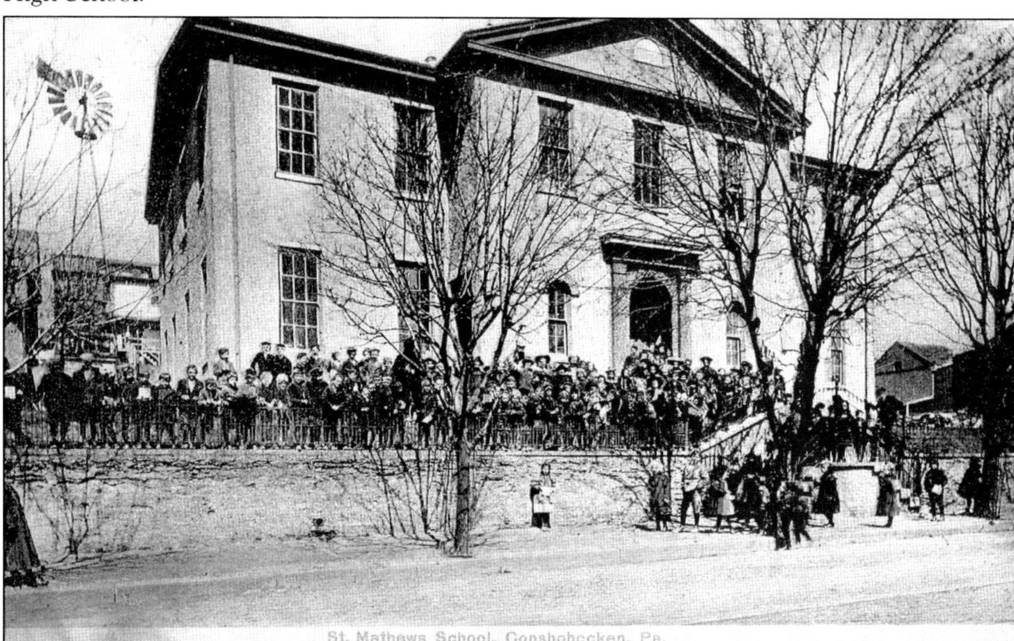

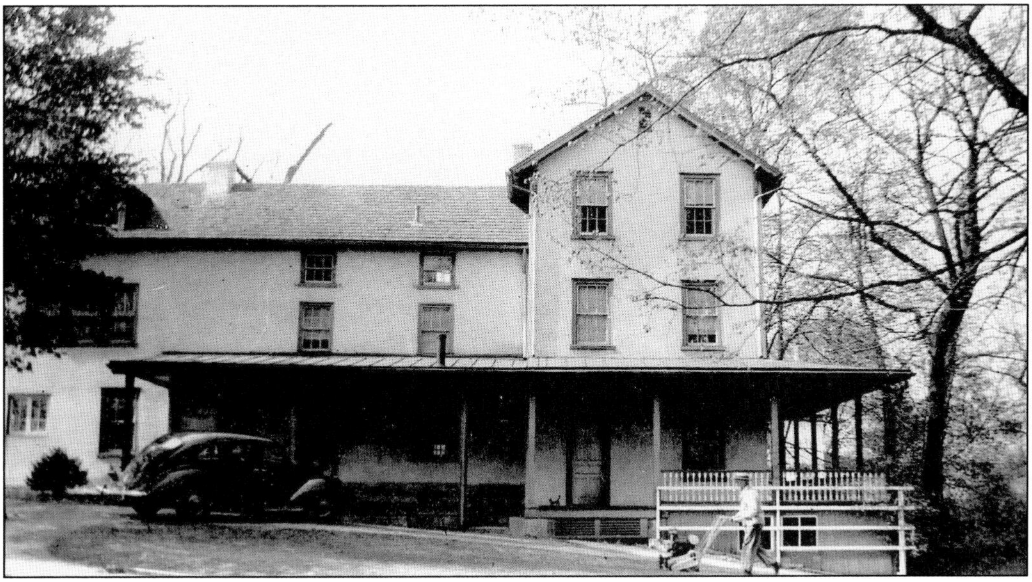

The Albertson House was originally built *c.* 1810 as a tenant farmhouse on the Dickinson Farmstead on Sierra Road in Plymouth Township. It was expanded in 1900 to fit a growing family. The large wraparound porch and window detailing were late-Victorian additions. The Albertson family owned the Dickinson Farmstead from Jacob Albertson's purchase of it in 1800 until the 1940 death of Alice Albertson Price and the subsequent 1941 sale of the property.

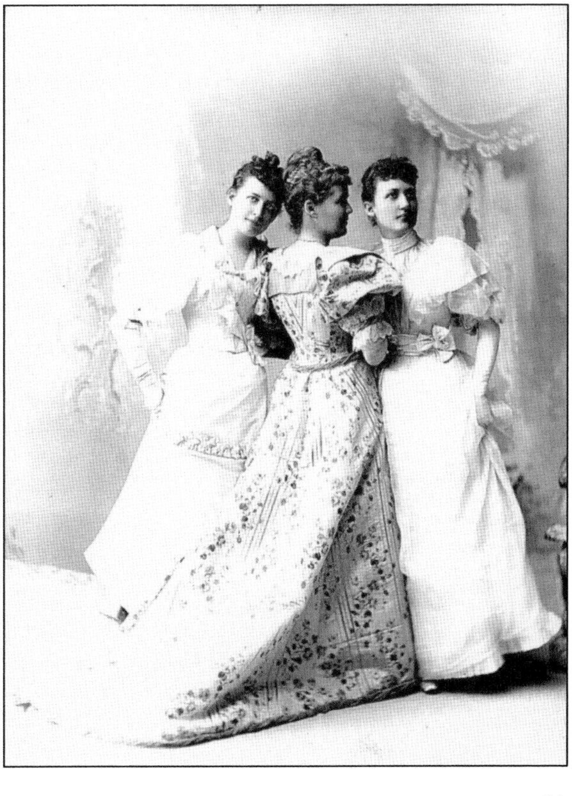

The Albertson girls are dressed in their finest in April 1894. The woman on the right is Alice Albertson, who later married Charles Coale Price.

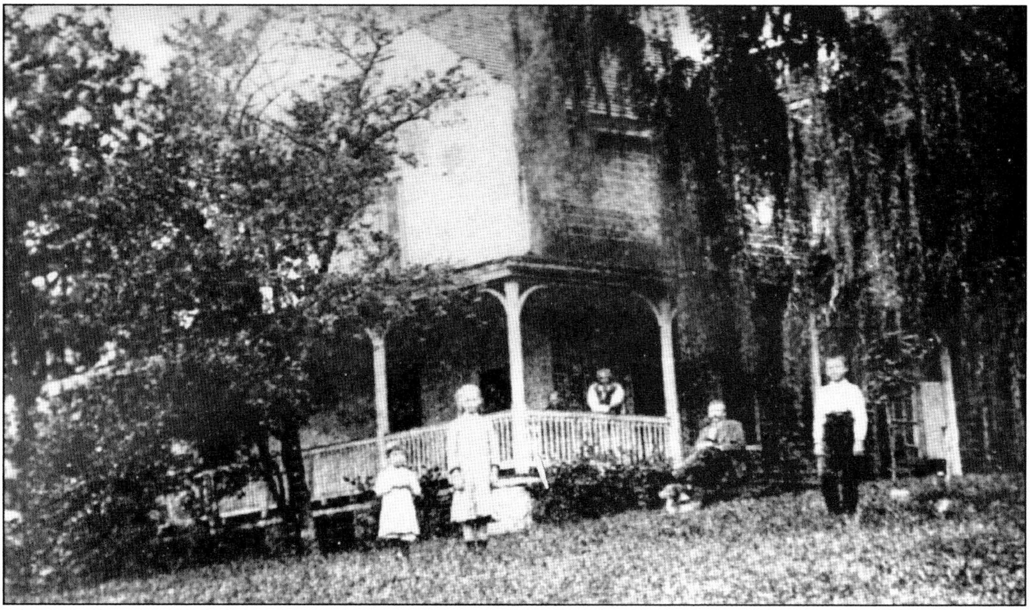

The Dickinson House, the main residence on the Dickinson Farmstead, was constructed c. 1754 for the marriage of Joseph Dickinson and Hannah Wright, making it one of the oldest surviving houses in Plymouth Meeting. In the late 1960s, the property faced destruction for the construction of the Blue Route. Through the efforts of the Plymouth Meeting Historical Society, the highway was rerouted and the house, as well as the historic village of Plymouth Meeting, were saved.

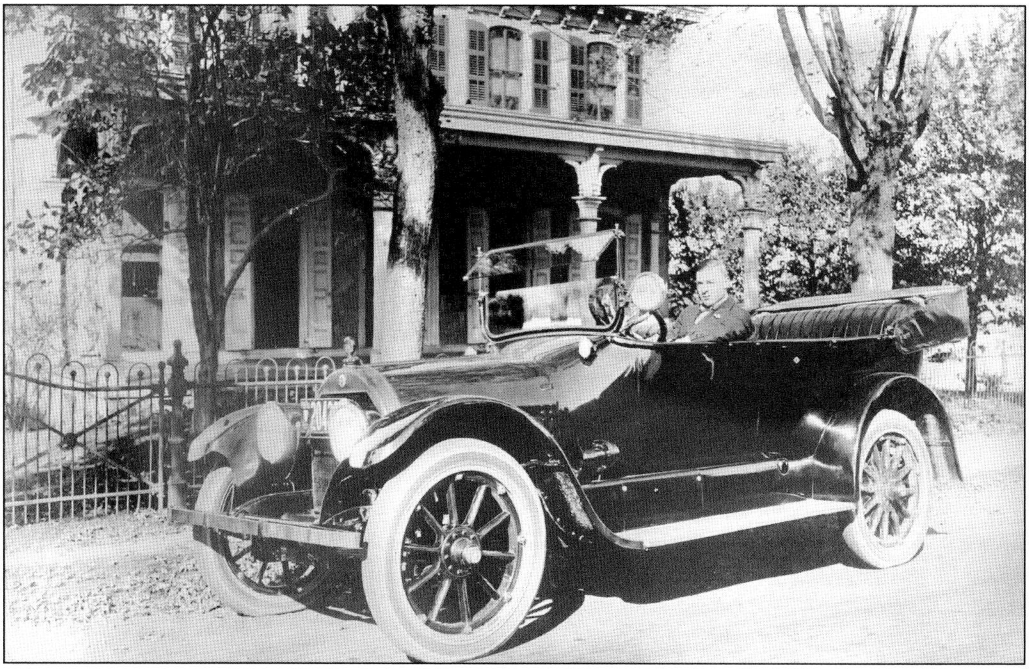

George Ragine poses proudly with his new 1917 Cadillac outside his house, which is now the Lownes Funeral Home, on Germantown Pike in Lafayette Hill. (Courtesy of the Lownes Family Funeral Home.)

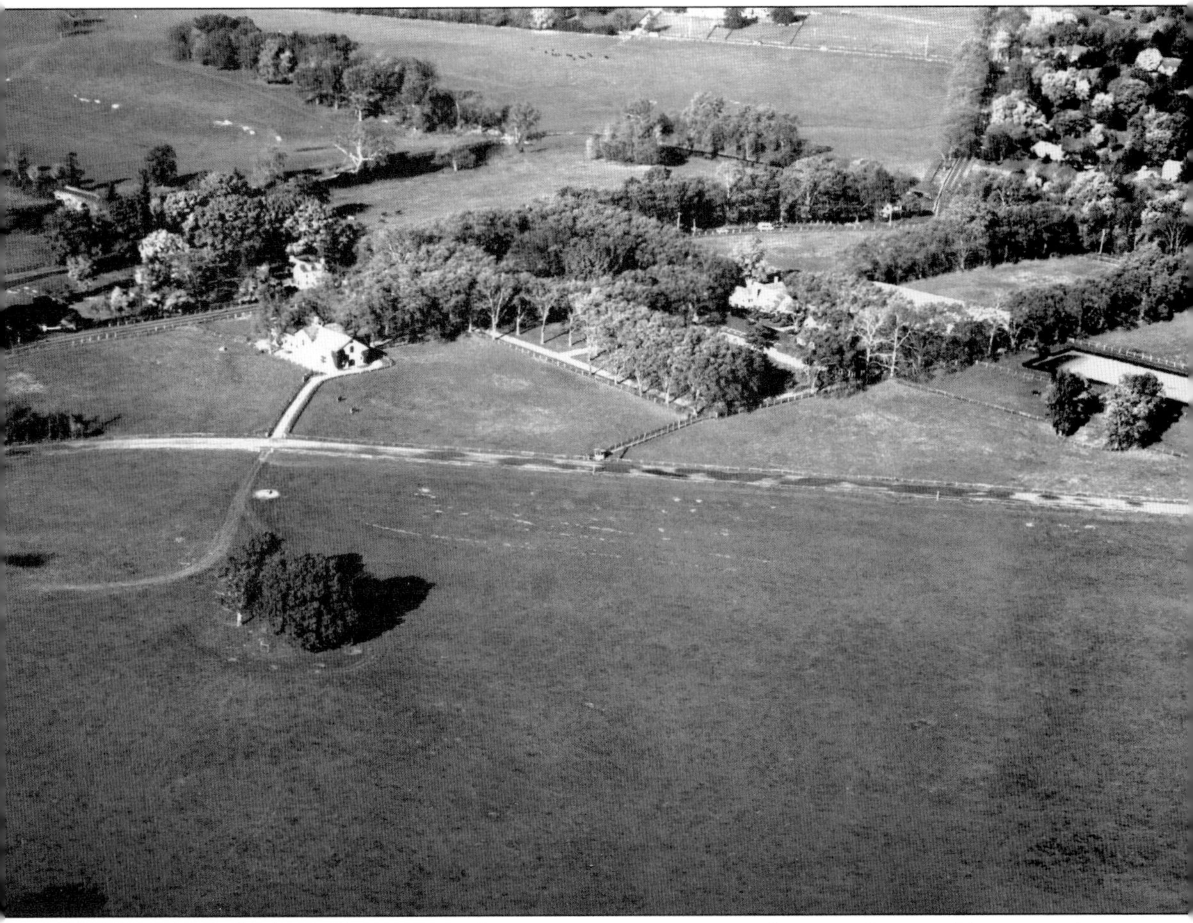

The 500-acre Erdenheim Farms estate forms a scenic entrance to the townships and is a central feature in the nearly 3,000 acres of contiguous open space running from upper Chestnut Hill through Fort Washington State Park. The first owner was Johann Georg Hocker, a German immigrant who settled there in 1751 and named his new home Erdenheim, meaning "earthly home." In the early 1860s, the farm was owned by Aristides Welch, whose finely bred racehorses were renowned for first-place showings at the Kentucky Derby, Ascot in England, and many other courses. The racetrack, which is still in use today, can be seen at the center of the photograph; at the top, the Wissahickon Creek winds through the farm. (Courtesy of Mr. and Mrs. F. Eugene Dixon Jr.)

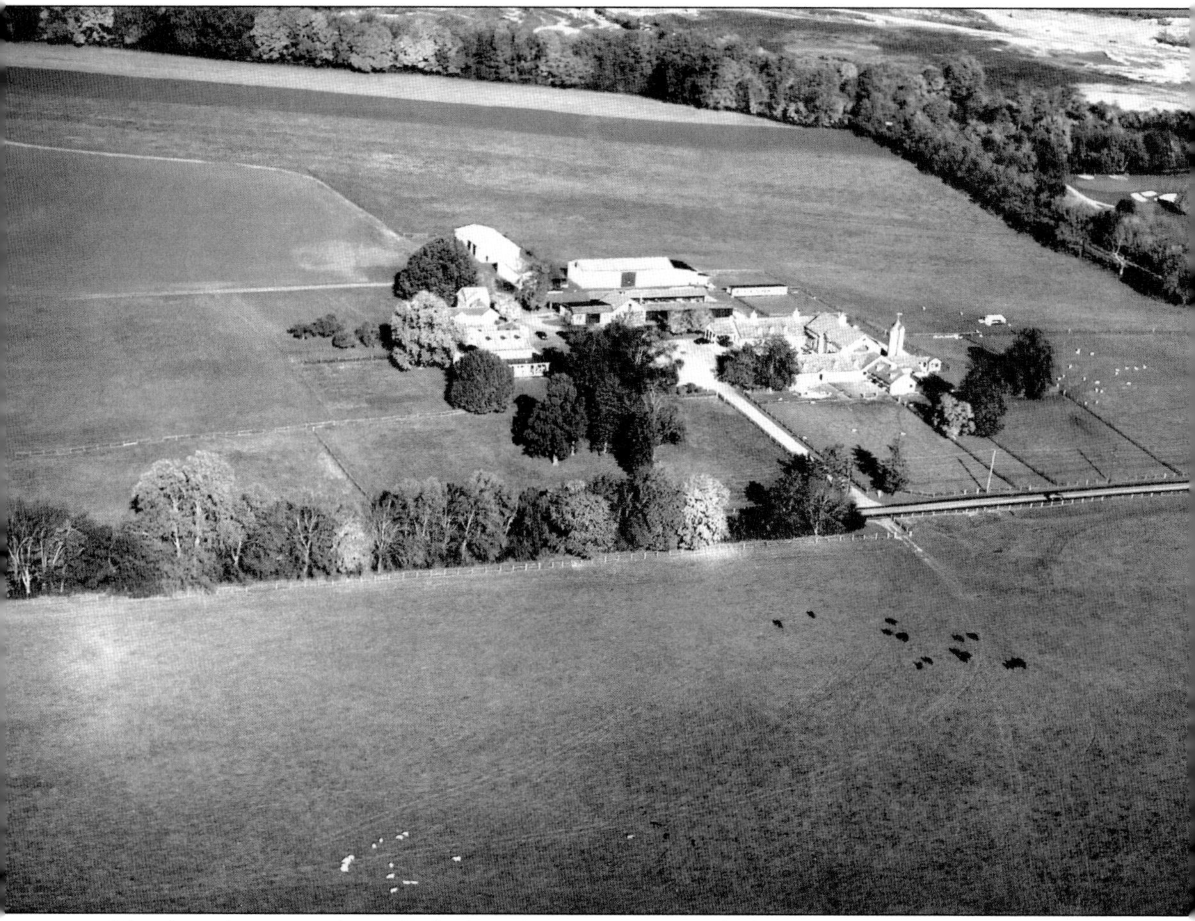

The sheep barn complex at Erdenheim Farms is composed of numerous slate-roofed outbuildings with fancy cupolas. The sheep graze on the site of an old burial ground, used as early as 1722 and formally established in 1746 by Henry Bartleson, Peter Knight, and James Stroud. No house of worship was built—which was the original intent—probably because several nearby churches were established at about the same time. (Courtesy of Mr. and Mrs. F. Eugene Dixon Jr.)

Four

SCHOOLS AND HOUSES OF WORSHIP

The earliest schools in the townships were private or sponsored by religious institutions. When public schools were established in the mid-1800s, they had to be distributed widely in order to be within walking distance for their pupils. The advent of the school bus in the early 20th century allowed the townships to close the small one-room schoolhouses and to create larger consolidated schools. A variety of religious denominations provided spiritual comfort as well as many social activities for members.

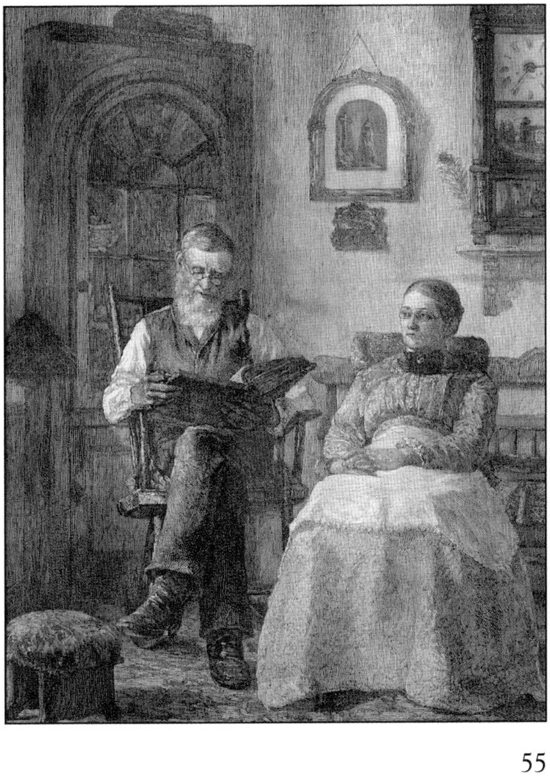

The Old Version, Thomas Hovenden.

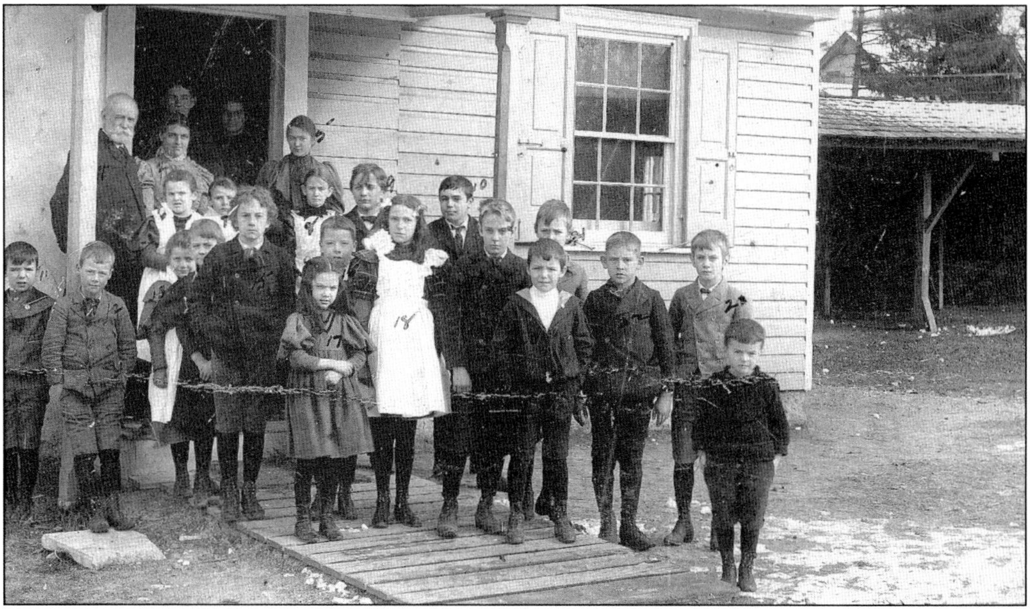

The Plymouth Meeting Friends School was officially established in 1780, although the Friends probably educated children prior to that date. For a time, it was the only school in Plymouth Township. In this 1898 photograph, students at the Plymouth Meeting Friends School pose in front of their typical one-room schoolhouse.

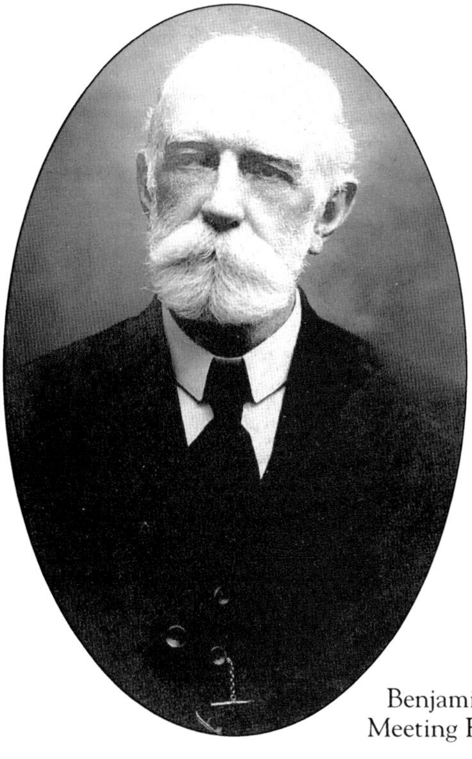

Benjamin Smith, venerable headmaster of the Plymouth Meeting Friends School, served from 1895 to 1911.

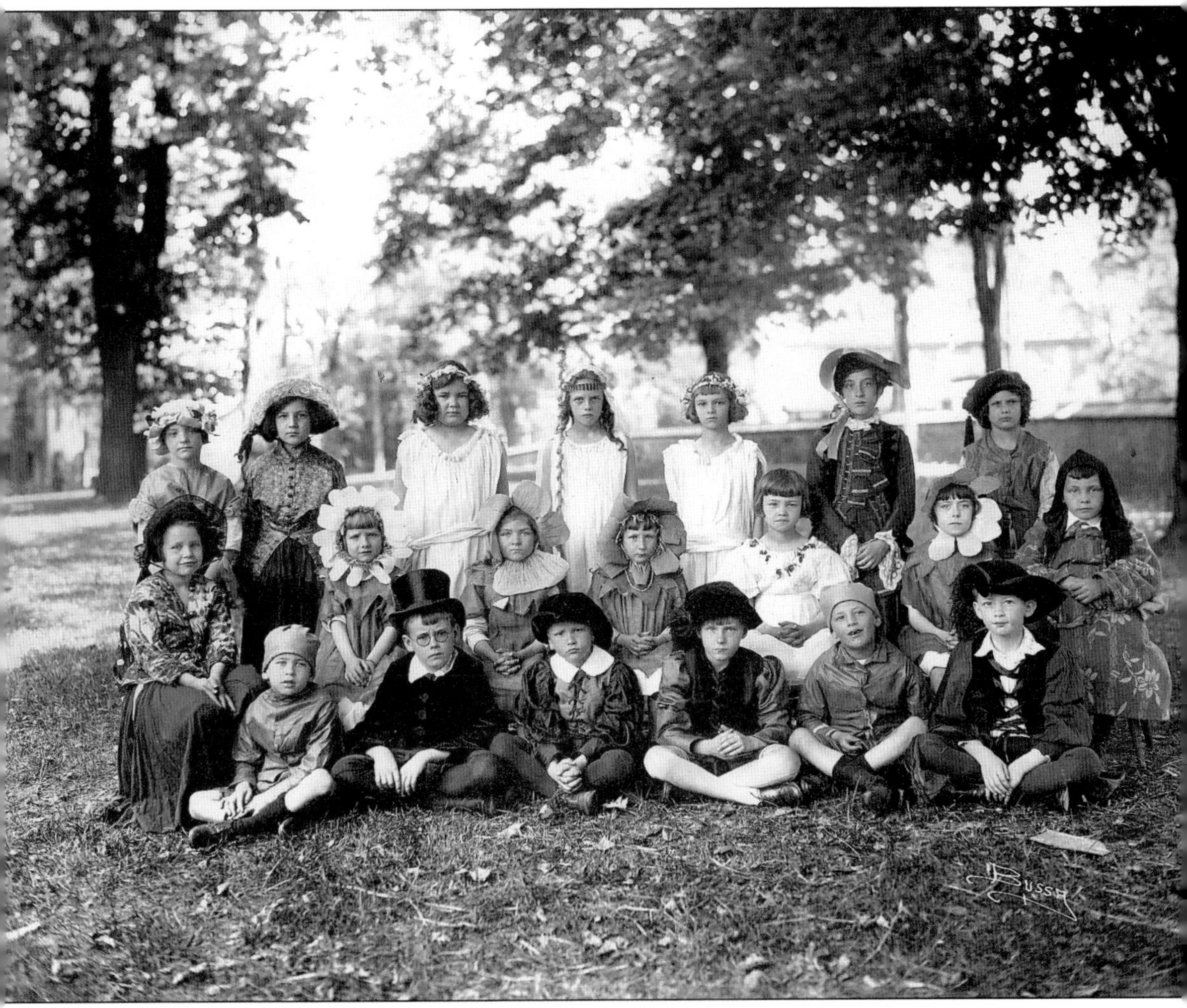

Students at the Plymouth Meeting Friends School are possibly dressed for a May Day pageant c. 1920. What was the rather serious boy in the top hat and spectacles thinking?

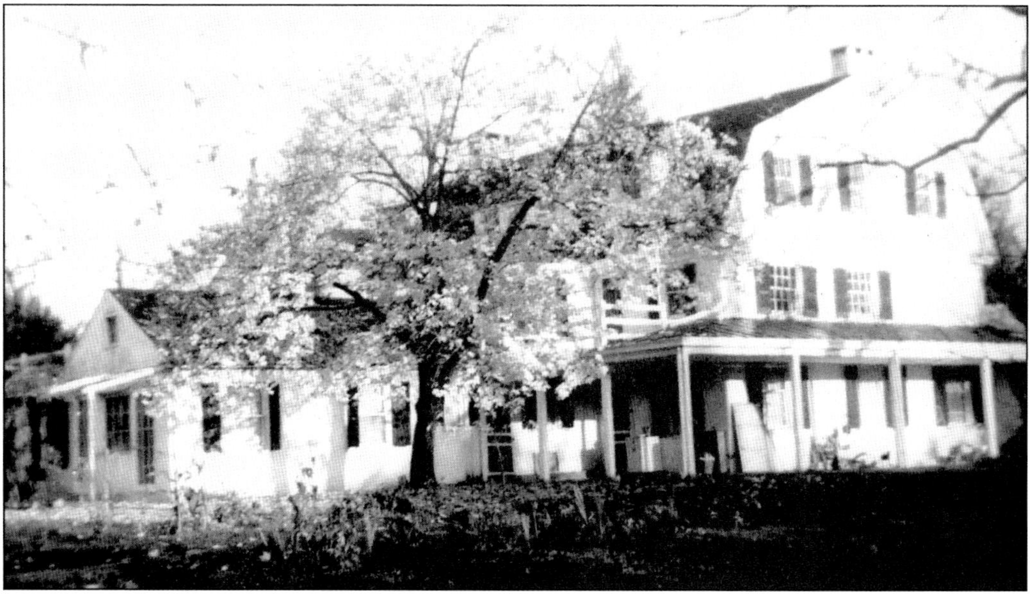

This building at 4 Germantown Pike is now home to several offices, but it once housed groups of young ladies attending the Hannah Williams School. On April 20, 1845, the following advertisement appeared in the *Norristown Herald*: "Plymouth Boarding School for Girls, HANNAH WILLIAMS' Boarding School, under the care of ABIGAIL WILLIAMS, with the assistance of a Teacher, will be ready for the reception of Scholars the 1st of the fifth mo."

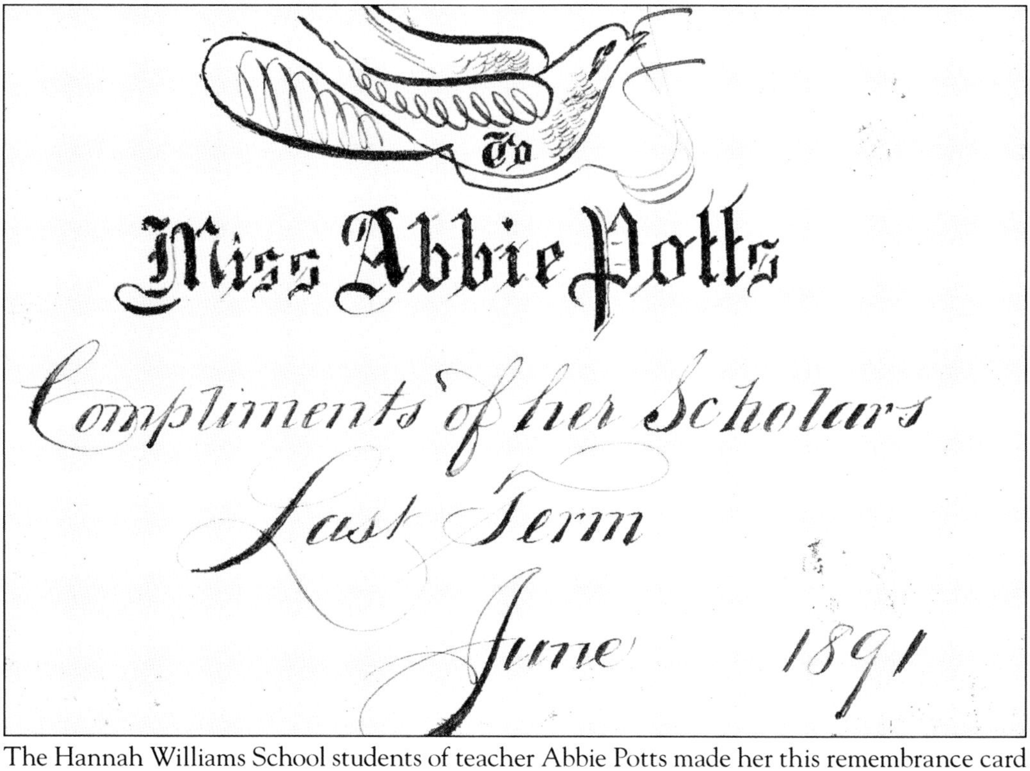

The Hannah Williams School students of teacher Abbie Potts made her this remembrance card in June 1891.

Shown in the late 1800s, the Sandy Hill School served the students of the Black Horse area of Plymouth Township. Teachers' salaries at the time averaged $32 per month; the annual school budget for Plymouth Township was $2,500 to $3,000.

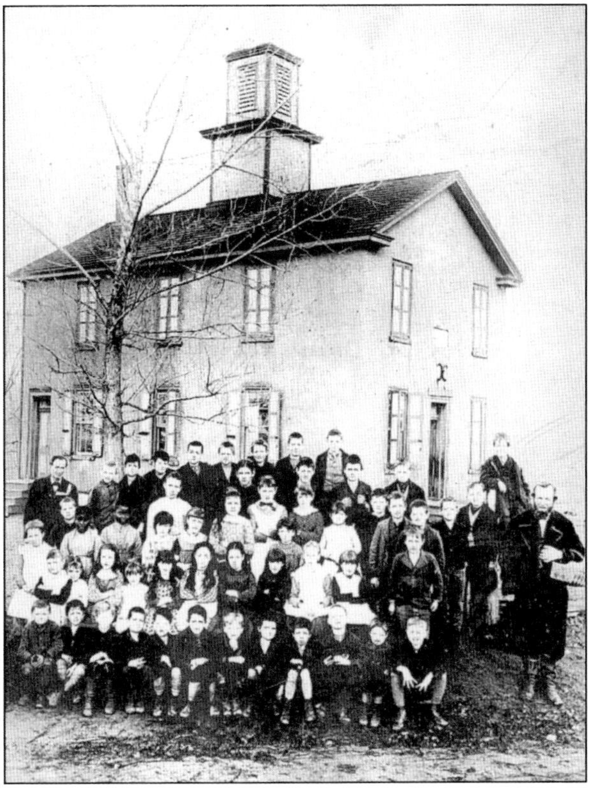

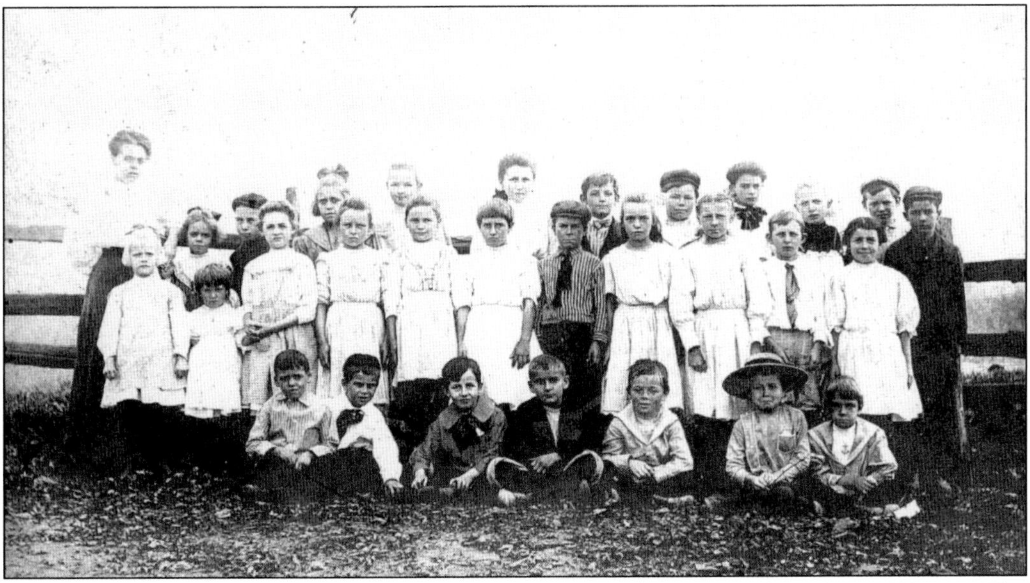

Students of the 8-Square School are pictured in 1907 with their teacher, Anna Weaver. The aptly named school was a one-room schoolhouse built in the then-popular eight-sided shape, on North Lane in Plymouth Township. It was believed that octagonal buildings helped conserve heat. A well for drinking water was located in the middle of the schoolyard. The school was closed in 1915 and used as a residence until being demolished in 1947.

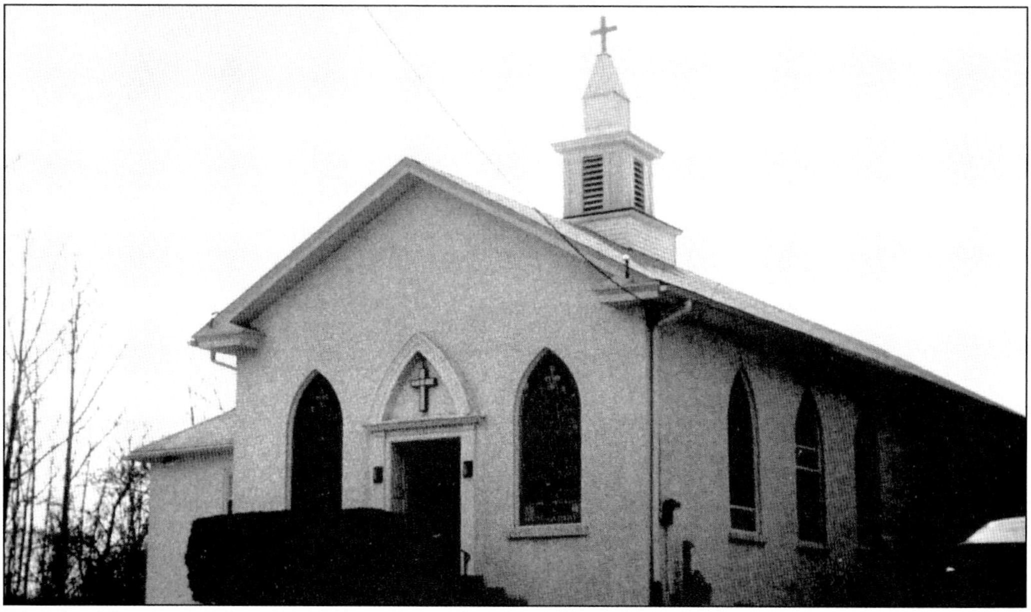

This building, now the Christ Evangelical Free Church, originally housed the North Star or Hickorytown Grade School from 1840 to 1915. Through the efforts of S. Powell Childs, a farmer and civic leader, Plymouth Township's first high school was started here in 1890. Previously, Plymouth Township had provided education only through the eighth grade. The school was closed in 1915, and the high school students were sent to nearby schools.

Dedication and Flag Raising Exercises

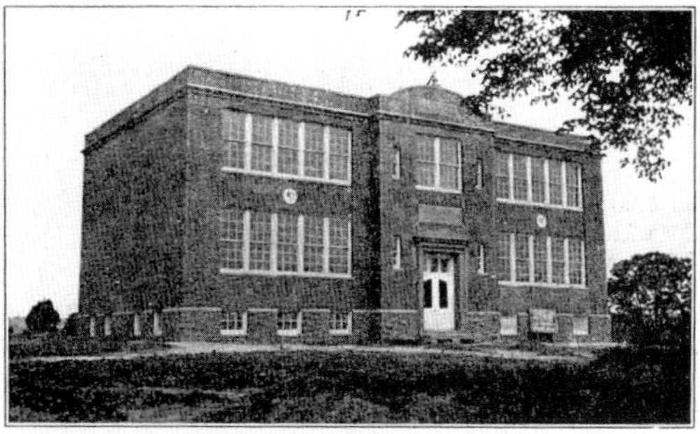

"Built by the people, and dedicated to our youth, the hope of our country."

Consolidated School

Plymouth Township, Montgomery County, Pa.

Saturday, June 12th, 1915

2.30 P. M.

The Plymouth Consolidated School, on Butler Pike between Ridge and Germantown Pikes, opened in 1915. Educating students from first through eighth grades, it replaced several small village schools. The Consolidated School served Plymouth Township until the mid-1970s, when it was closed and used for storage. In 1981, it was sold to the Harmonville Fire Company, whose engine house now stands on the site.

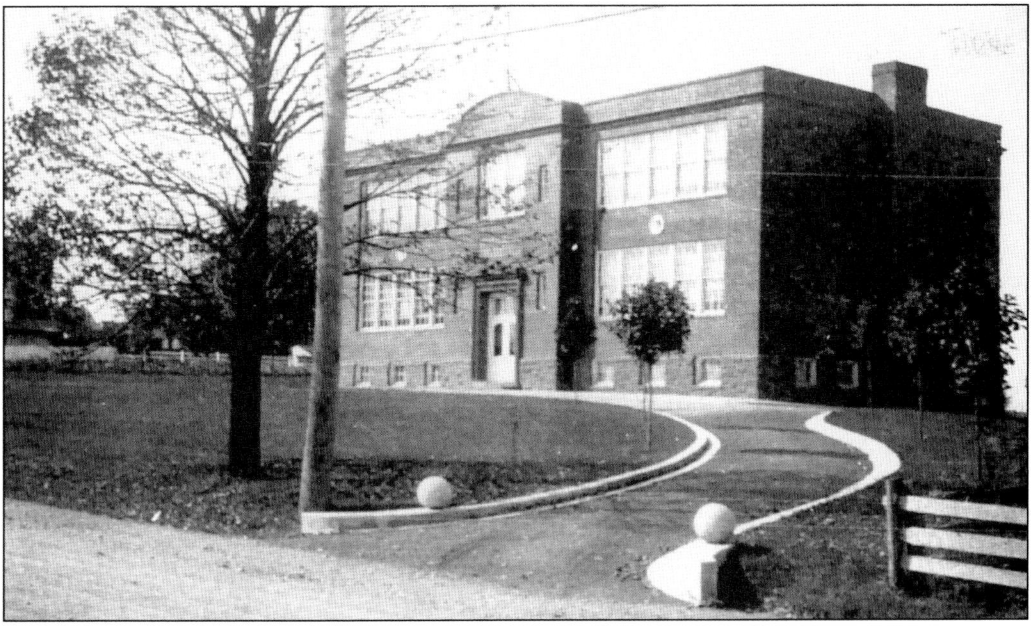

In rural townships from *c.* 1910 to 1930, a wave of consolidations ended the days of the one-room schoolhouse—part of a larger nationwide movement to provide more modern facilities. With the advent of the school bus, schools no longer needed to be within walking distance for students.

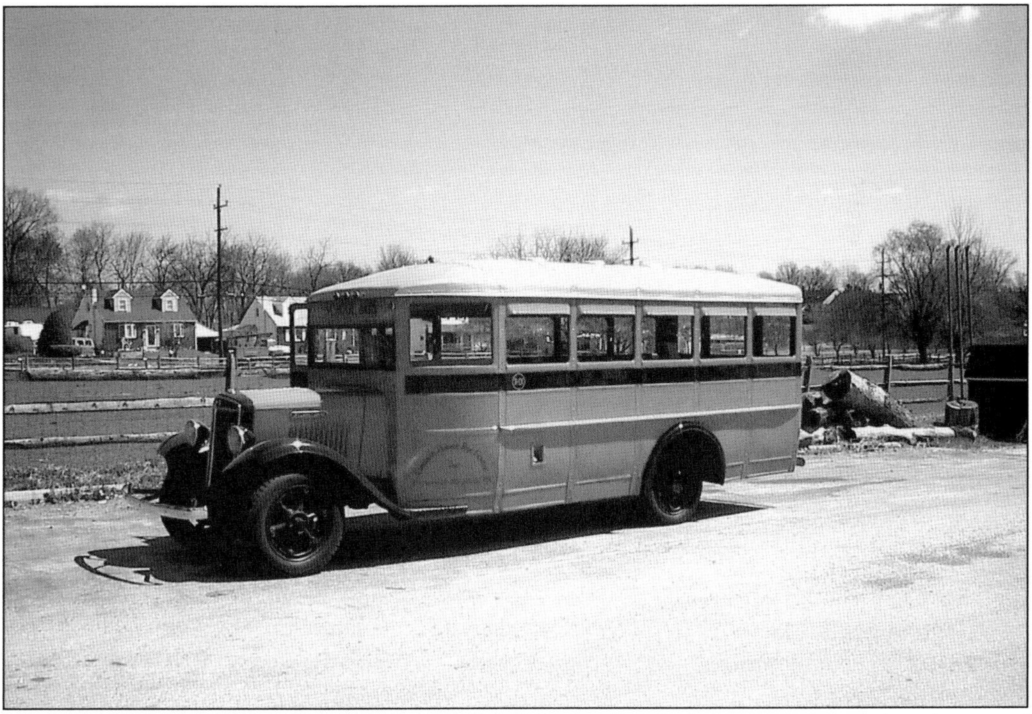

A 1935 bus, now owned by Romano School Bus Service, transported students after the era of school consolidation. (Courtesy of the Romano School Bus Service.)

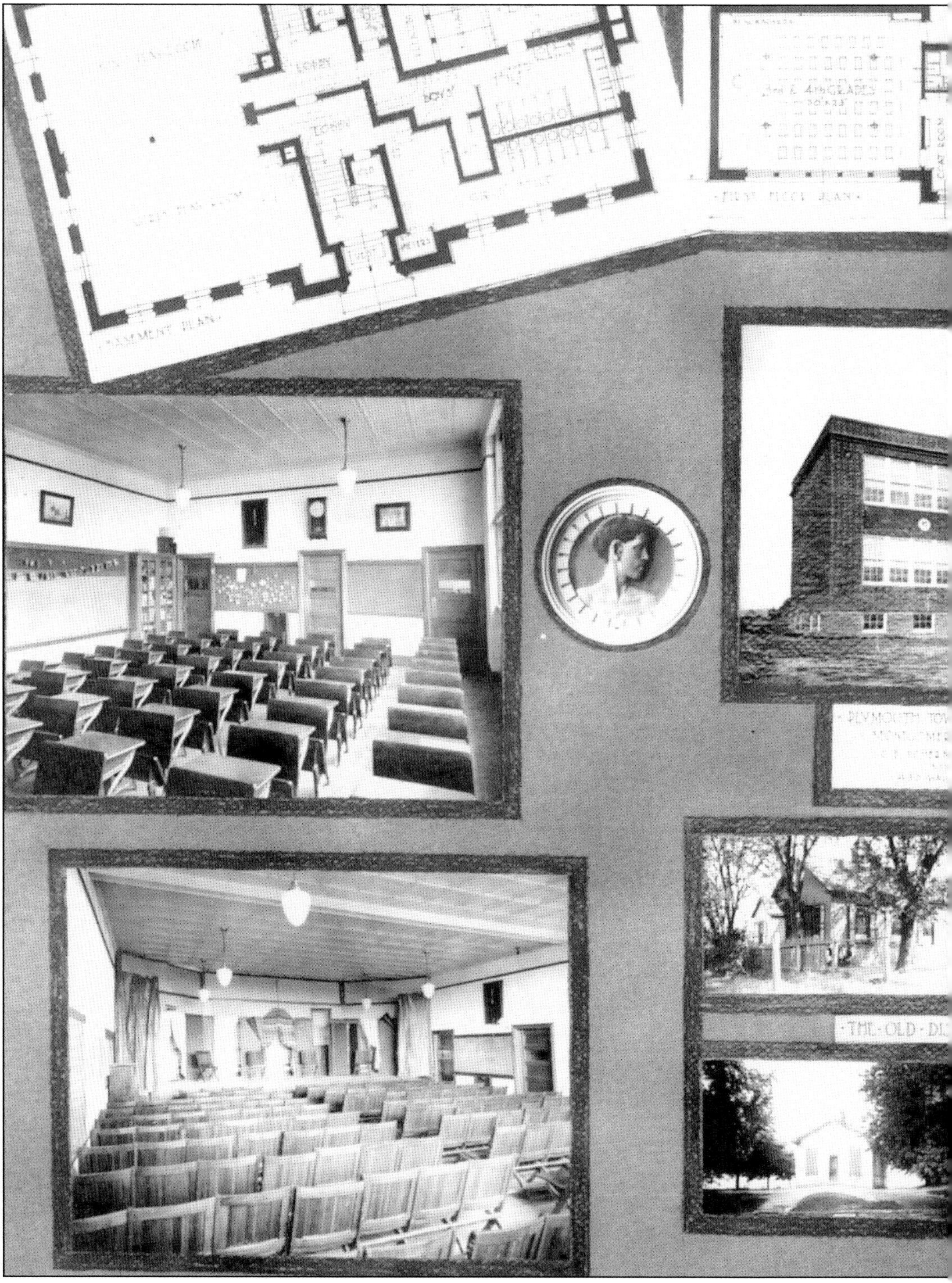

The Plymouth Consolidated School, designed by architect Watson K. Phillips of Philadelphia, was constructed at a total cost of $24,266.79. The general contractor was Alexander Chambley, plumbing was installed by Ira Bickhart, and the electricians were Crisman & Quillman. A far

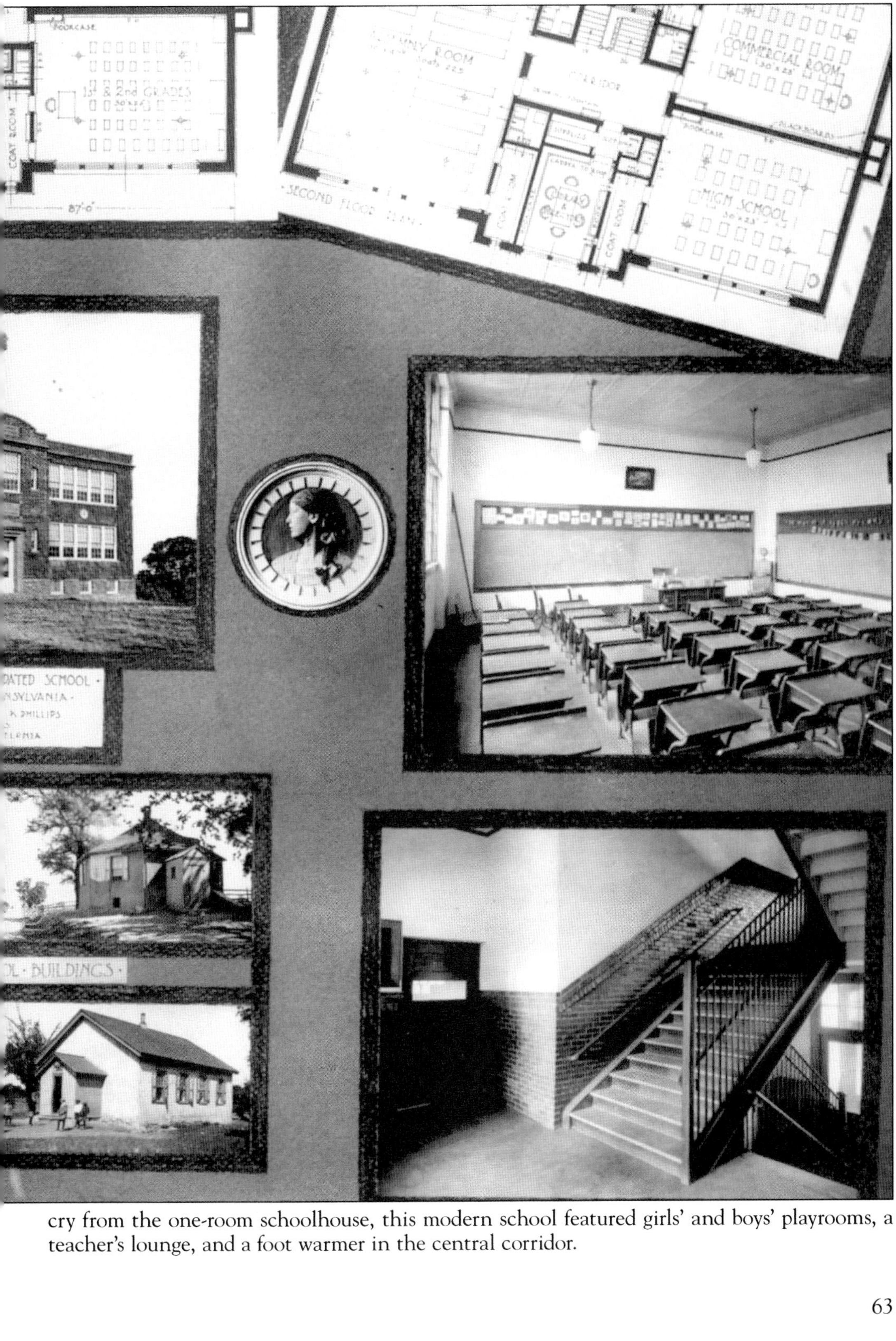

cry from the one-room schoolhouse, this modern school featured girls' and boys' playrooms, a teacher's lounge, and a foot warmer in the central corridor.

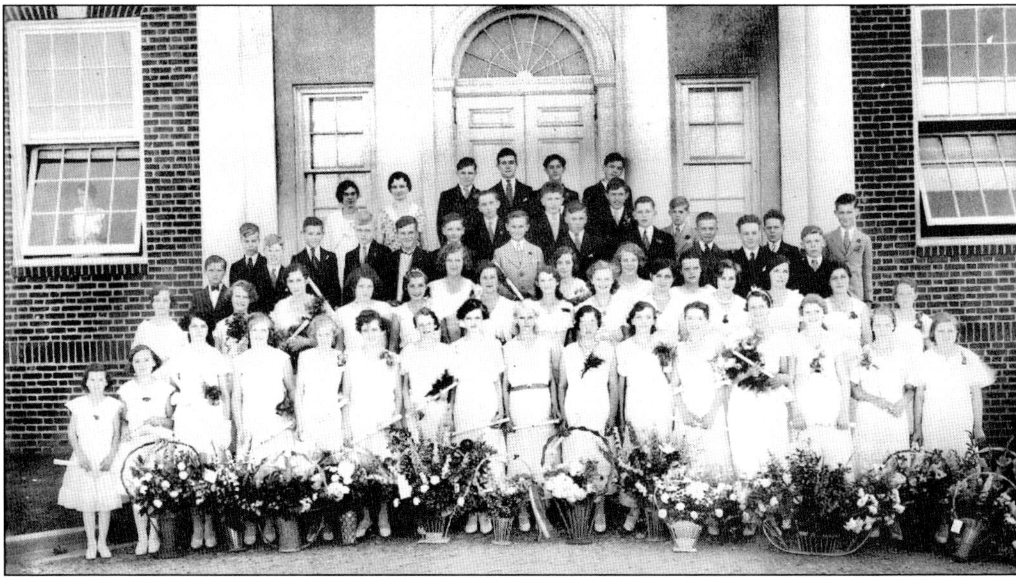

In 1921, the Whitemarsh School District built the Barren Hill Consolidated School at Germantown Pike and Crescent Avenue to serve students through eighth grade. Before the Plymouth Whitemarsh High School was built, students could choose to continue their education, after graduation from Barren Hill, at one of four neighboring community schools: Conshohocken, Ambler, Springfield, or Norristown. Shown is the Barren Hill School class of 1921 on their graduation day. (Courtesy of the Lownes Family Funeral Home.)

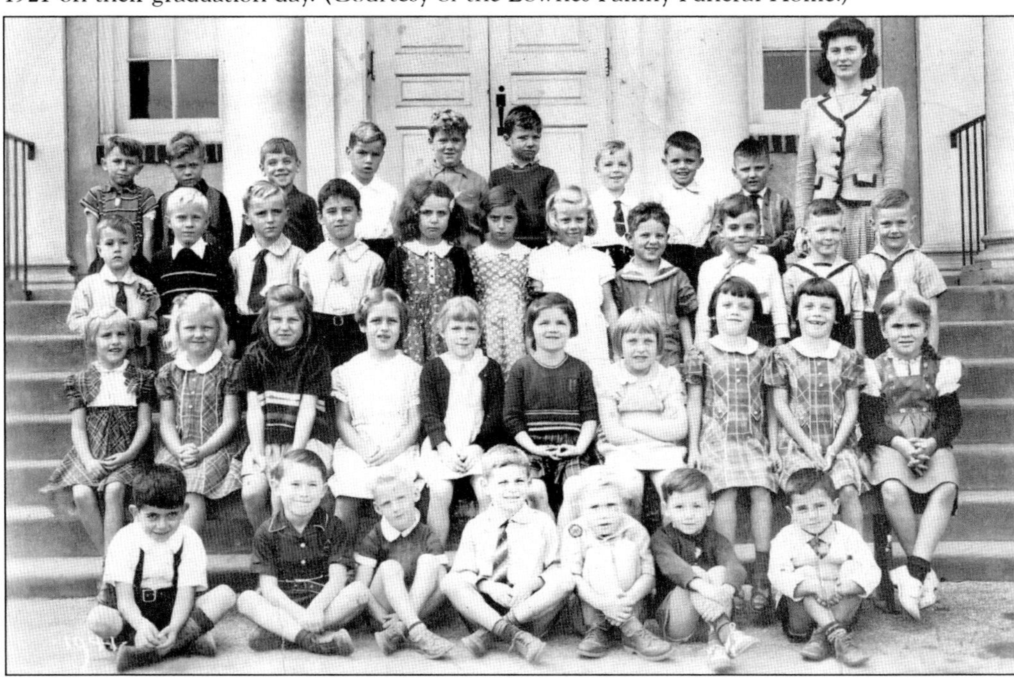

The students of Barren Hill Consolidated pose in front of the school in 1941. The school was renamed the Lafayette Consolidated Elementary School in 1957 in honor of the Marquis de Lafayette. It was closed in 1977. The offices of Whitemarsh Township and a commercial bank are currently housed here. (Courtesy of Virginia E. Ottey.)

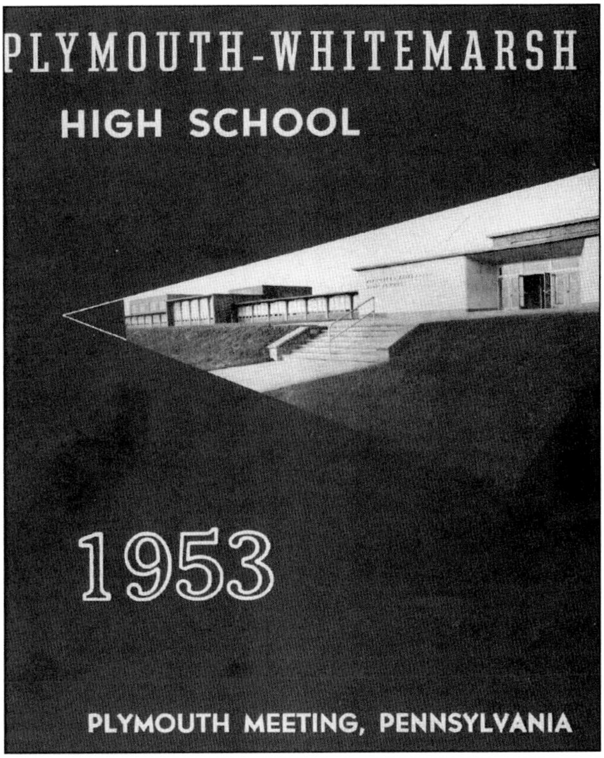

After World War II, rapid population increases in Plymouth and Whitemarsh Townships created a demand for a complete school system for grades 1 through 12. On March 25, 1947, the school districts of the two townships entered into an agreement for the joint operation of their schools. Plans were made for a shared high school in 1950, and ground was broken for the Plymouth Whitemarsh High School in May 1952. The high school officially opened on September 14, 1953, to 585 students in grades 7, 8, 9, and 10. During the next two years, grades 11 and 12 were added.

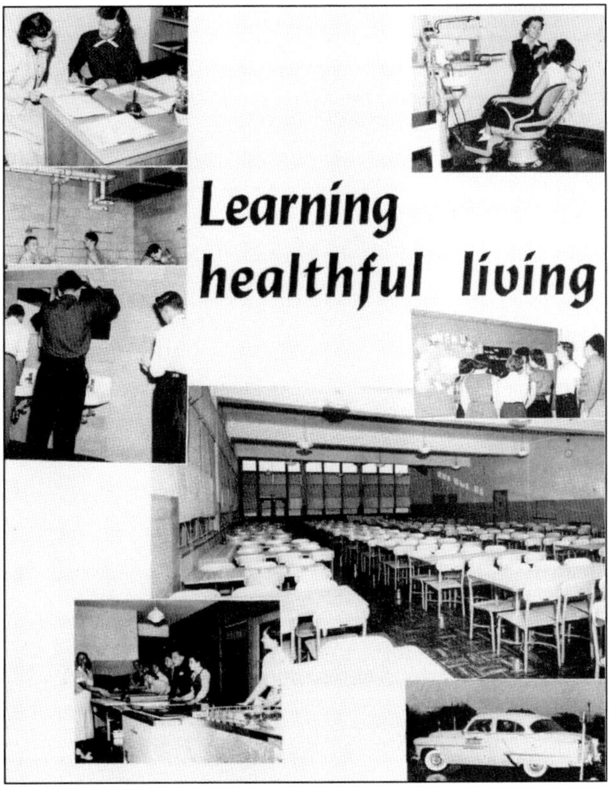

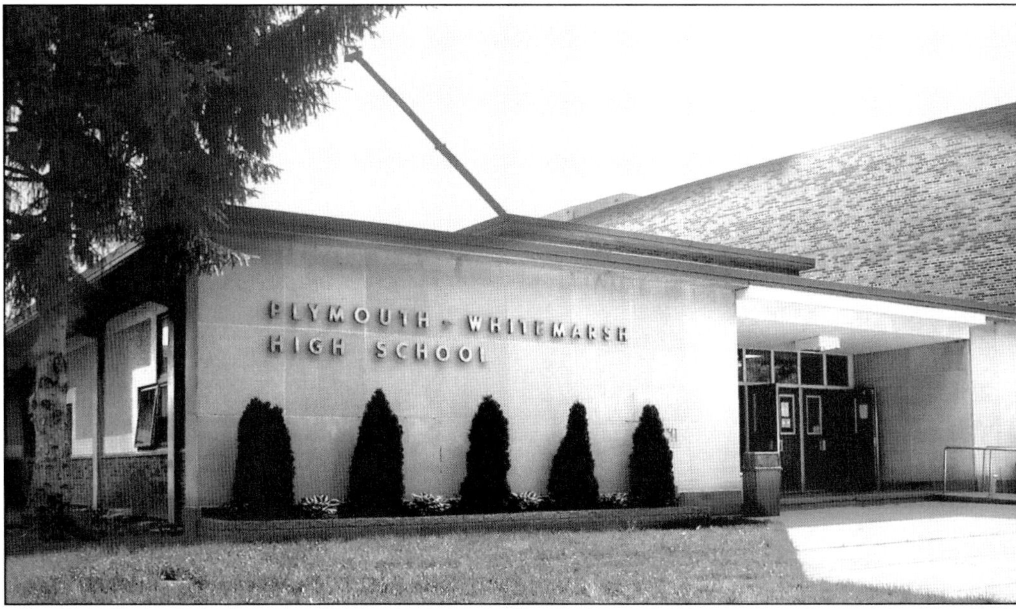

Designed by architects Davis, Dunlop & Carver of Philadelphia, the 80,937-square-foot Plymouth Whitemarsh High School was constructed by McCloskey & Company for about $1.5 million. The modern building featured 13 academic classrooms, a full shop, homemaking and science areas, and a mimeograph room, along with two stores and snack bars.

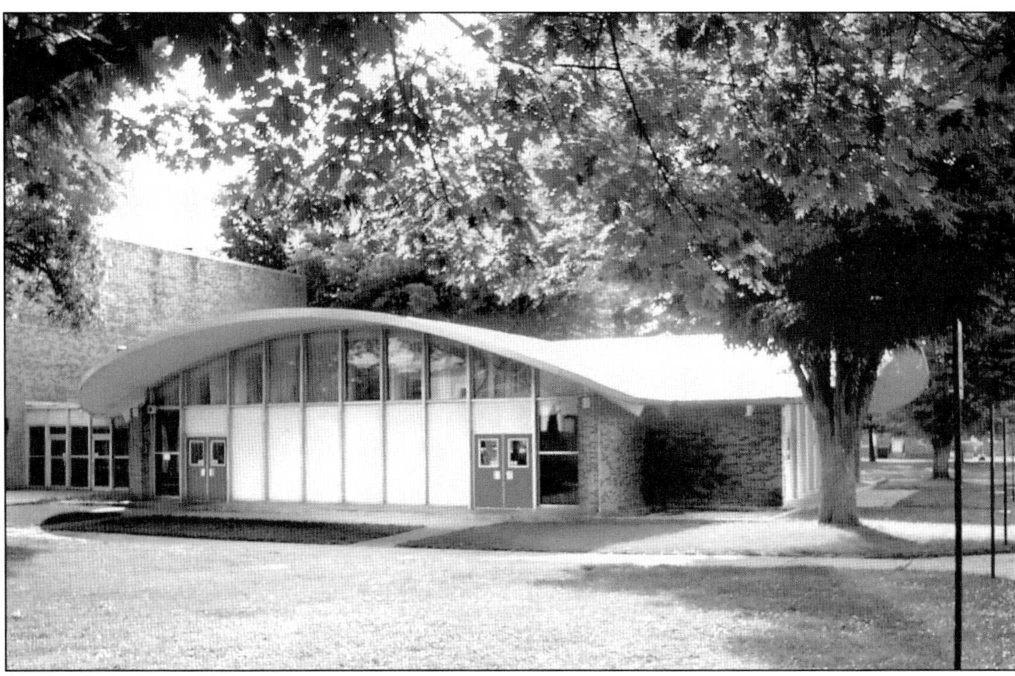

The futuristic cafetorium was among the first of many additions as the high school expanded to serve the growing population. The sleek, undulating roof reminds one of a 1950s space-age fantasy.

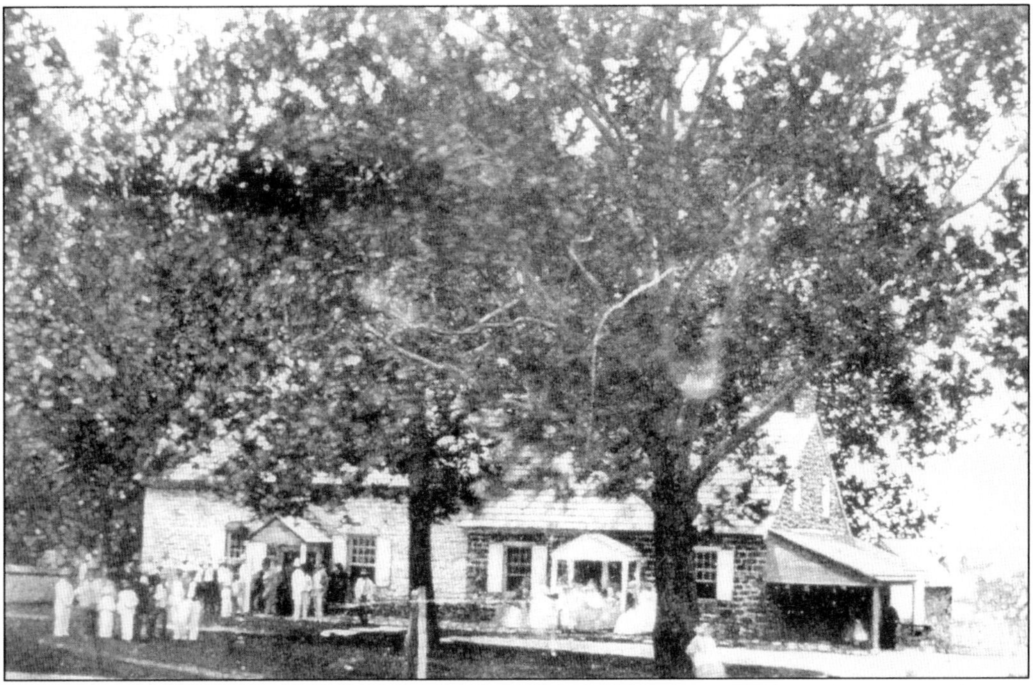

The first religious meetings in the region were held by the Society of Friends in private homes in Plymouth, beginning *c.* 1686. The deed to the land of their meetinghouse dates from 1704, and the building was constructed shortly thereafter.

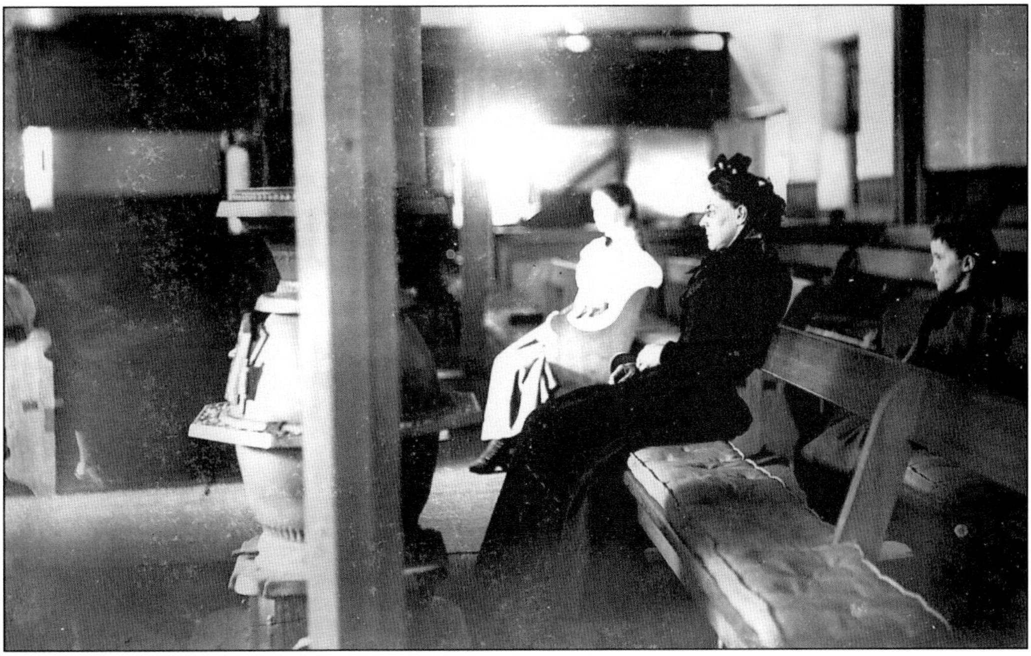

The interior of the Plymouth Friends Meeting House has changed little over the years, except perhaps the replacement of the potbelly stove by a modern heating system in 1945. People arrived early to get a seat near the stove, while latecomers brought blankets.

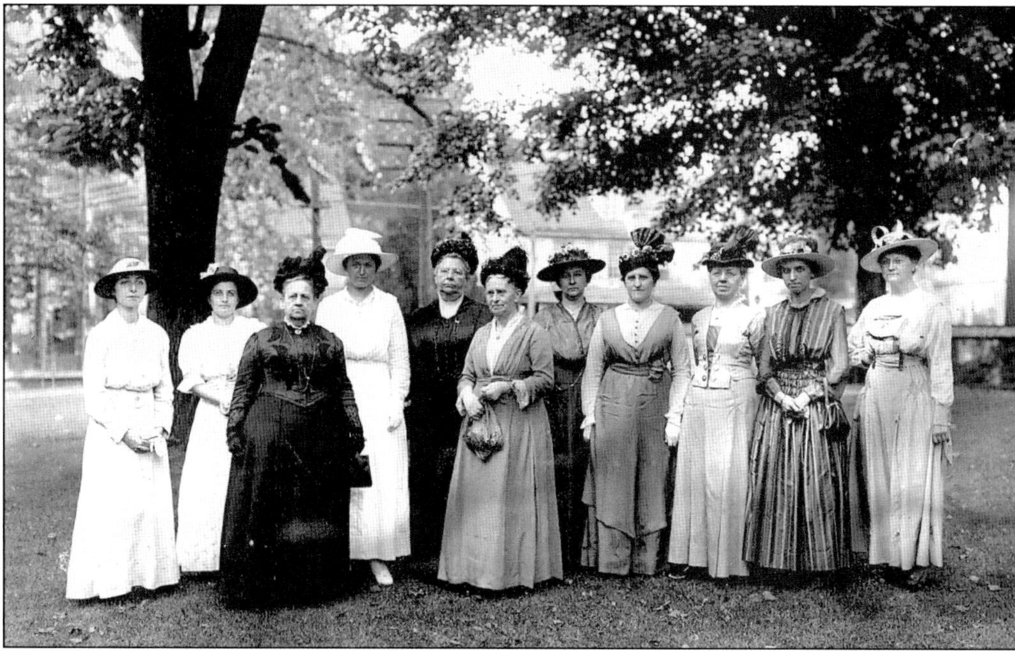

Pictured in 1902, these women are dressed in their finest to celebrate the 200th anniversary of the Plymouth Friends Meeting. From left to right are Helen Williams, Alice H. Ambler, Mary Livezey, Emma Hibbs, Mary R. Livezey, Anna Cadwallader Pennock, Emily Tomlinson, Amy Thompson Thomas, Lidie Norrell, Mabel Cooper, and Helen C. Livezey.

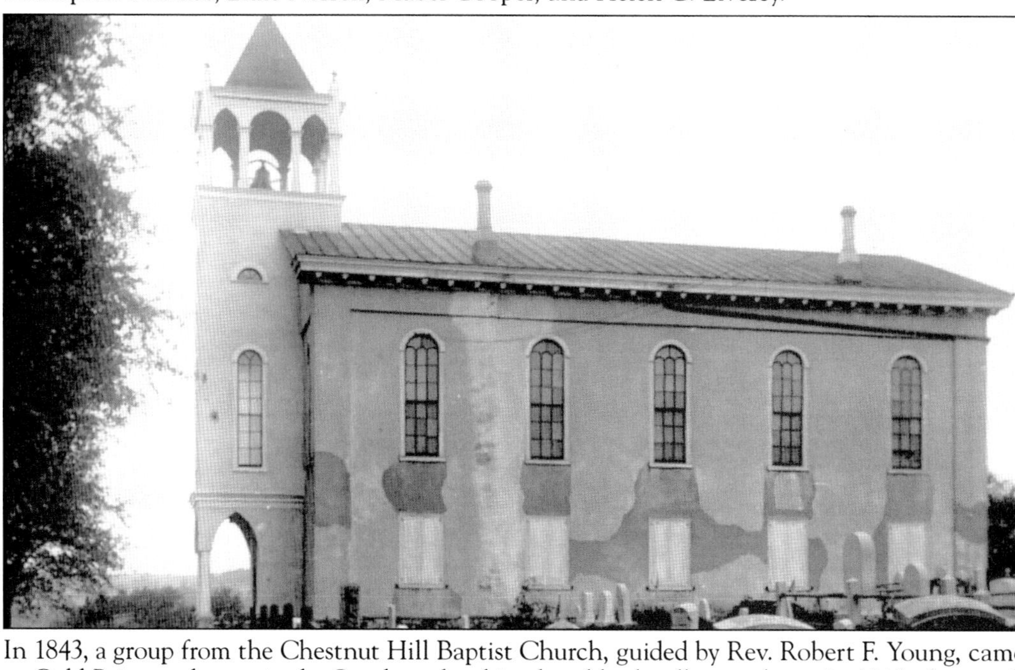

In 1843, a group from the Chestnut Hill Baptist Church, guided by Rev. Robert F. Young, came to Cold Point and organized a Sunday school in the old schoolhouse there. In 1845, this small contingent purchased a lot with a view on which to build a church. Cold Point Baptist Church, the "little white church on the hill," was officially founded in 1854. The present church building was constructed in 1868.

The Plymouth Meeting Evangelical Congregational Church—begun by a mission organized by the Methodist church and later attached to the Evangelical church—traces its local roots to a meeting in an old saddle shop in 1861. In 1876, the foundation was laid for the present building on Germantown Pike in Plymouth Meeting; members and friends of the church finally completed the building in 1884. (Courtesy of the Plymouth Meeting Evangelical Congregational Church.)

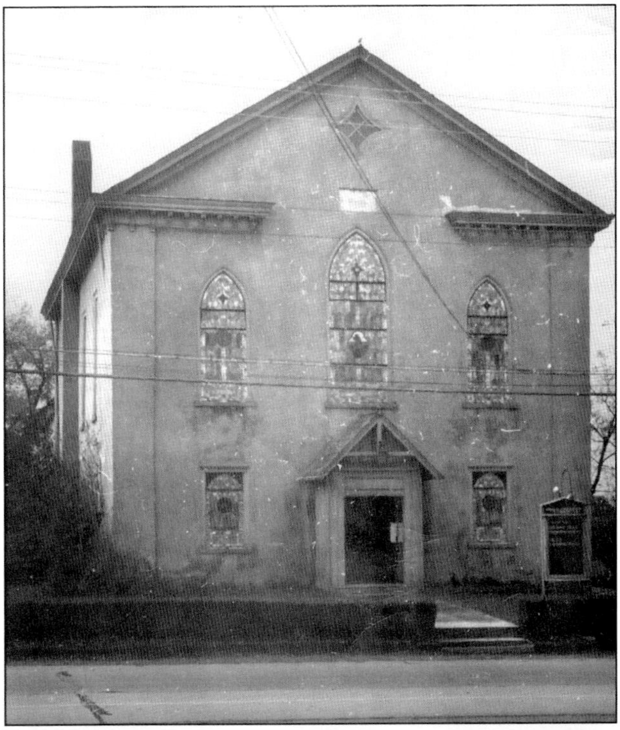

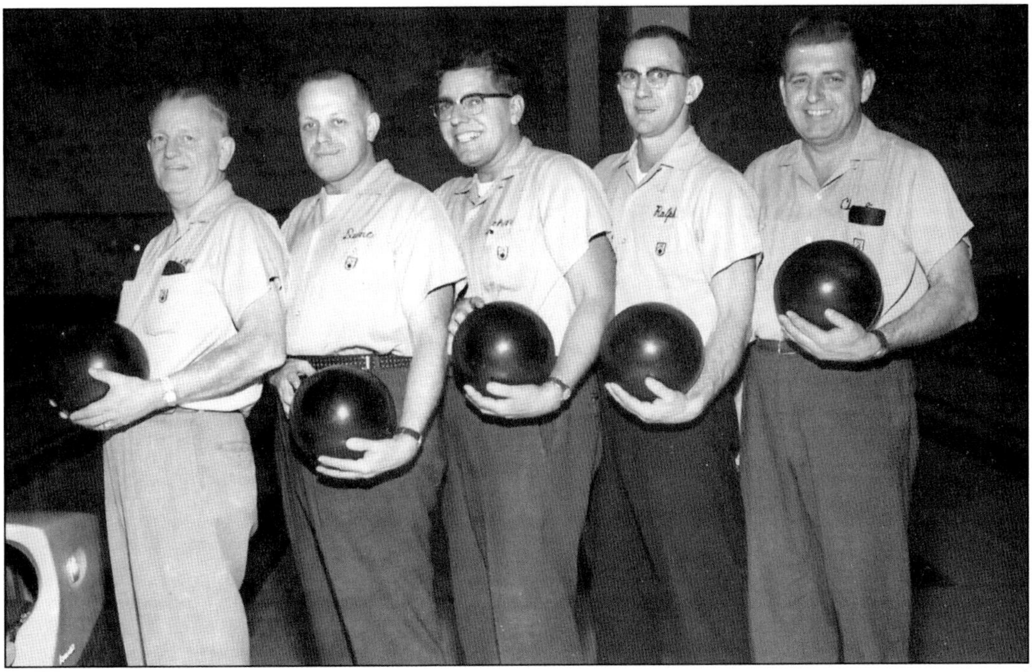

Besides worshiping together, church members enjoyed each other's company during various social activities. In the 1962–1963 season, the bowling team of the Plymouth Meeting Evangelical Congregational Church won first place at Plymouth Lanes. Shown, from left to right, are George Neal, Duncan Forsyth, John Haub, Ralph Smith (captain), and Charles Staley. (Courtesy of the Plymouth Meeting Evangelical Congregational Church.)

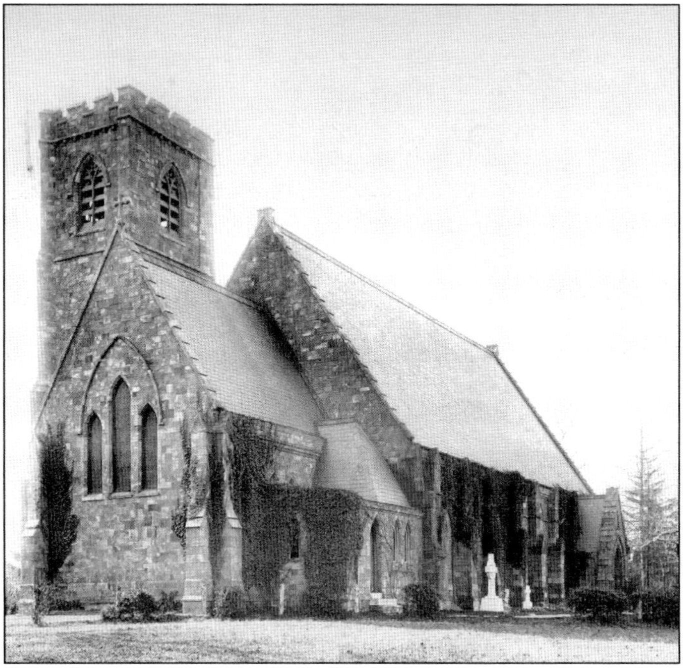

St. Thomas Episcopal Church was founded in 1698 and first occupied a log cabin on Church Road in Fort Washington. Shown here *c.* 1900 is the fourth church structure, built in 1881. Legend has it that during the Revolutionary War, British soldiers used the tombstones for target practice and stabled their horses in the church sanctuary. (Courtesy of St. Thomas Episcopal Church.)

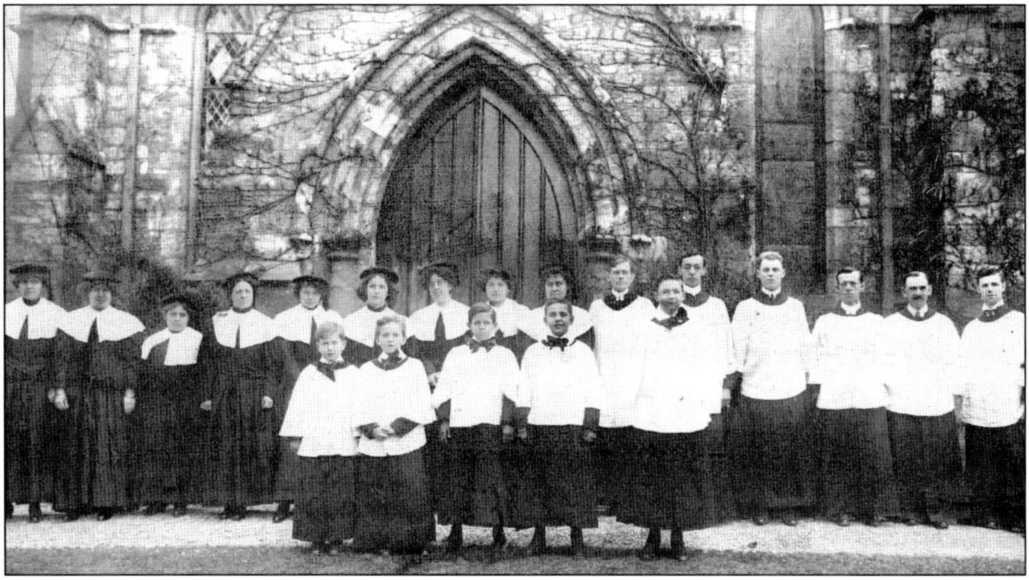

Shown is the choir at St. Thomas *c.* 1930. From left to right are the following: (front row) Heydrick Savin, Frank Angeny, George Snyder, William Leslie, and Robert Brundett; (back row) Edna Snyder, Clara Leslie, Elsie Scheetz, Florence Houlhouser, Margaret Bauer, Edith McGregor, Emma Comly, Dorothy Campbell MacFarlan, Bessie Smith, unidentified, Joseph Hamilton, Russell Savin, Thomas Robinson (organist), and two unidentified individuals. (Courtesy of St. Thomas Episcopal Church.)

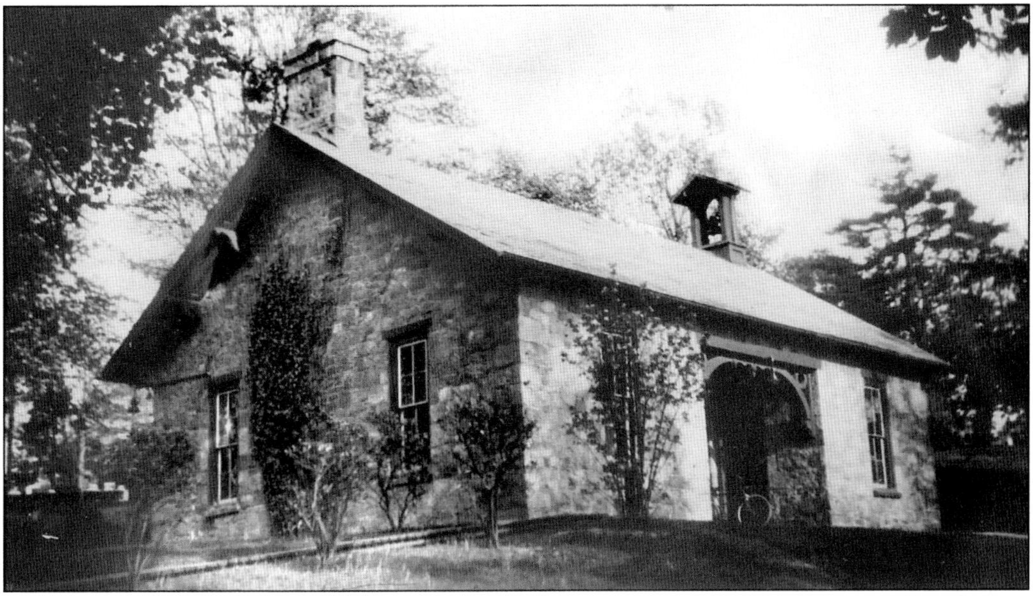

In 1855, Ellen Sheaff built the schoolhouse at St. Thomas as a memorial to her brother, Henry, who had died two years before. The schoolhouse became Sheaff's primary concern and interest, and she was its sole financial supporter. It housed St. Thomas's Sunday and parochial schools until the early 1900s. (Courtesy of St. Thomas Episcopal Church.)

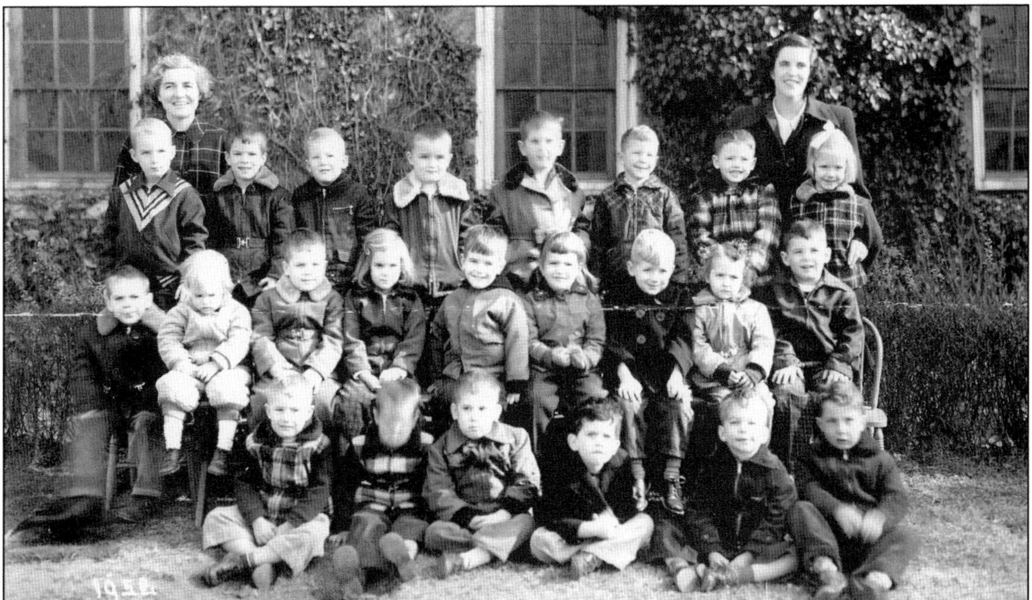

The nursery school class at St. Thomas sat still (most of them) for a photograph in 1952. From left to right are the following: (front row) Rickey Lazarick, Eddy Roberts, Charlie Zimmerman, Andy McAleer, Tim Greenwood, and Robin Cox; (middle row) Dickie Fitzgerald, Cathy Cross, Frankie Melograna, Sally Reichner, Bruce Gibby, Gretchen Lippincott, Stan Allsopp, Evie Curran, and Cliffy Cutler; (back row) Daniel Sadler, Dickie Pitman, Herb Black, Luke Lucard, Chris Zimmerman, Timmy Napier, Steve Hubler, and Barbara Murdoch. The teachers are Mrs. Newhall and Mrs. "Groton-to-be." (Courtesy of St. Thomas Episcopal Church.)

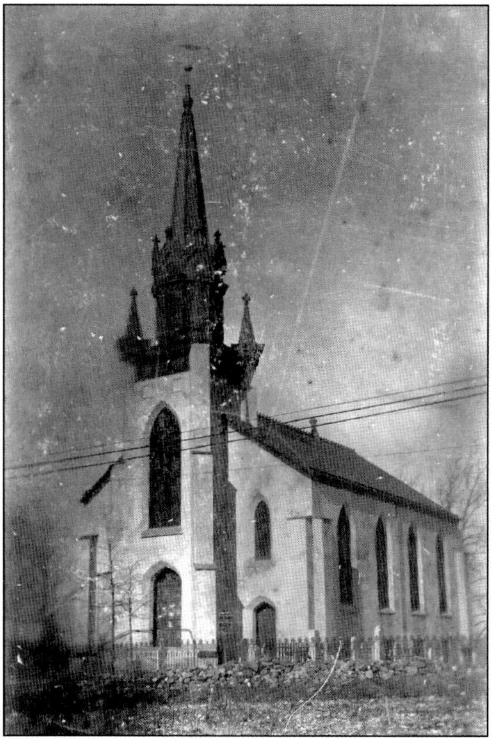

The first St. Peter's was built in 1767 and could be seen for miles around. Because of this vantage, the tower of the church was used during the Revolutionary War by General Lafayette to observe British and Hessian troops approaching from Cold Point, and he was able to plan a hasty retreat. The second church building, shown here, was constructed in 1849. (Courtesy of St. Peter's Lutheran Church.)

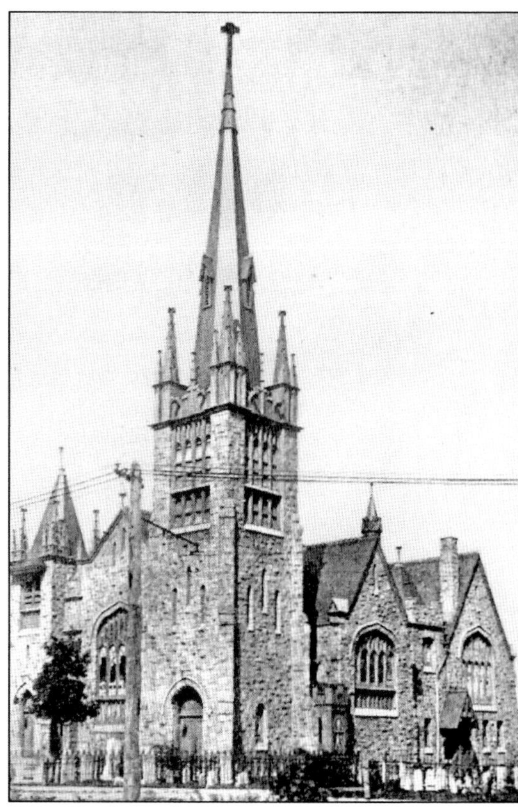

On September 28, 1899, a fire of unknown cause began in the basement Sunday school room at St. Peter's. The entire church was destroyed. A new church building, which has been much modified over the years, was constructed in 1900. (Courtesy of St. Peter's Lutheran Church.)

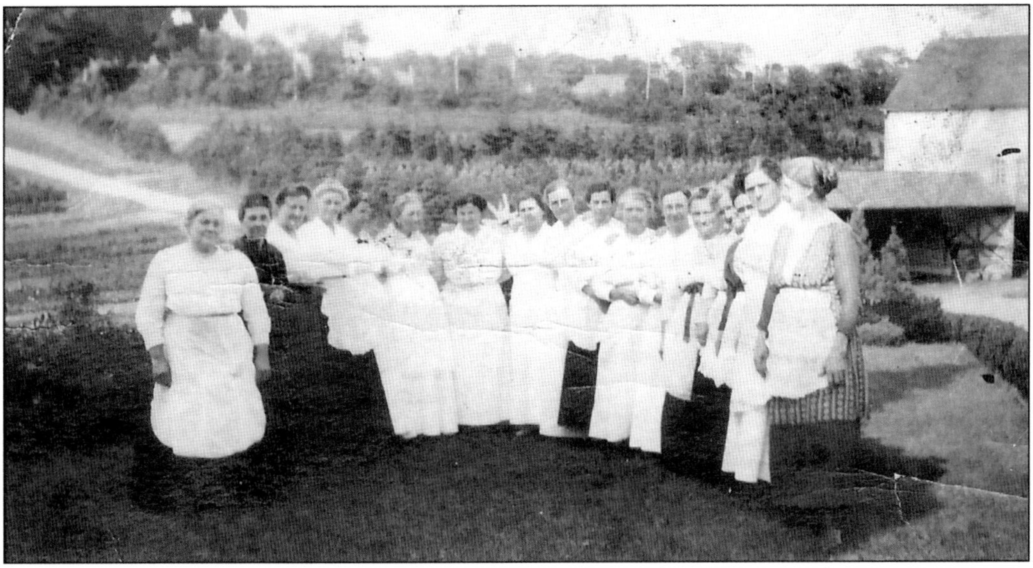

St. Peter's Helping Hand Sewing Circle was organized on February 9, 1916, by Mrs. Grayson L. Stup, wife of the pastor. Meeting the second Thursday afternoon of each month, the group sewed for the Loysville Orphanage of Loysville, Pennsylvania. Members of the Helping Hand (meeting in 1937) included Mrs. A.G. Carver (president), Mrs. William Stacke (vice president), Mrs. John Sague, Mrs. H. Gilinger, and Mrs. Walter Coulston. (Courtesy of St. Peter's Lutheran Church.)

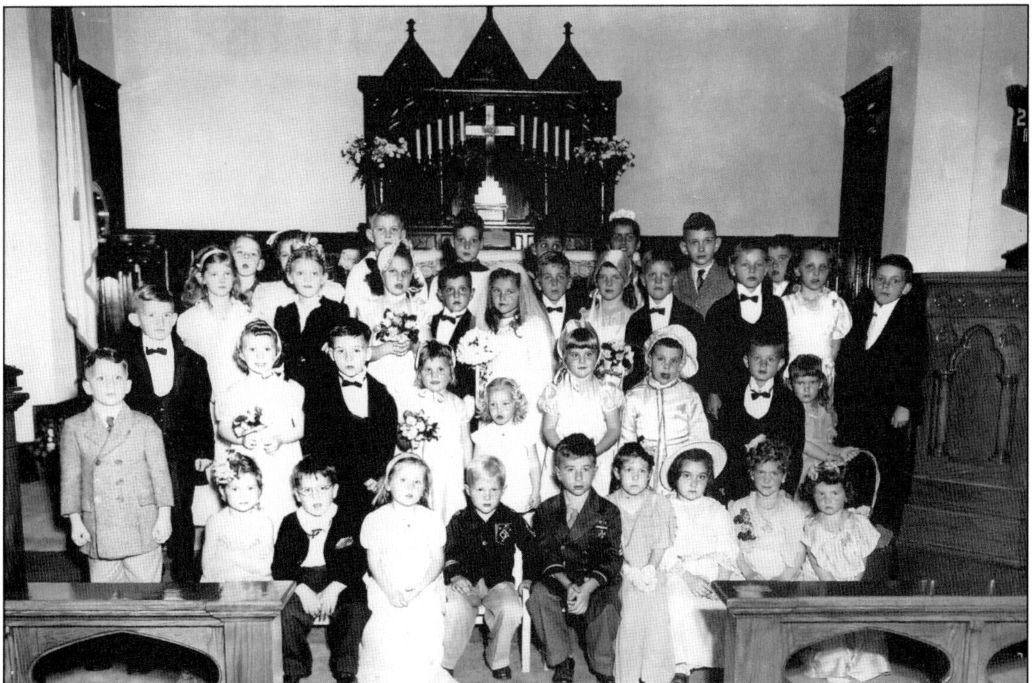

Like many churches and social organizations, the members of St. Peter's held a Tom Thumb wedding as a social event at the church. This 1945 photograph shows children of church members dressed as the bride, groom, and various attendants. (Courtesy of St. Peter's Lutheran Church.)

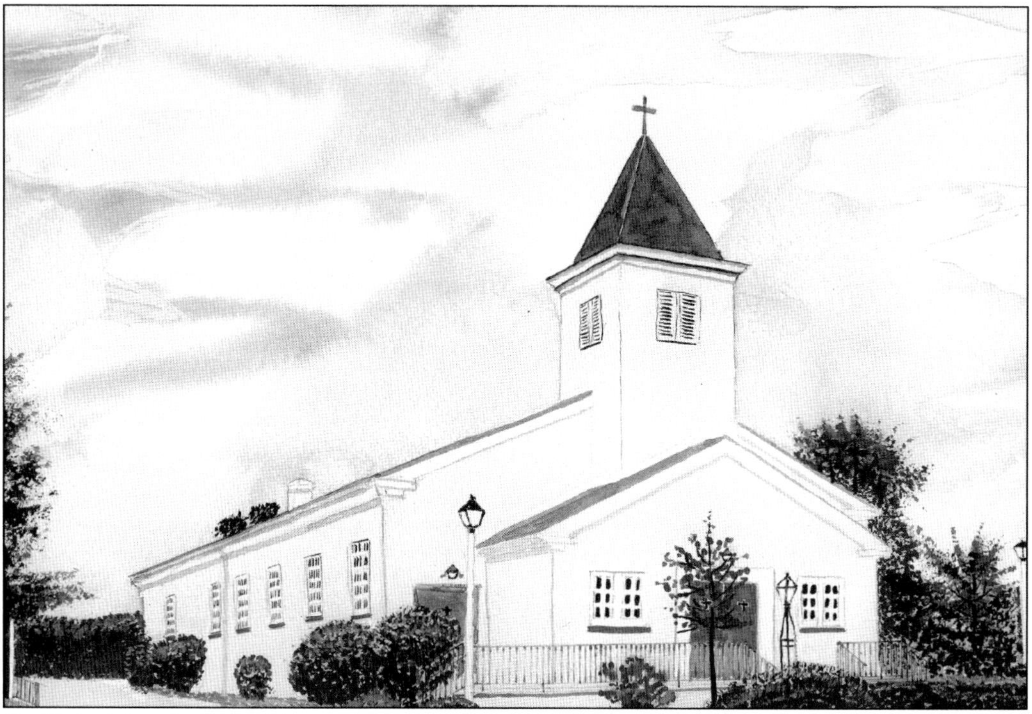

St. Philip Neri Catholic Church began as a mission of St. Matthew's in Conshohocken, meeting in private homes in the 1920s and 1930s. Property on Germantown Pike was purchased in 1936, and in 1946, a mission chapel was constructed of government-surplus wood, formerly the barracks of Fort Dix. (Painting by William Anderson, courtesy of St. Philip Neri Catholic Church.)

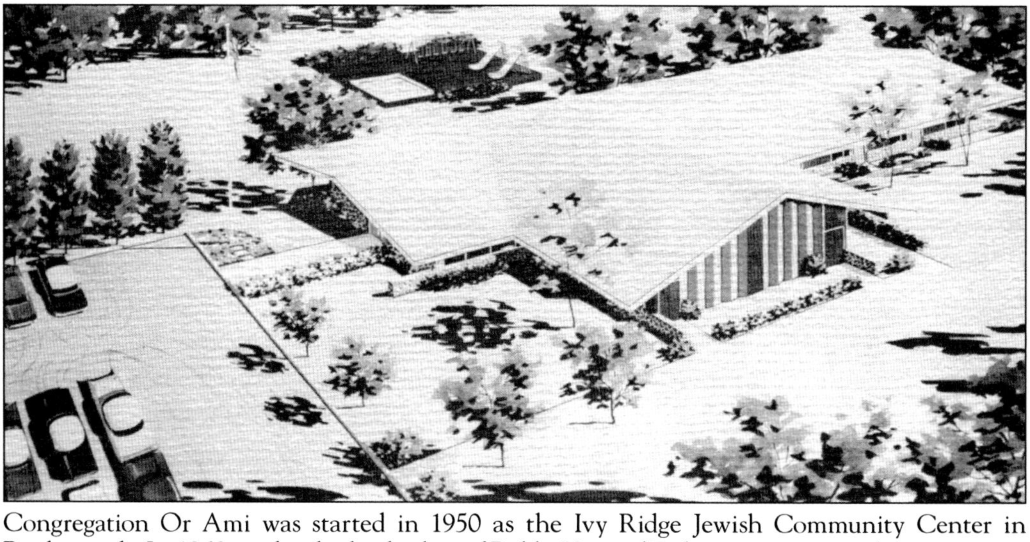

Congregation Or Ami was started in 1950 as the Ivy Ridge Jewish Community Center in Roxborough. In 1960, under the leadership of Rabbi Howard Rabinowitz, it moved to its present location on Ridge Pike in Lafayette Hill. Shown is an artist's rendition of the Ridge Pike building from the May 1960 dedication program. (Courtesy of Congregation Or Ami.)

Five

LIFE IN PLYMOUTH AND WHITEMARSH

Township residents have always found ways to relax, socialize, and enjoy themselves. The manner in which they did so depended on age, gender, location, economic means, and the state of technology at a particular time. Some activities, such as playing in the snow, have changed little over the years, while reading in the evening or smoking a pipe as a pastime have both declined, the first because of new electronic media and the second because of health concerns.

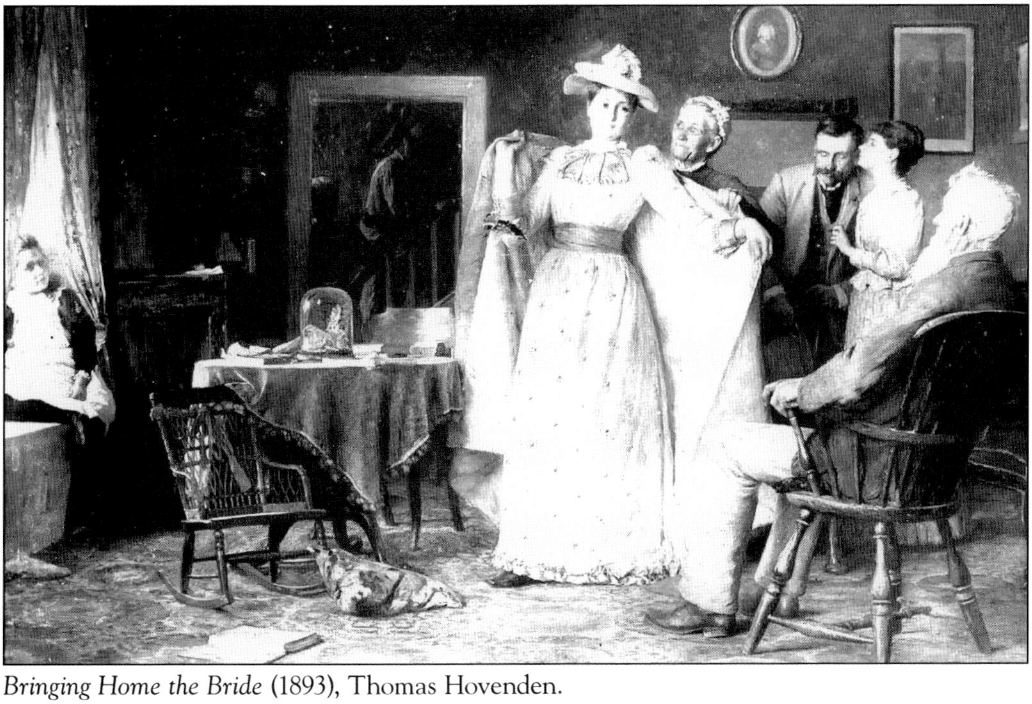

Bringing Home the Bride (1893), Thomas Hovenden.

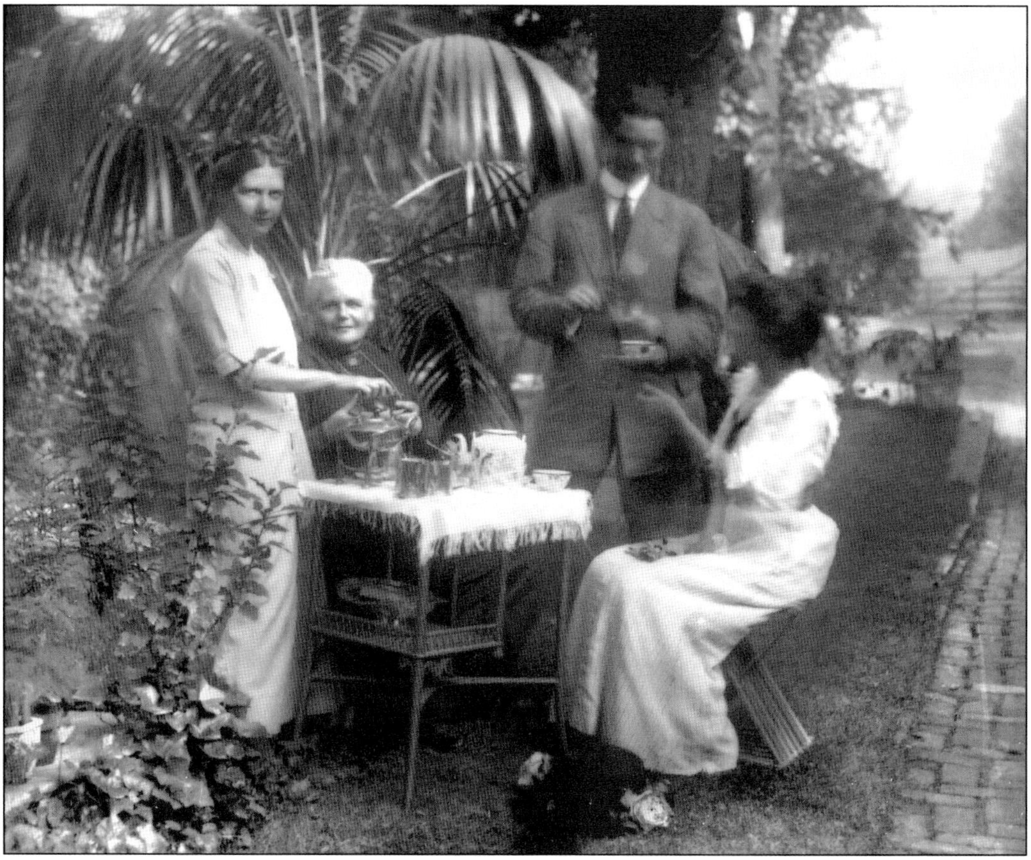

Afternoon tea was a familiar ritual among prosperous families from Colonial days well into the 20th century.

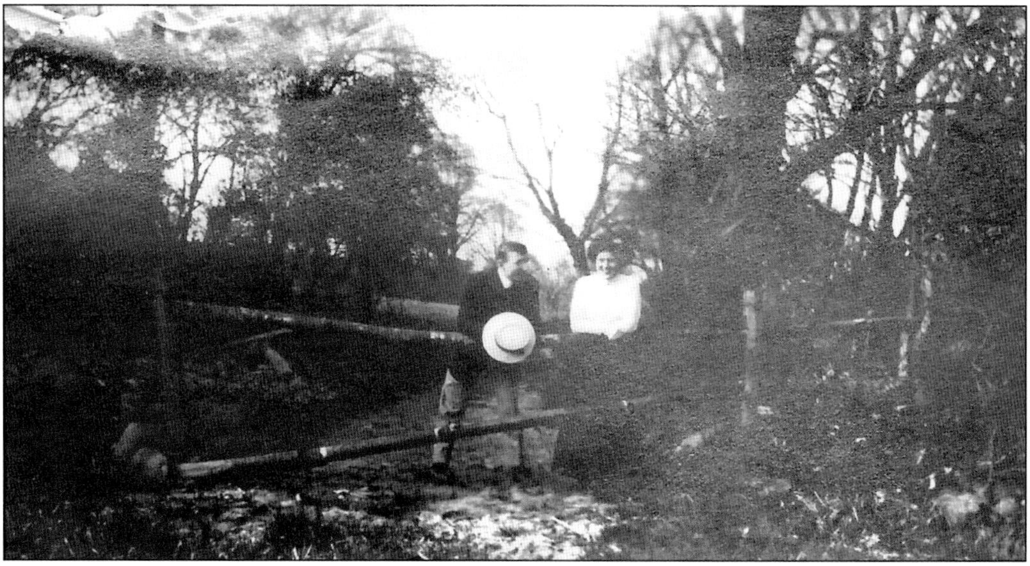

Another ritual at the beginning of the 20th century was courting. Young people enjoyed more freedom, as the once ever-present chaperone was becoming a rare sight.

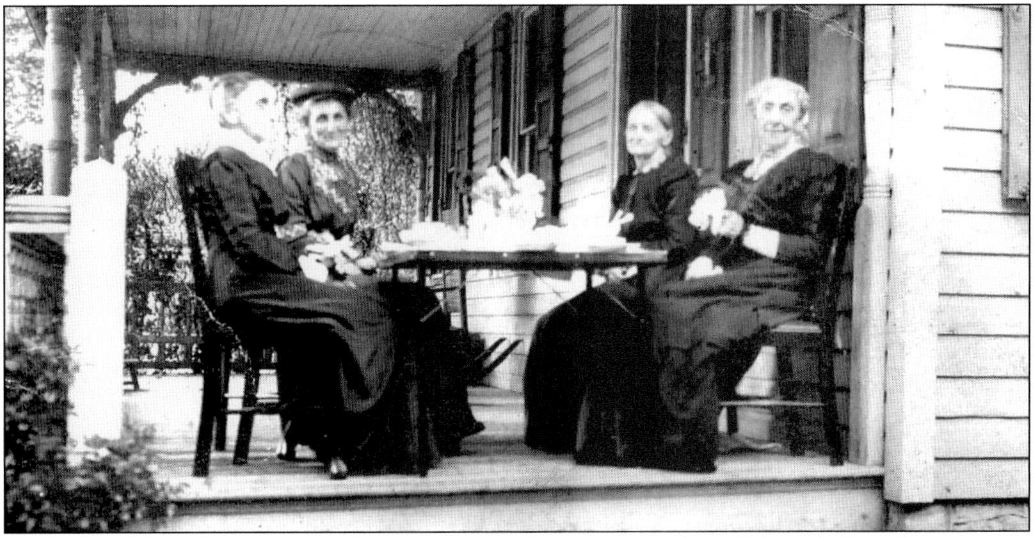

Handcrafts were a pleasant way of spending an afternoon on the porch with friends.

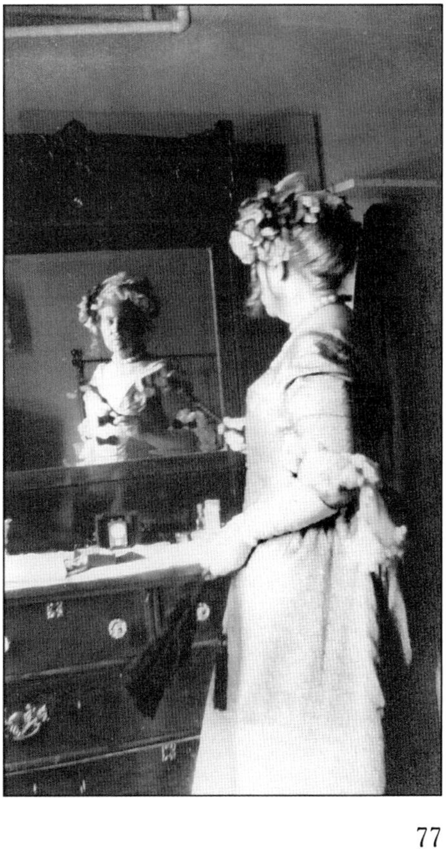

In the late 19th century, many members of old, established families became intensely conscious of their roots, partly as a result of the 1876 centennial celebrations. They founded lineage societies, such as the Daughters of the American Revolution, and dressed in Colonial costumes to attend balls and pageants.

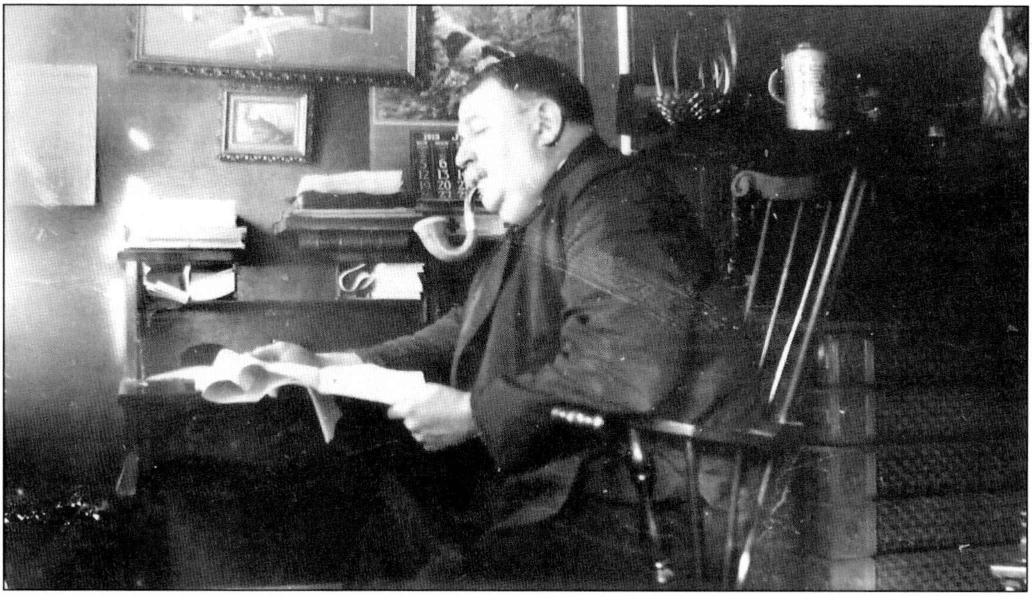

This man is shown smoking his pipe at a time when tobacco was not yet considered a serious health hazard and pipe smoking was thought to be both manly and genteel. One can almost hear the man of the house announcing after dinner, "I'll be in the study smoking my pipe."

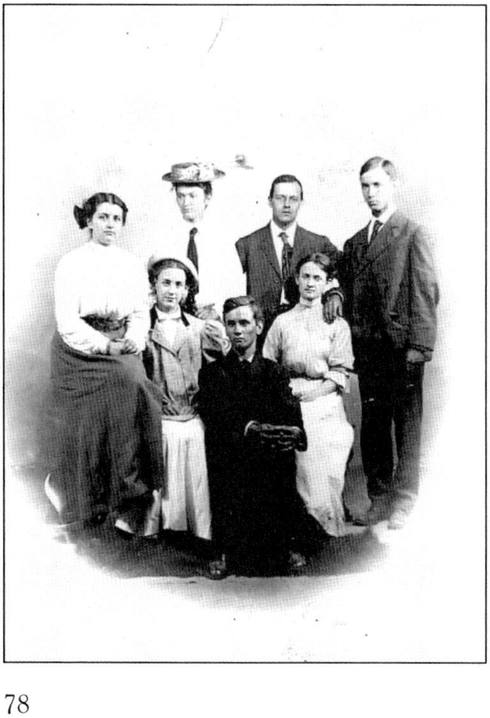

A treat for families living in Plymouth and Whitemarsh was a trip to the Willow Grove amusement park, located in Philadelphia's northeastern suburbs. Dressed in their best for the excursion, this family posed for a portrait, which was then printed as a postcard.

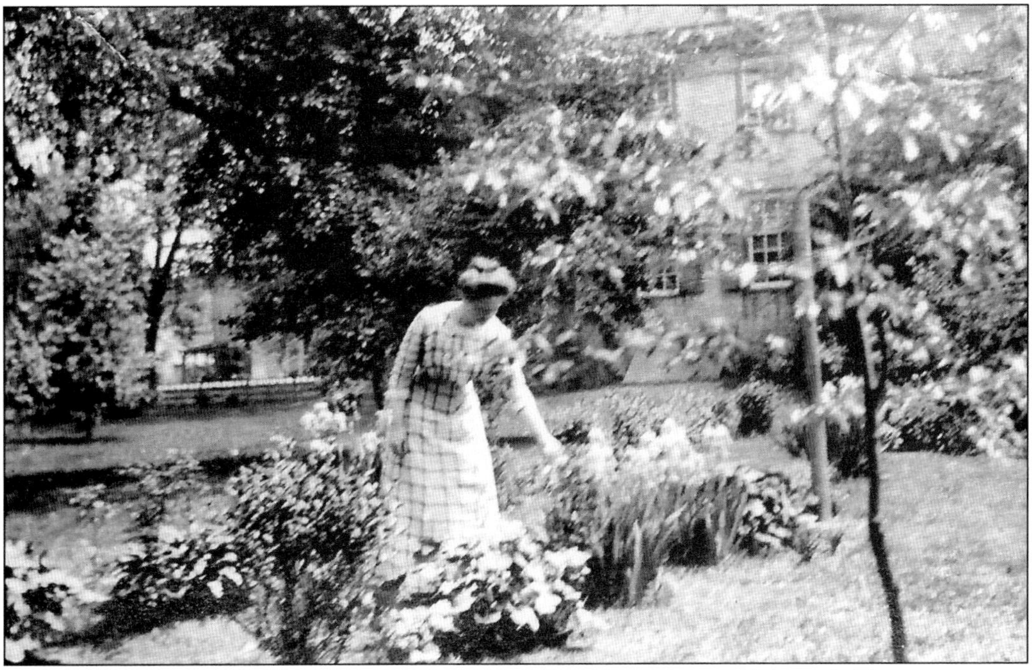

Gardening was a popular pastime, particularly for women. Here, a Plymouth Meeting woman tends her flower garden.

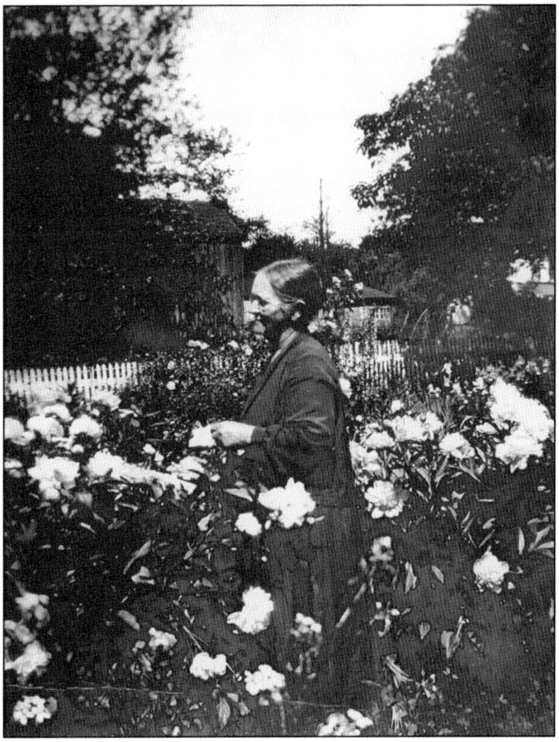

This woman is very proud of her roses—a familiar American scene, with a white picket fence in the background.

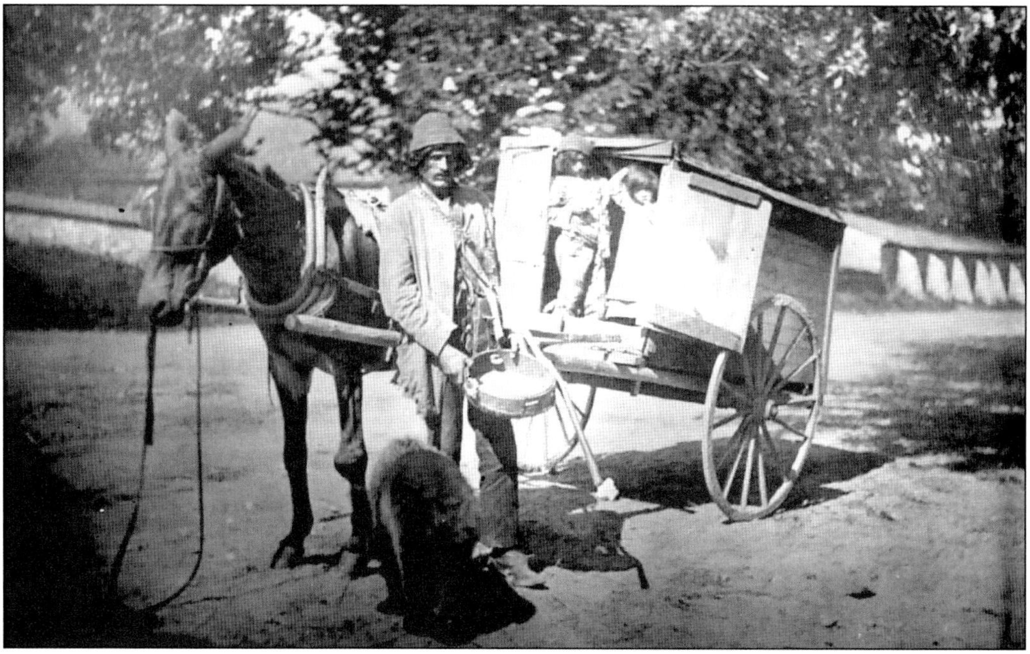

Traveling gypsies worked their way around the countryside, entertaining villagers with, among other novelties, trained bears. This man with his children and their bear visited the Friends Meeting in the 1880s.

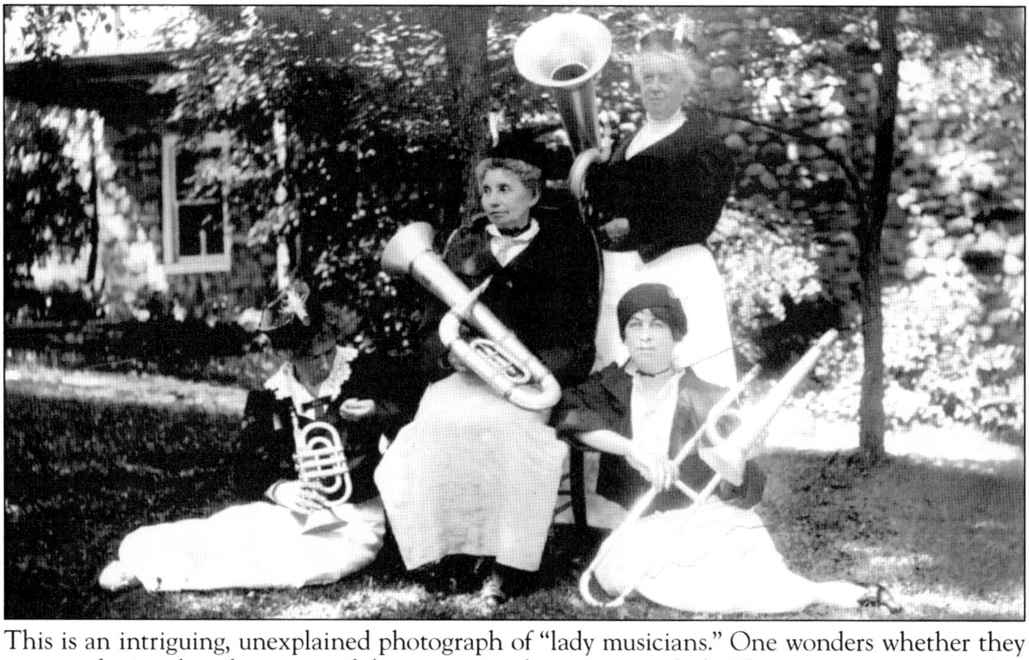

This is an intriguing, unexplained photograph of "lady musicians." One wonders whether they were professional performers or if they were simply posing as a lark. The woman examining her fingernails does not seem terribly interested in her trumpet.

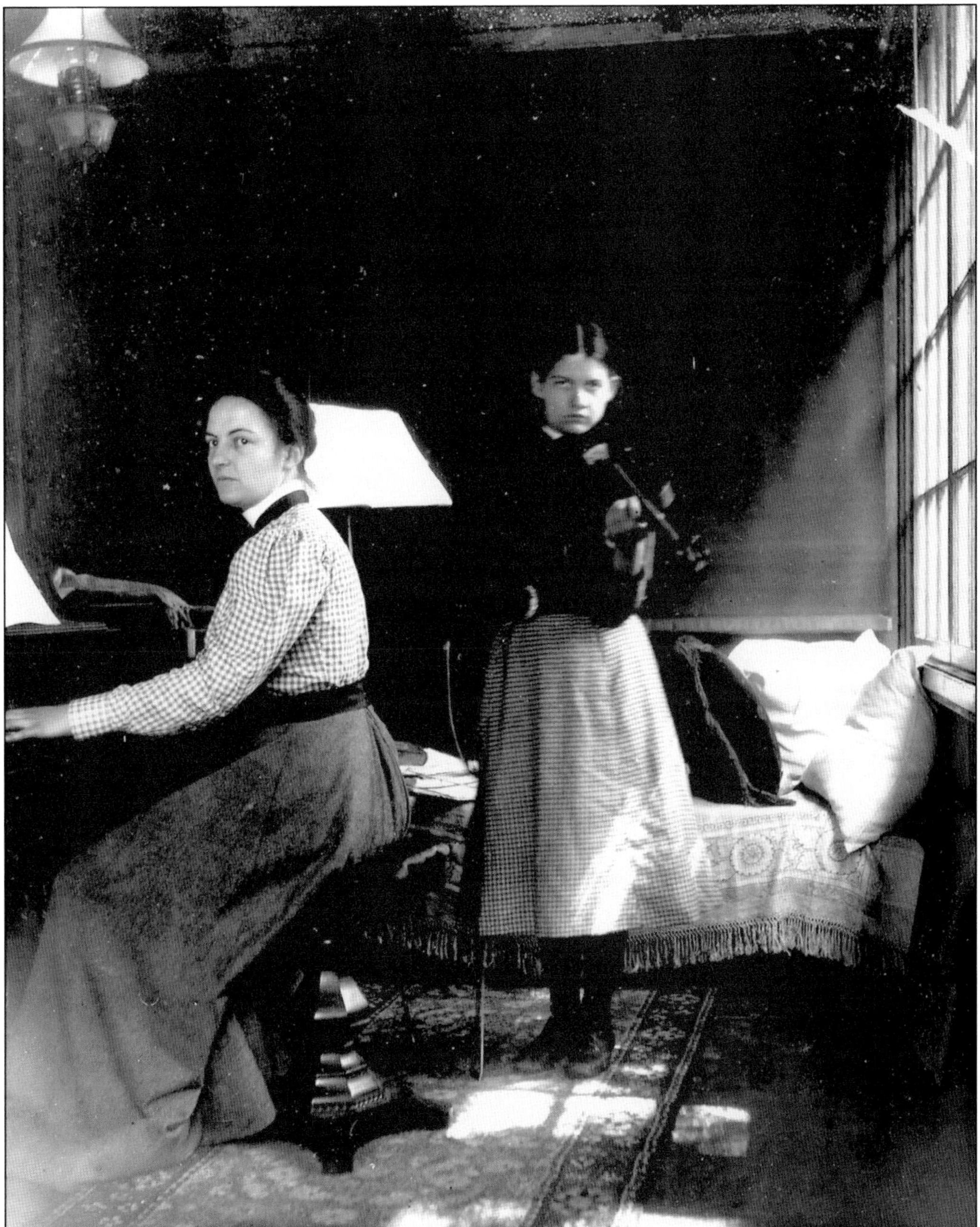

At a time before recordings, families provided their own musical entertainment. This Plymouth Meeting mother and daughter enjoy the piano and violin in a sunny music room. (Courtesy of the Nancy I. Corson Foundation.)

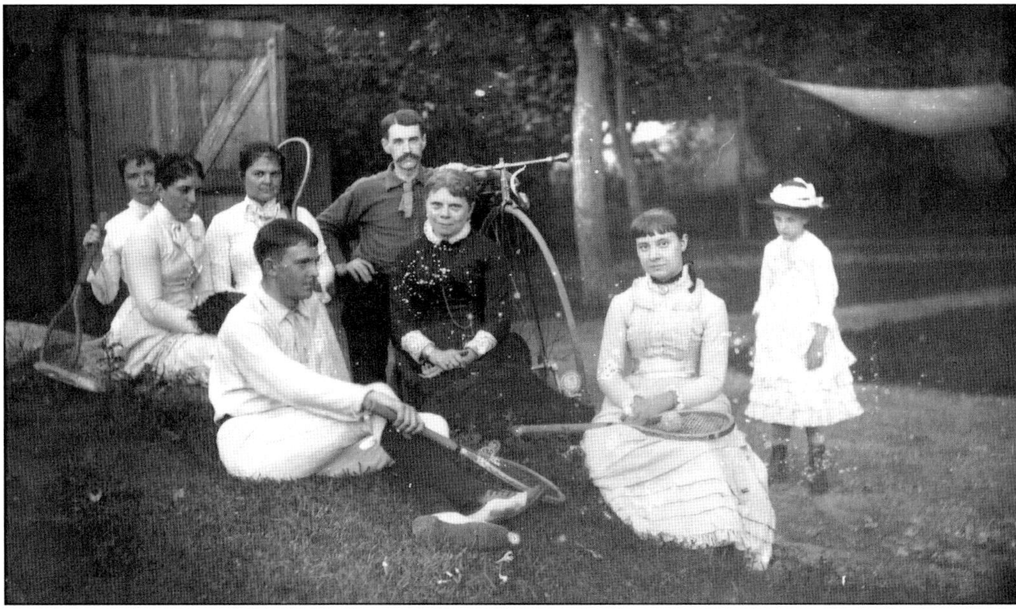

Tennis and bicycling were all the rage in the late 19th century. While bicycling was still considered a man's domain, tennis could be enjoyed by both sexes. (Courtesy of the Nancy I. Corson Foundation.)

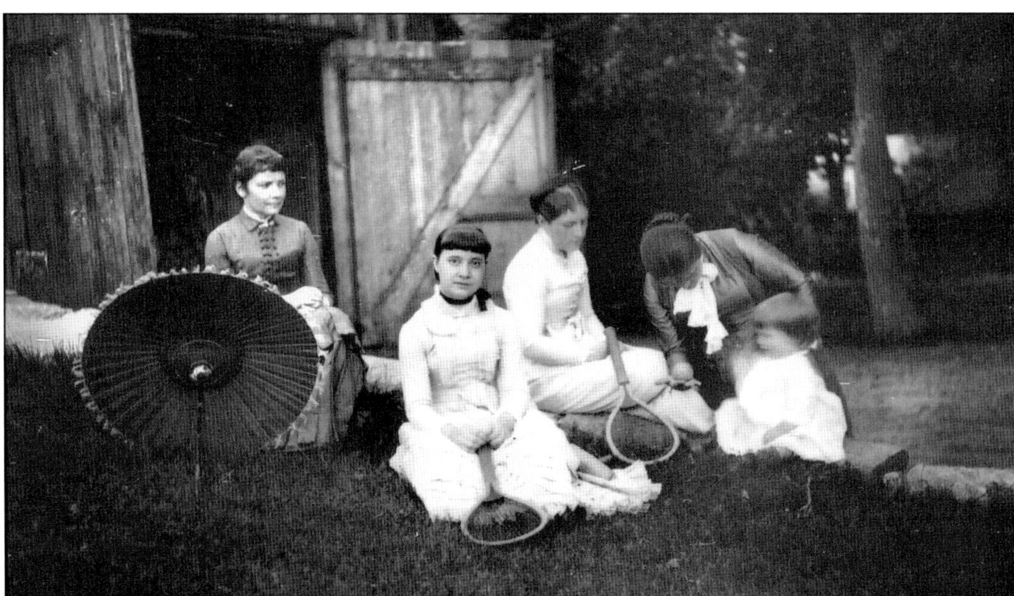

Having a suntan was not fashionable for well-to-do ladies in the Victorian age, since any trace of exposure to the sun would mark them as poor farm women who had to work in the fields or at other difficult outdoor tasks. Many used parasols to shield themselves from the summer sun. (Courtesy of the Nancy I. Corson Foundation.)

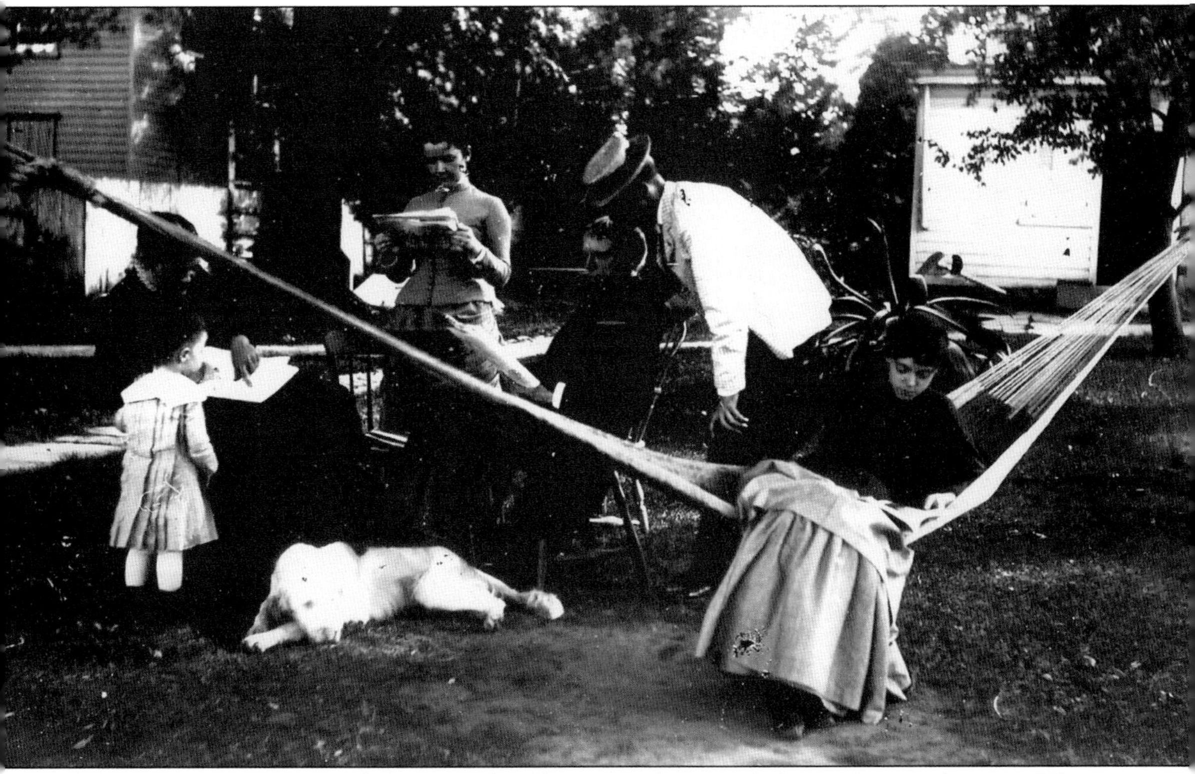

Reading was a favorite family pastime for all ages in the time before radio or television. The Hovenden family and some friends relax with a hammock, books, and newspapers behind the Hovenden House, at 1 East Germantown Pike. (Courtesy of the Nancy I. Corson Foundation.)

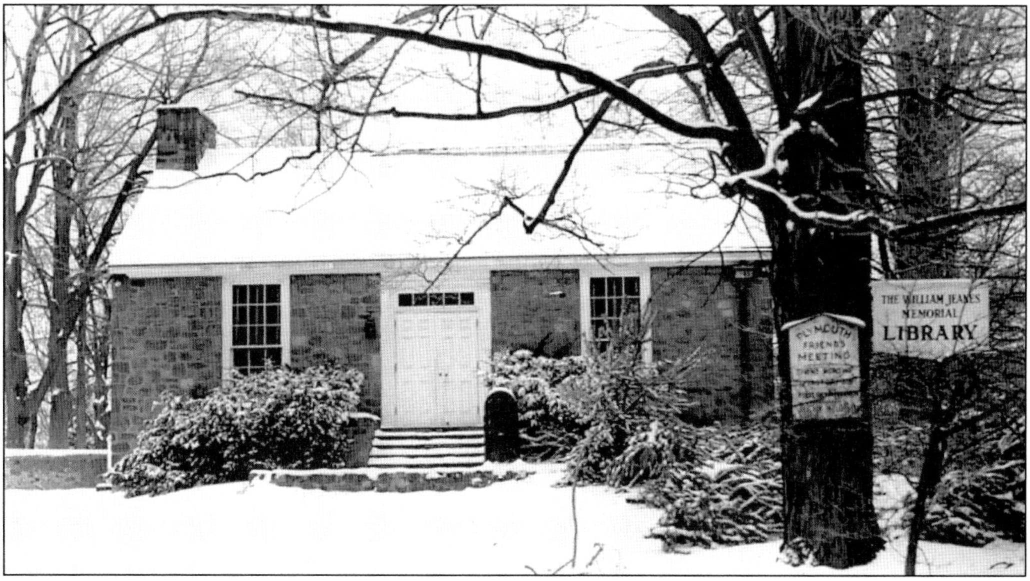

In 1868, citizens in Barren Hill raised funds to establish a library association, which was located in a building on Ridge Pike and in operation for approximately 20 years. In 1926, a trust fund was set up by the widow of William Jeanes to create a public library for the residents of Plymouth Meeting. The library opened in 1933 in a private home on Germantown Pike, and in 1935, it moved to a new building on the grounds of the Friends Meeting.

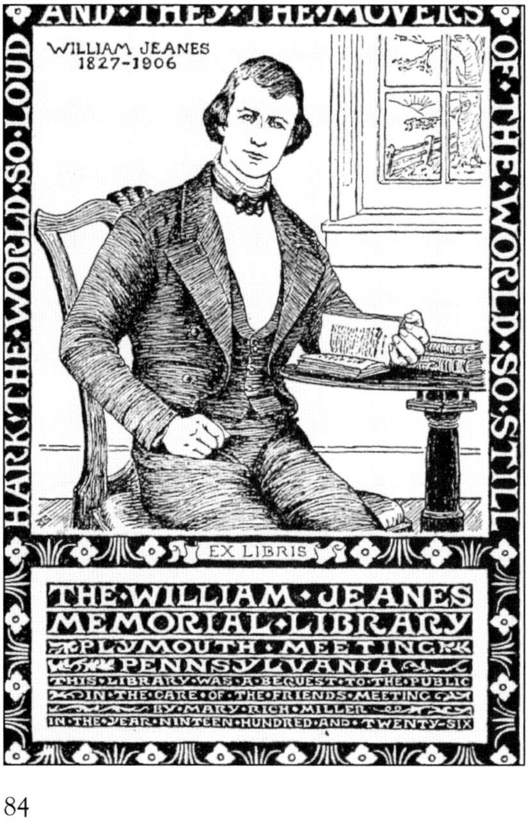

A version of the bookplate engraving by artist Martha Hovenden is still in use by the Friends of the William Jeanes Memorial Library.

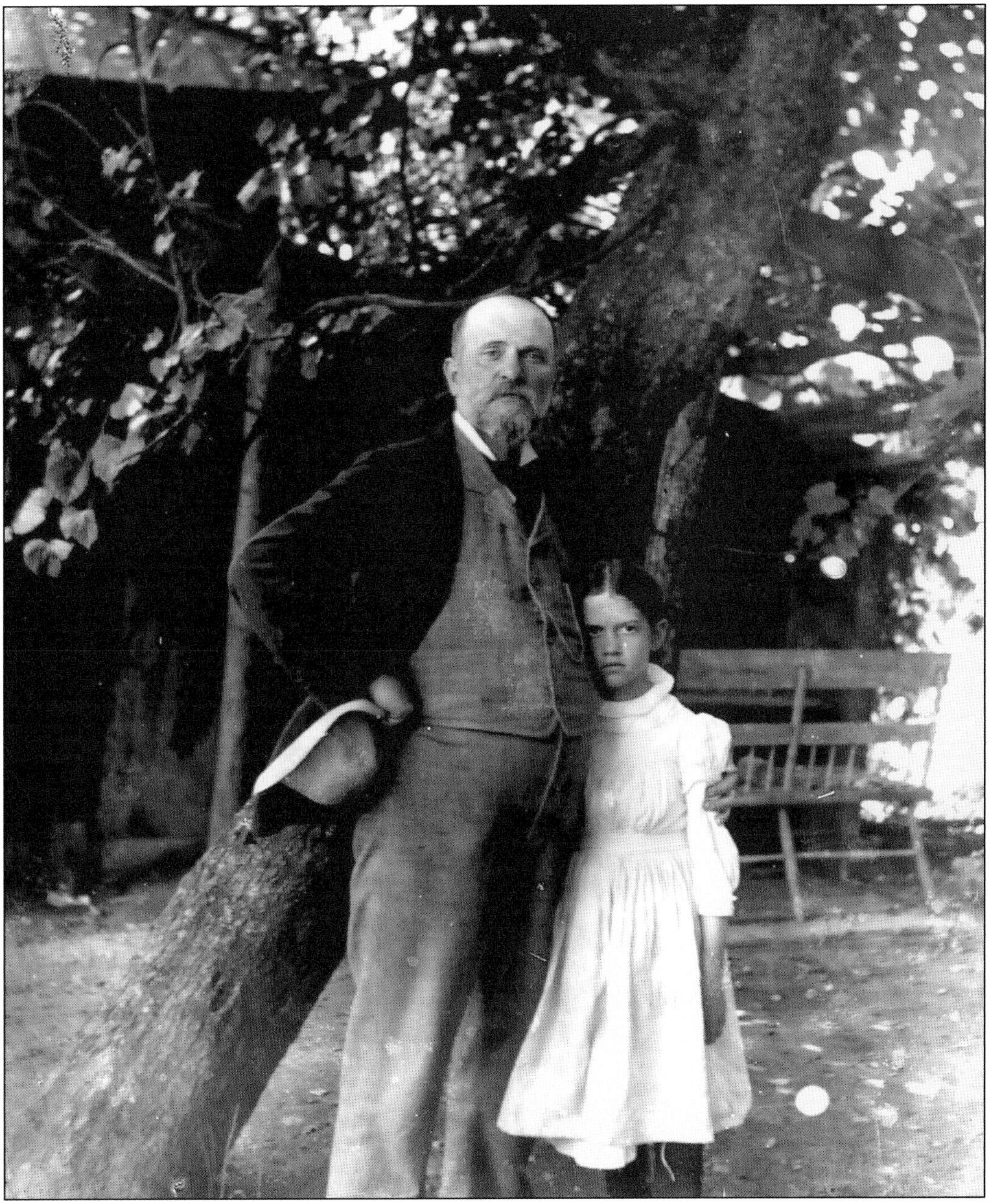

At the height of his career, Thomas Hovenden (1840–1895) was the most popular genre painter in the United States. Born in Ireland, Hovenden was orphaned at age six when both his parents died during the potato famine. This traumatic experience was one reason why the artist placed such a strong emphasis on the family and the passing down of important values.

After studying art in Cork, Hovenden immigrated to New York City to join his brother. He continued his studies at the National Academy of Design, followed by a six-year sojourn in France, where he studied under one of the masters of Paris's celebrated Ecole des Beaux-Arts. While in France, he met artist Helen Corson of Plymouth Meeting, whom he married in 1881, settling in the village the same year. They lived at the family homestead on the southeast corner of Butler Pike and Germantown Avenue. (Courtesy of the Nancy I. Corson Foundation.)

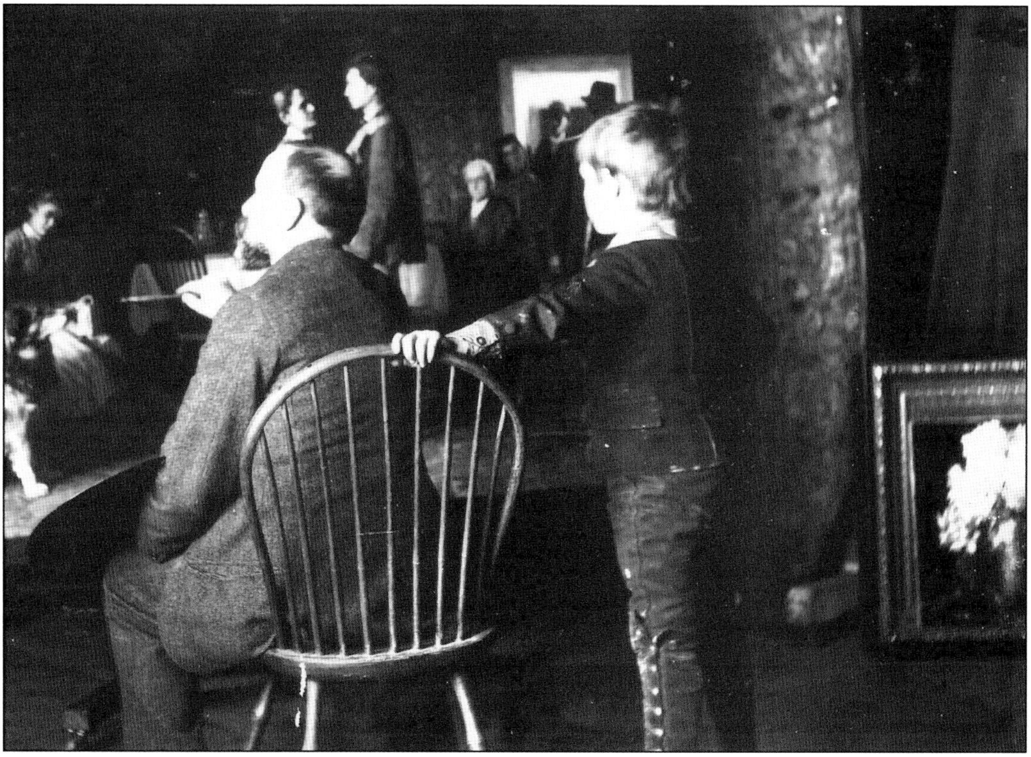

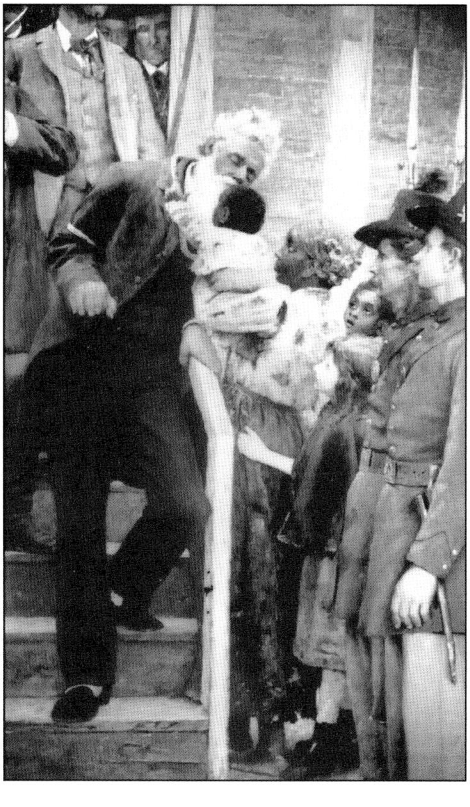

Using the old Abolition Hall behind the house as his studio, Hovenden created his most famous works at Plymouth Meeting, including *The Last Moments of John Brown* (left) and *Breaking Home Ties* (above, in progress). *Breaking Home Ties,* exhibited at Chicago's Columbian Exposition of 1893, was the most popular canvas at the fair. In 1895, Hovenden's life was cut short when he was struck by a train at a grade crossing near his home. A century later, Hovenden is viewed as an extraordinarily gifted artist whose works offer important insights into late-19th-century American life. (Courtesy of the Nancy I. Corson Foundation.)

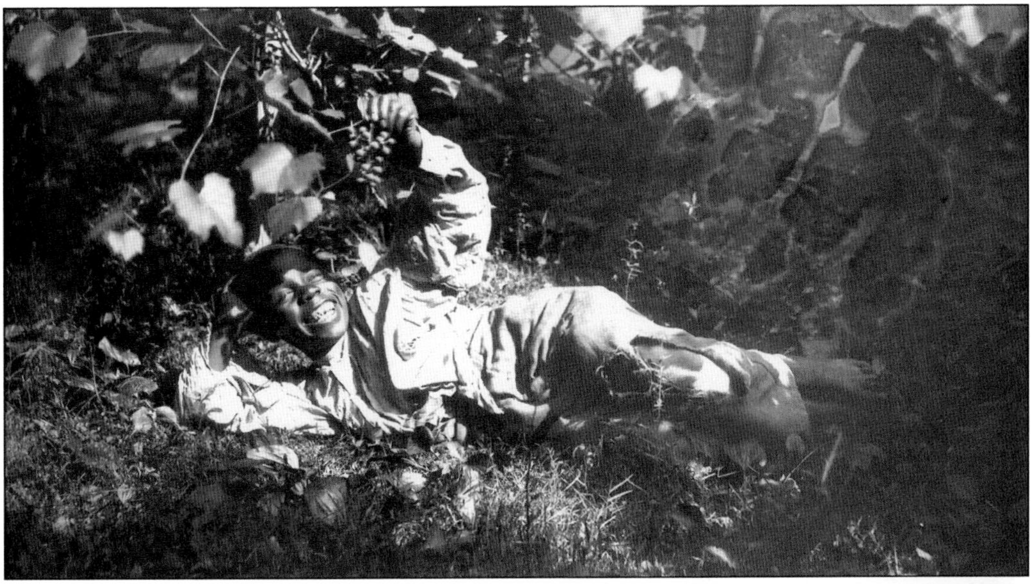

Hovenden's neighbors were often asked to pose for characters in his paintings. Here, a young Plymouth Meeting boy relaxes while taking a break from the taxing job of sitting motionless for long stretches of time. To the right is a photograph of the completed painting. (Courtesy of the Nancy I. Corson Foundation.)

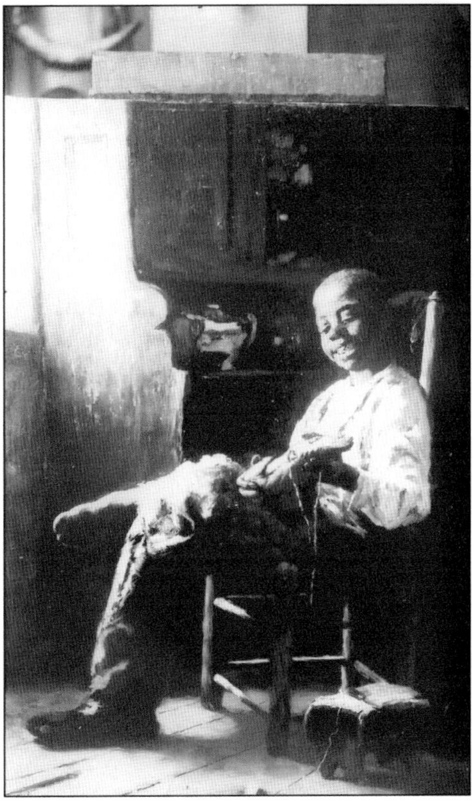

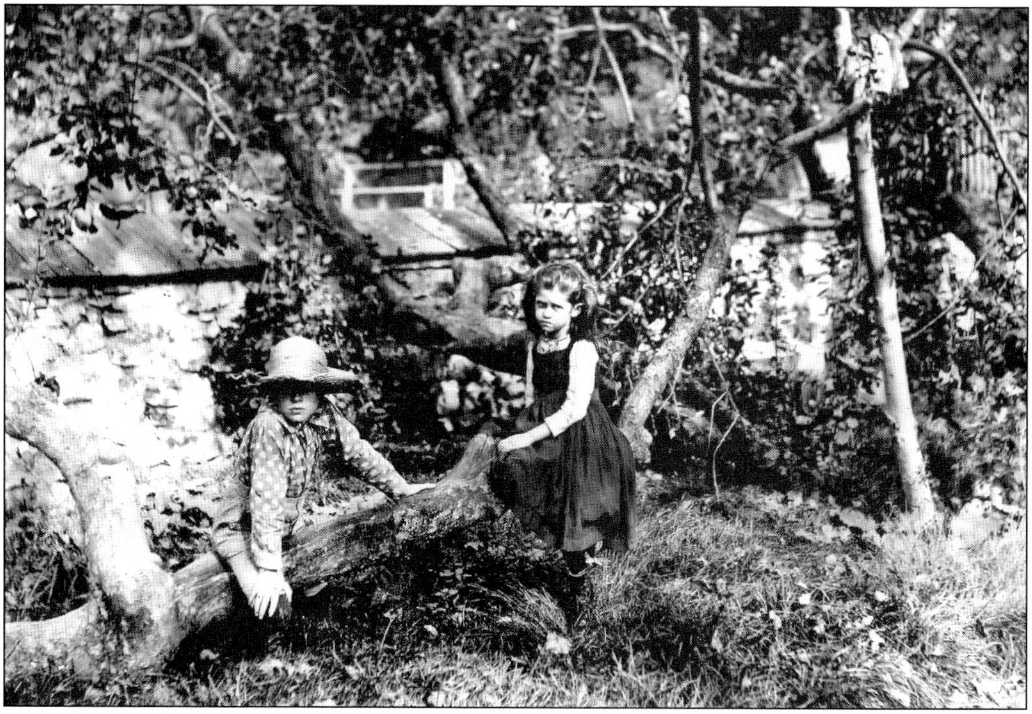

As today, children used imagination at play, creating their own games and adventures. Here, a Plymouth Meeting boy and girl play on a fallen limb near the Friends Meeting. (Courtesy of the Nancy I. Corson Foundation.)

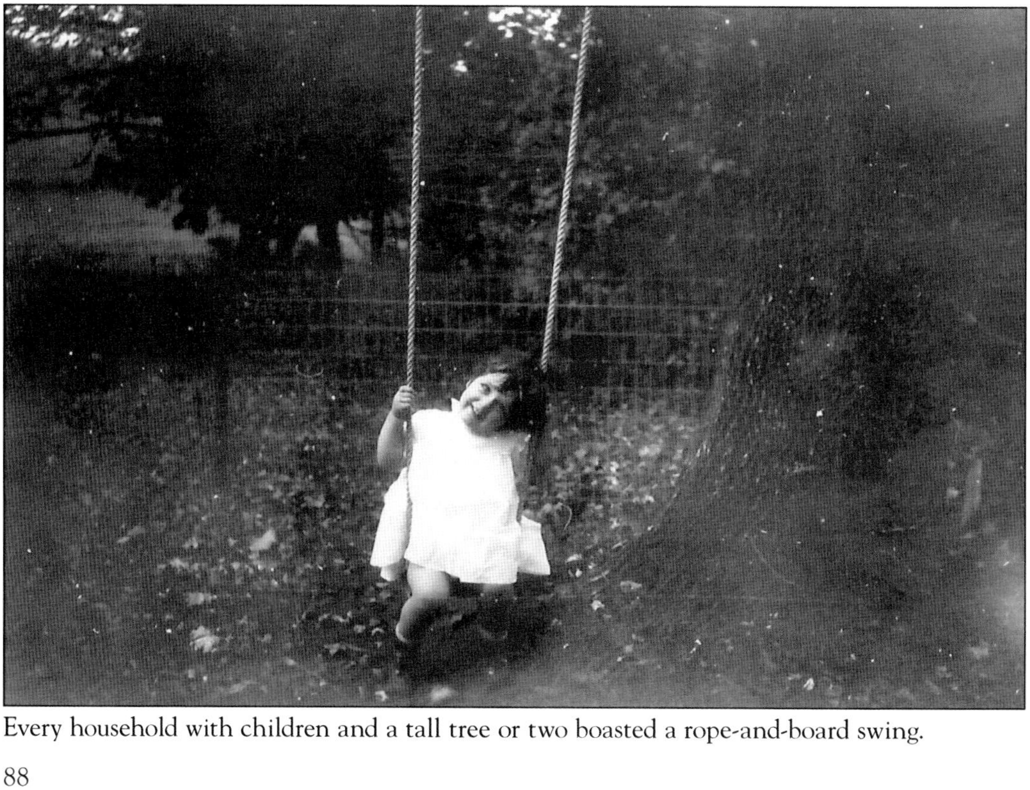

Every household with children and a tall tree or two boasted a rope-and-board swing.

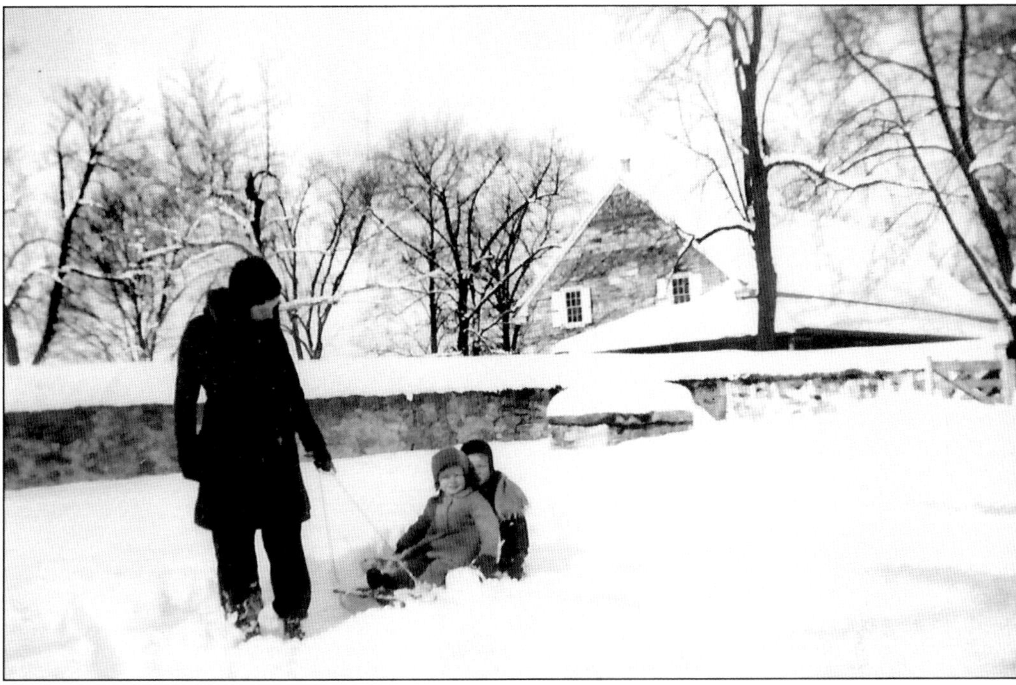

Children have always loved to play in the snow. In February 1941, a blizzard hit Plymouth and Whitemarsh, creating enormous drifts and leaving behind days of fun for children and days of cleanup for their parents.

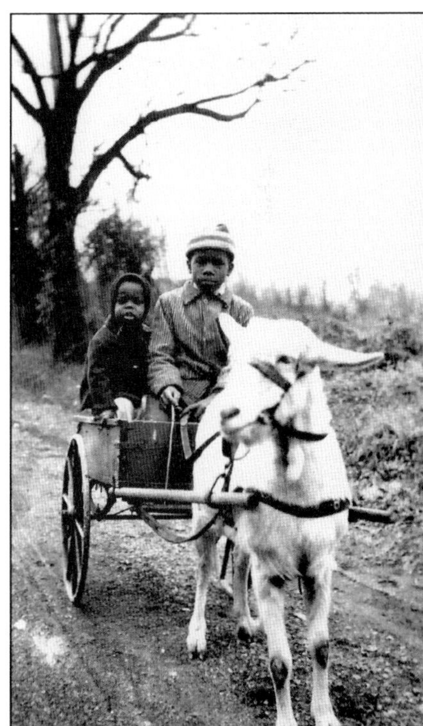

Toys have long reflected aspects of adult life. Two Plymouth Meeting children play in a goat cart, perhaps imitating their own parents' horse and cart. (Courtesy of the Nancy I. Corson Foundation.)

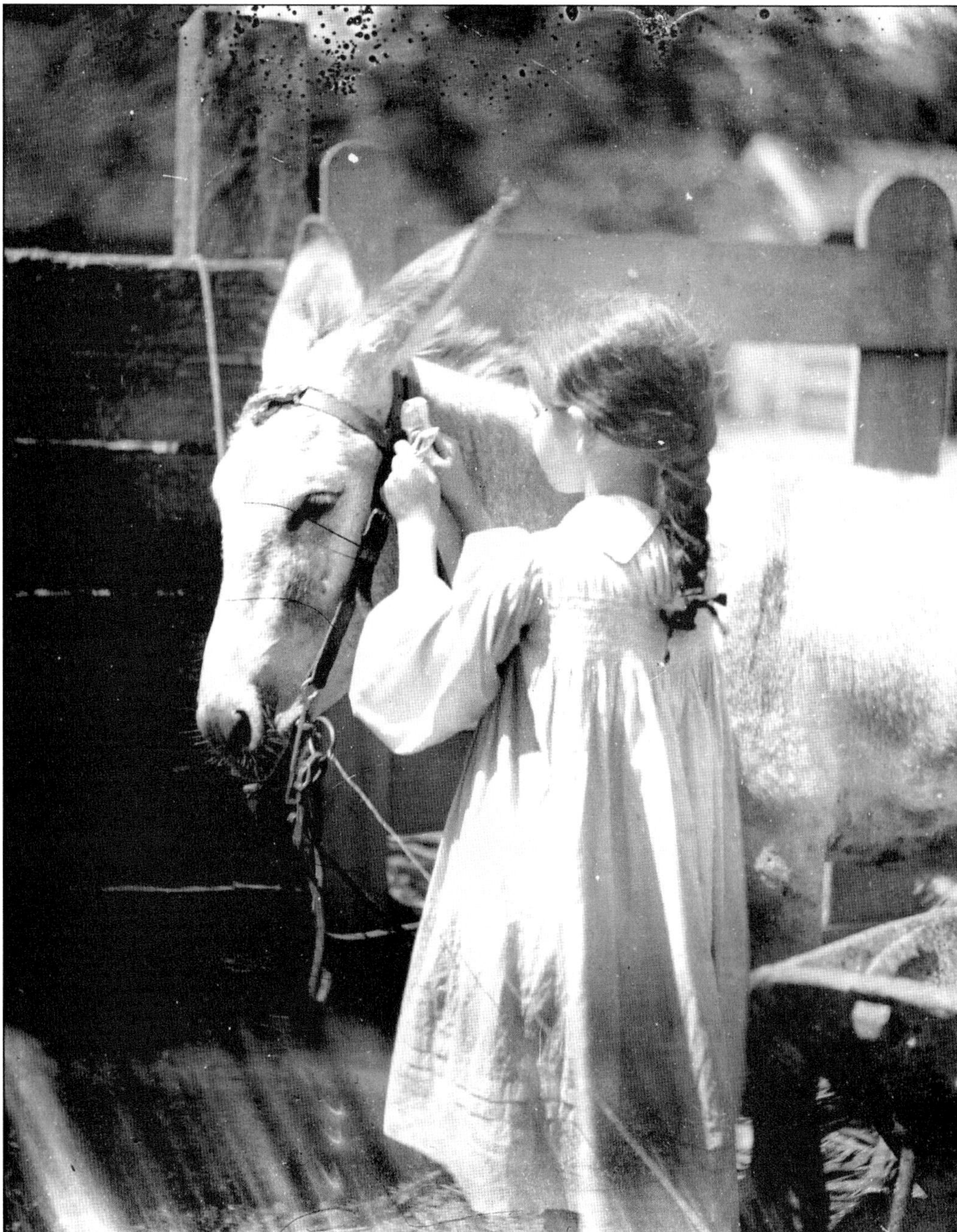

Horses were a part of everyday life as work animals, transportation, and pets. This little girl is tying a ribbon on her favorite pony. (Courtesy of the Nancy I. Corson Foundation.)

Children who managed to master the art of walking on stilts enjoyed a powerful new perspective. (Courtesy of the Nancy I. Corson Foundation.)

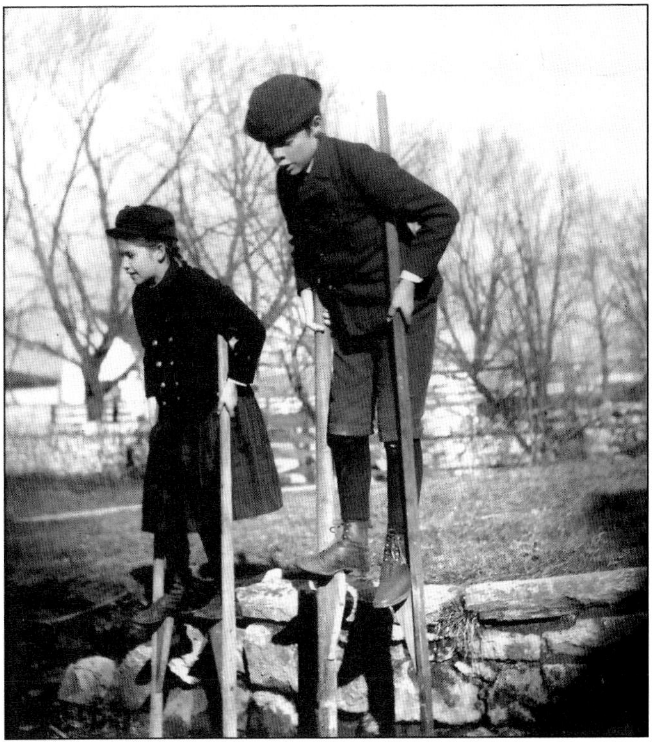

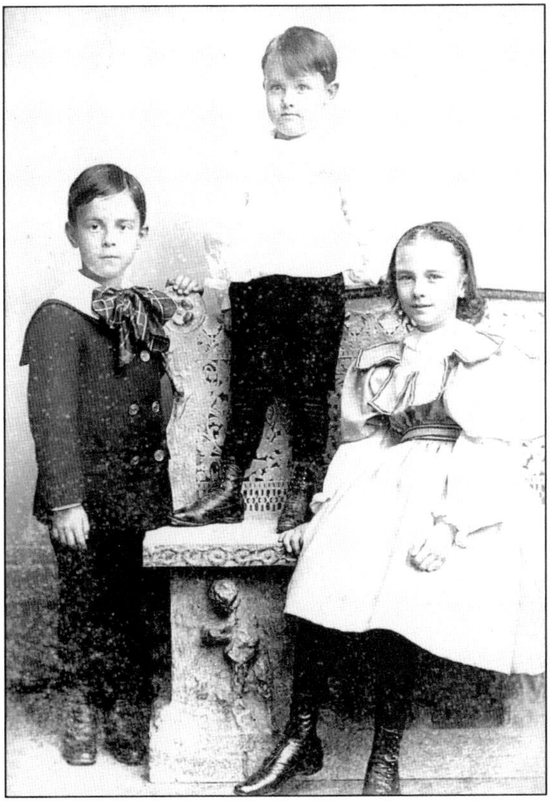

Children's clothing in the late 19th century appears rather fussy to modern eyes, as evidenced by Corson Poley's floppy bow tie and Emily Poley's elaborate collar. Children often struggled with a special hook needed to fasten the long rows of buttons on boots.

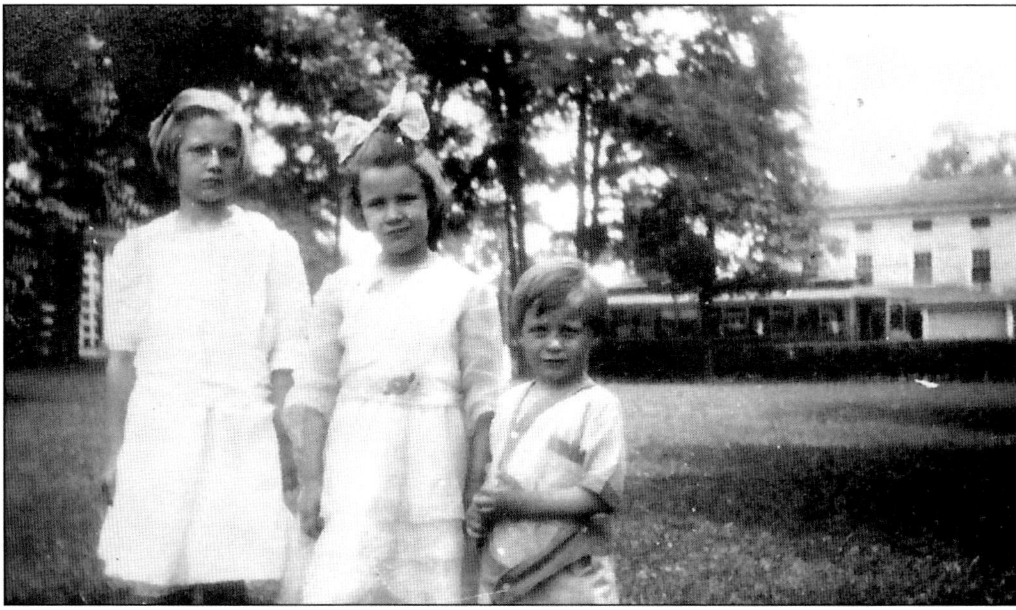

Enormous hair bows were a popular accessory in the 1920s. In the background is the trolley that ran along Germantown Pike.

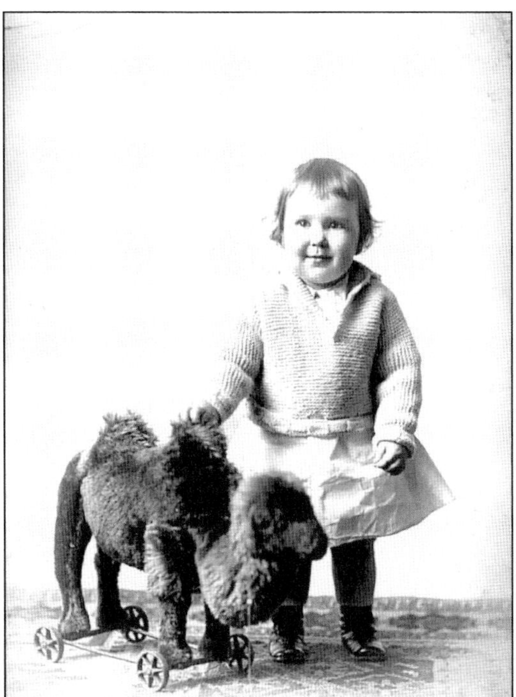

This young boy, in a hand-knit sweater and sturdy boots, seems quite proud of his stuffed camel.

May Day was a popular way to celebrate the coming of spring. Many schools and organizations held elaborate affairs, featuring Maypole dances, costumes, and sporting events.

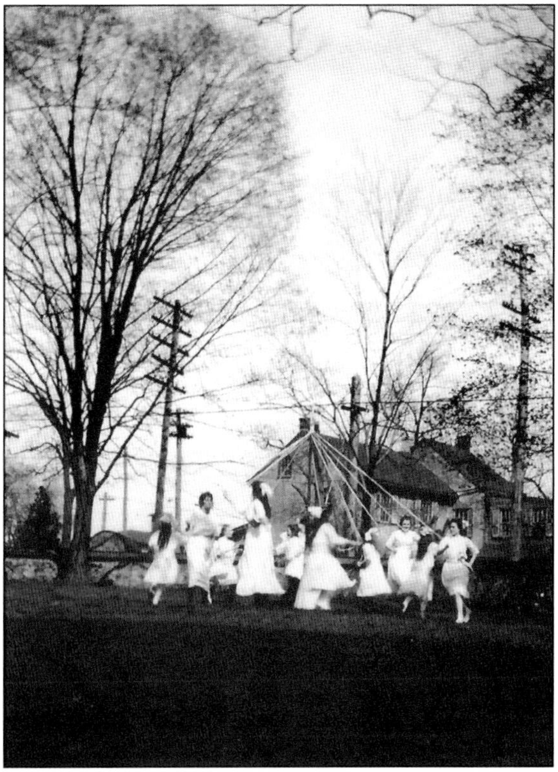

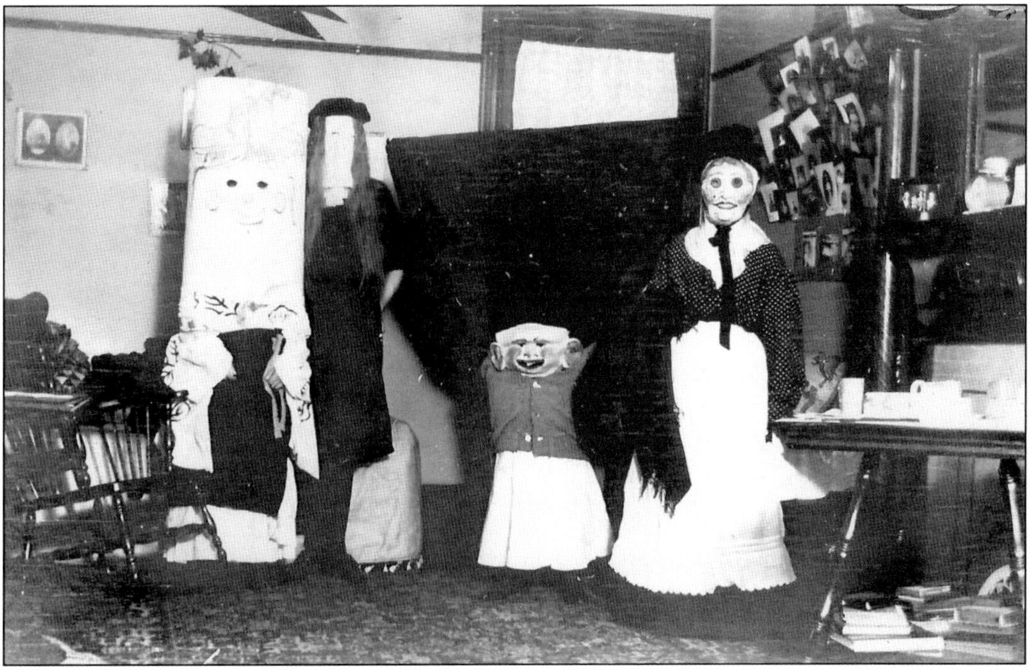

As in most communities, dressing up for Halloween is a tradition in Plymouth and Whitemarsh.

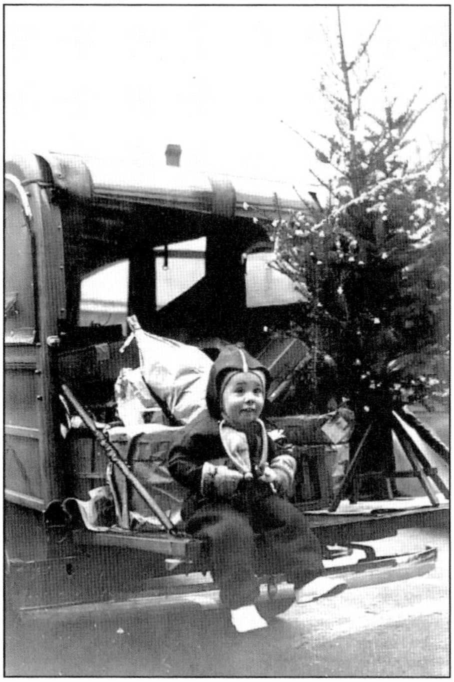

This young boy, perched on the back of the family "station wagon," is eager to get home for Christmas. Station wagons were originally wooden, horse-drawn wagons used to drive to and from train stations. Later, motorized station wagons retained the style of a wood-sided wagon—even if the wood was fake—into the late 20th century.

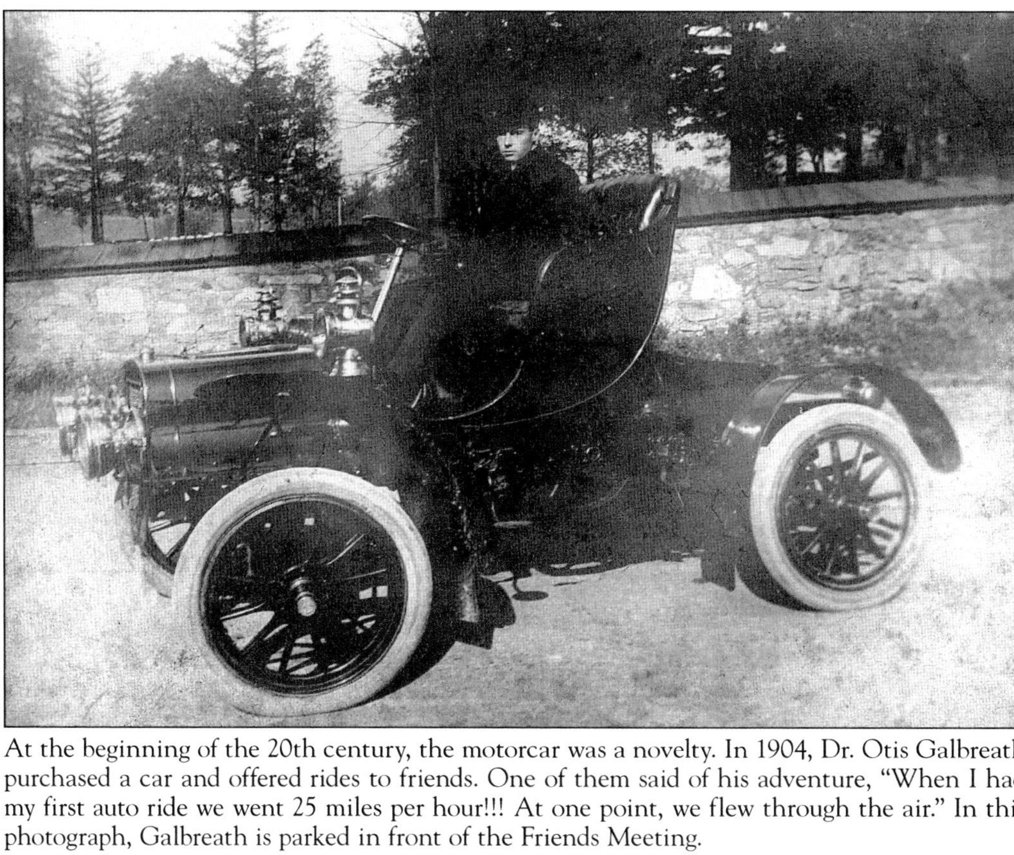

At the beginning of the 20th century, the motorcar was a novelty. In 1904, Dr. Otis Galbreath purchased a car and offered rides to friends. One of them said of his adventure, "When I had my first auto ride we went 25 miles per hour!!! At one point, we flew through the air." In this photograph, Galbreath is parked in front of the Friends Meeting.

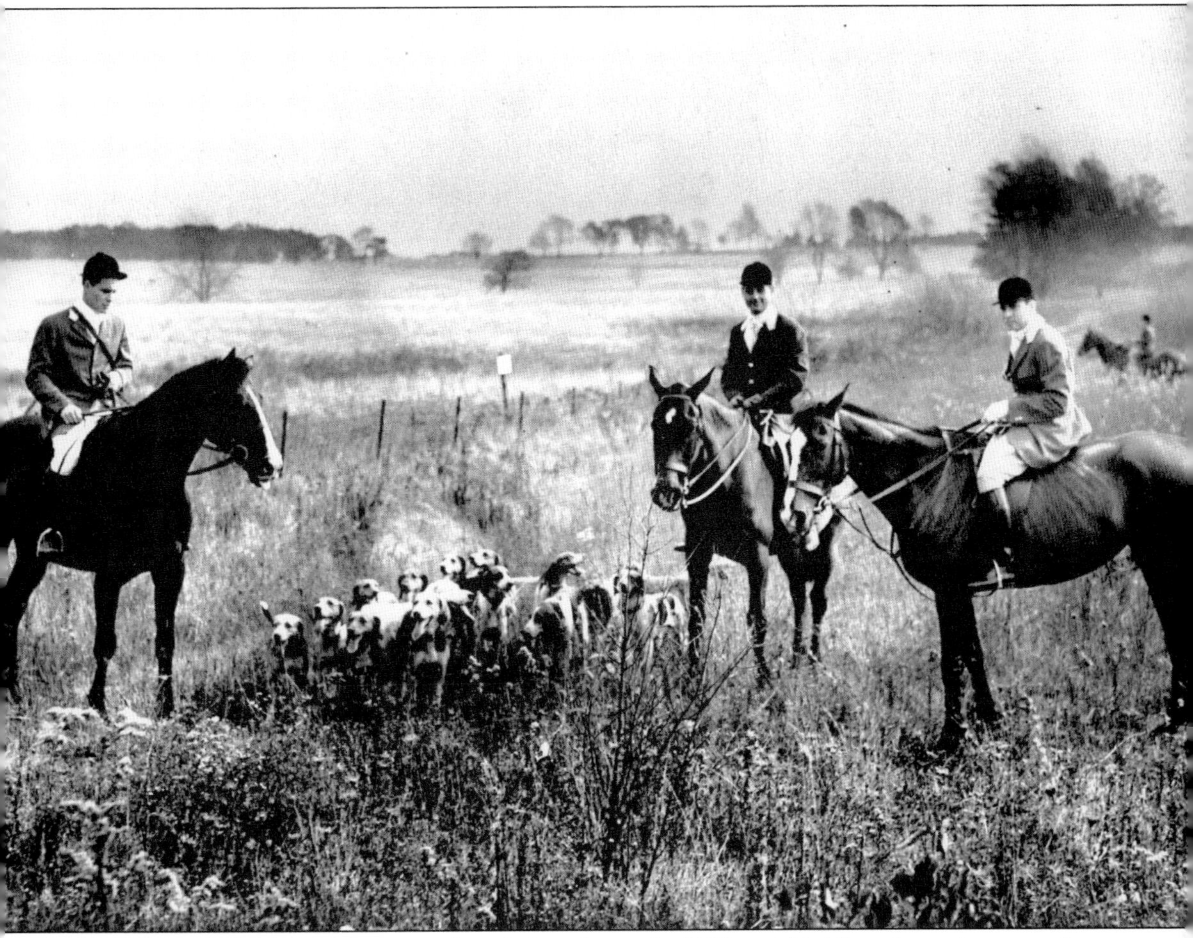

The Whitemarsh Valley Hunt was founded in the early 1900s, with riding three days a week, fall and winter, across Montgomery County, through both Plymouth and Whitemarsh, as well as nearby Whitpain, Springfield, and Upper and Lower Gwynedd Townships. In 1925, the *Chestnut Hill and Mount Airy Herald* described one of the more formal hunts: "Throngs of men and women prominently identified in social, club, financial and professional circles, were augmented by many of the hunting set, from New York, Long Island, Washington and Baltimore. . . . Several officials . . . met on horseback, in their pink riding coats." (Courtesy of the Highlands Mansion and Gardens.)

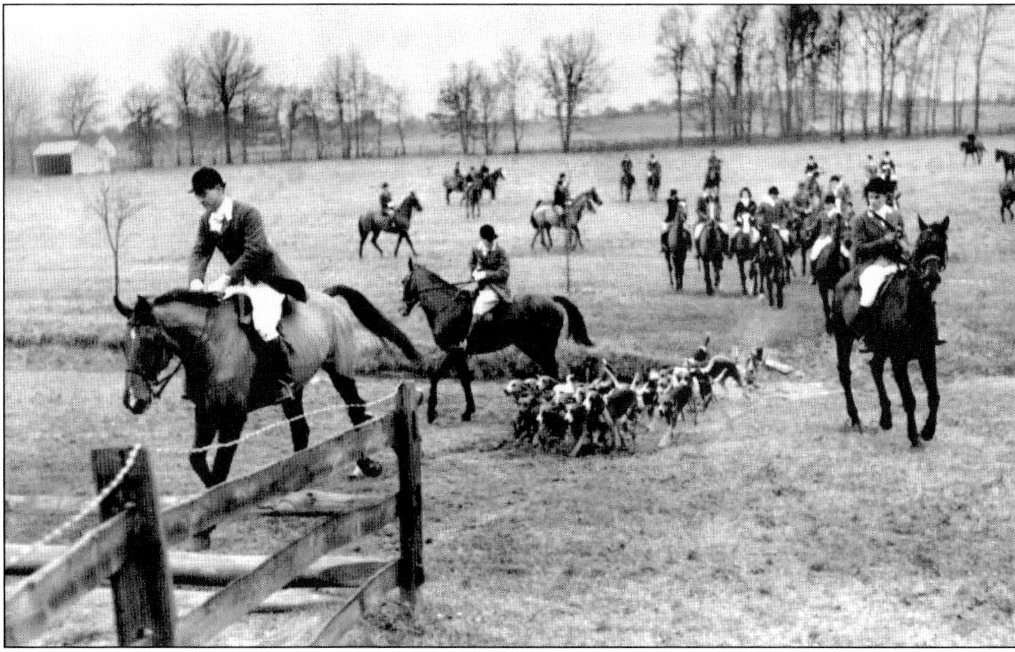

In 1953, the Pennsylvania Turnpike separated the clubhouse, stables, and kennels from most of the hunting grounds of the Whitemarsh Valley Hunt, ending the days of riding across the countryside. When the club decided to disband, several members in Pennlyn took charge of the dogs and formed the Wissahickon Hounds. (Courtesy of the Highlands Mansion and Gardens.)

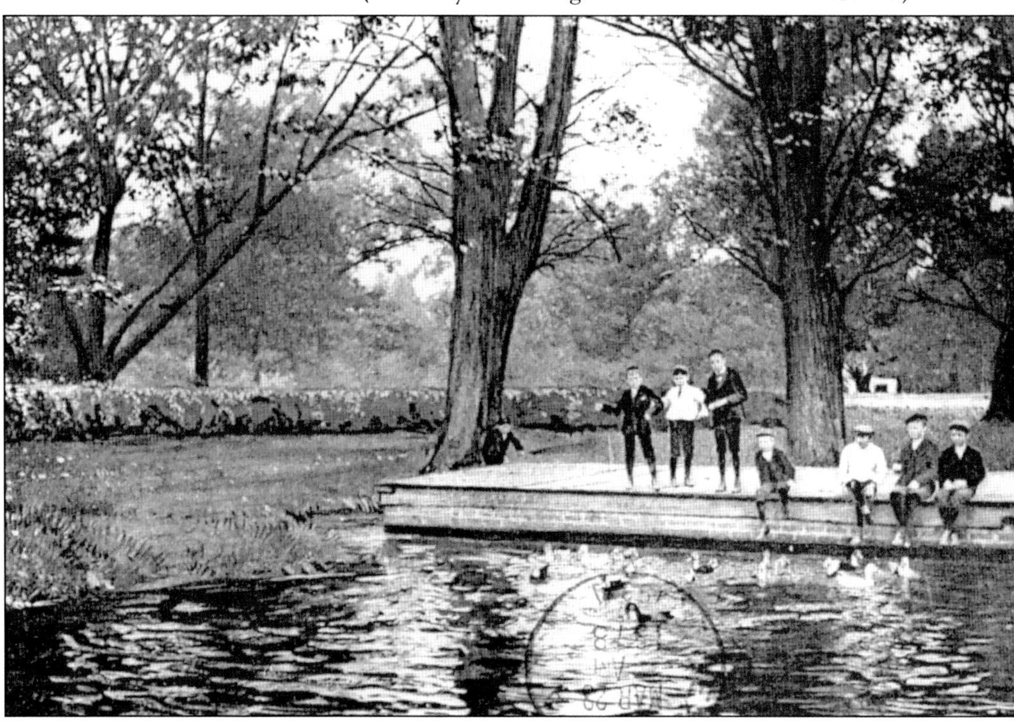

The Bubbling Springs, in Spring Mill, were a popular spot for picnicking and skipping stones. A group of boys feeds the ducks *c.* 1910.

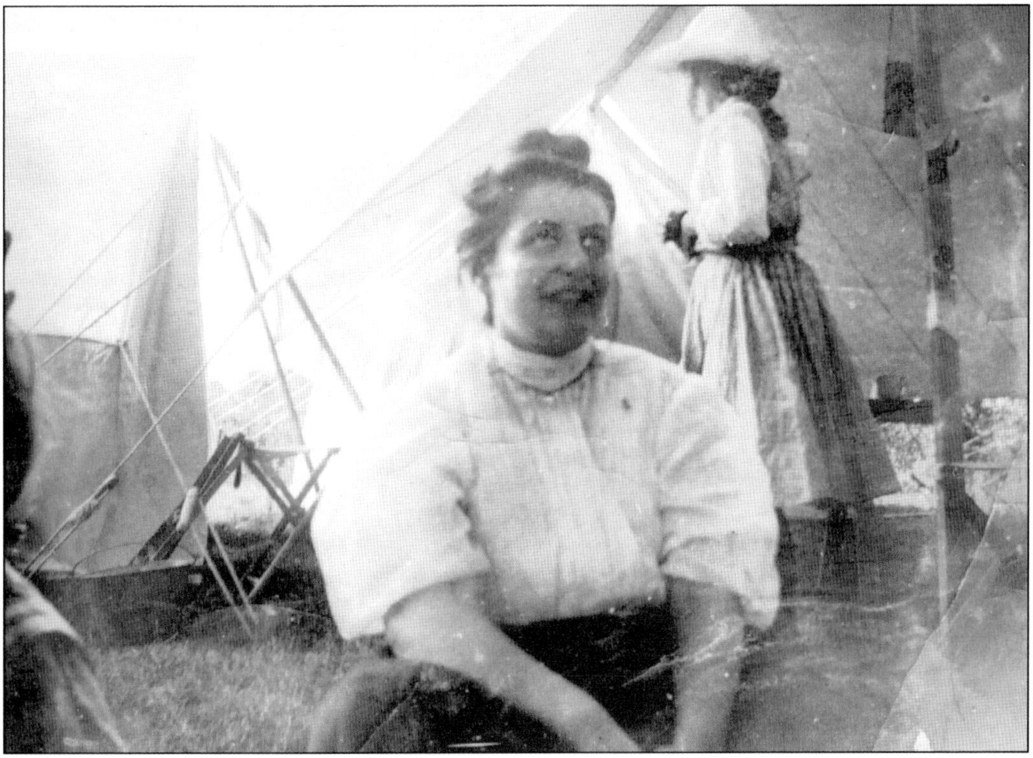

The "new woman" of the 1920s enjoyed outdoor activities as a welcome part of the growing emphasis on a healthy lifestyle. These women take in the fresh air while camping in a tent.

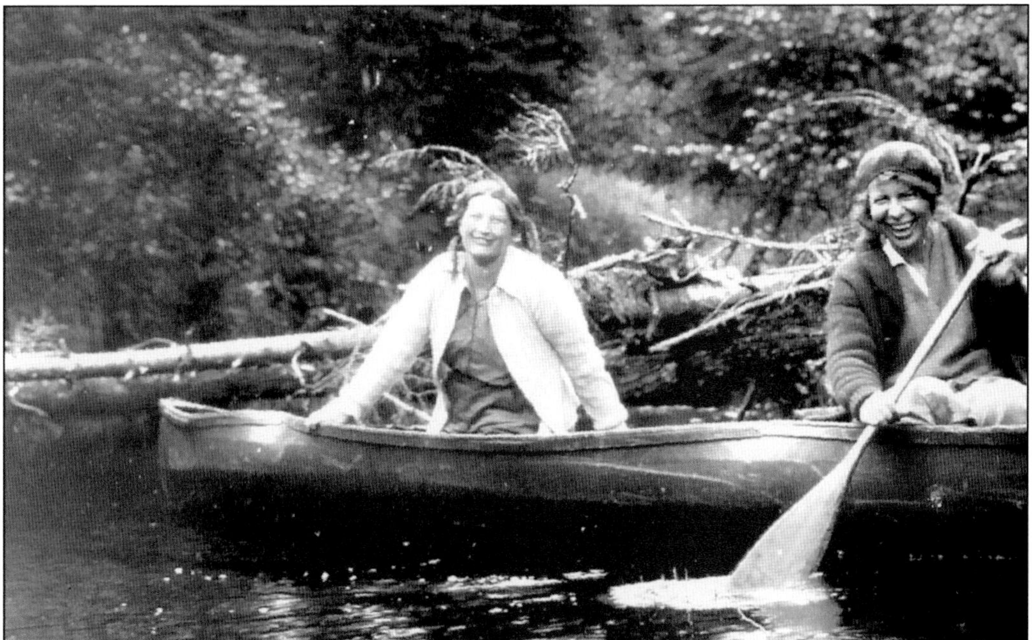

Both men and women enjoyed canoeing on the scenic Wissahickon Creek, which wound its way through the area.

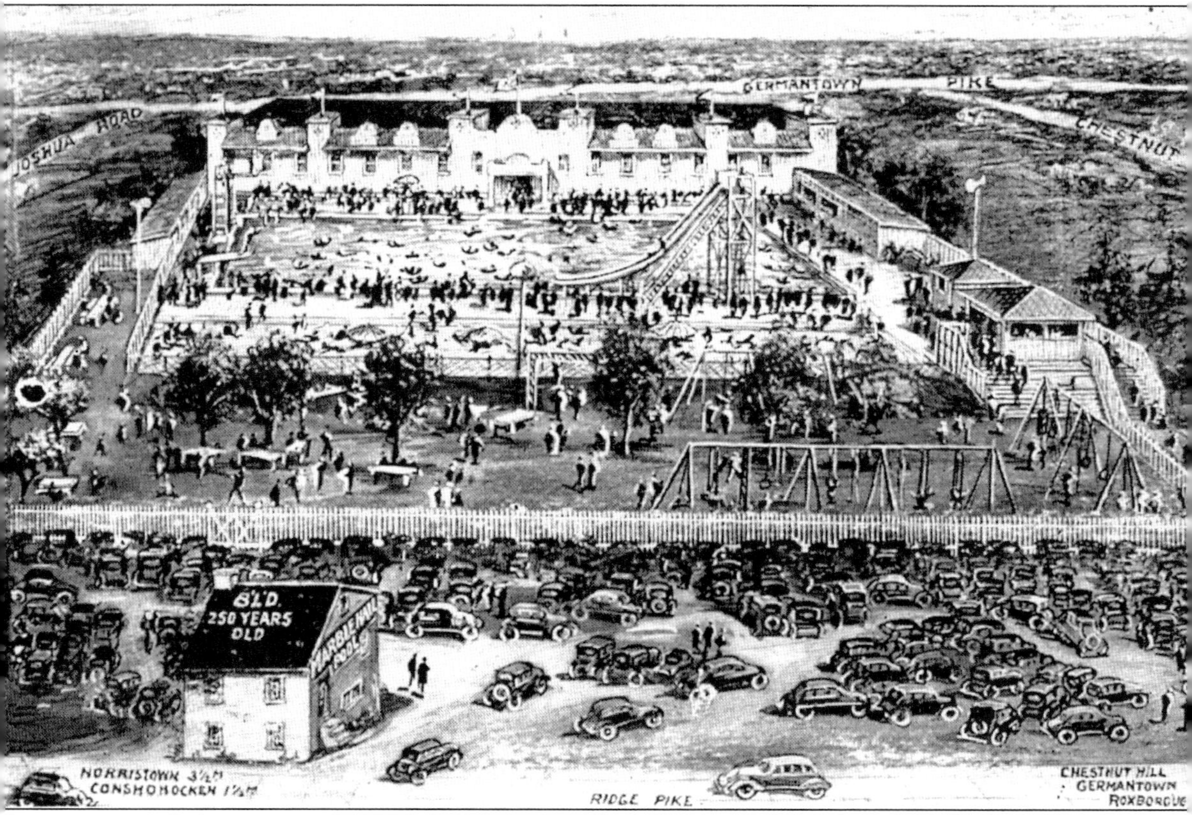

A popular local resort for many years was the Marble Hall Pool, located along Ridge Pike between Joshua Road and Chestnut Street. The swimming pool was built by W. Warner Harper, also the builder of the Marble Hall Golf Course and the head of the Andorra Nurseries for many years. During World War II, student admission to the pool was a special rate of 27¢, plus a 3¢ war tax.

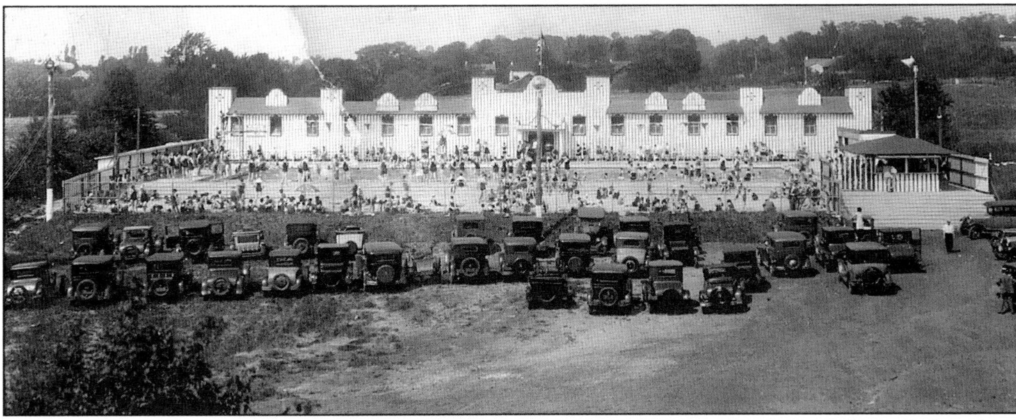

Shown here in 1929, the Marble Hall Pool featured a castlelike bathhouse and sandy beach.

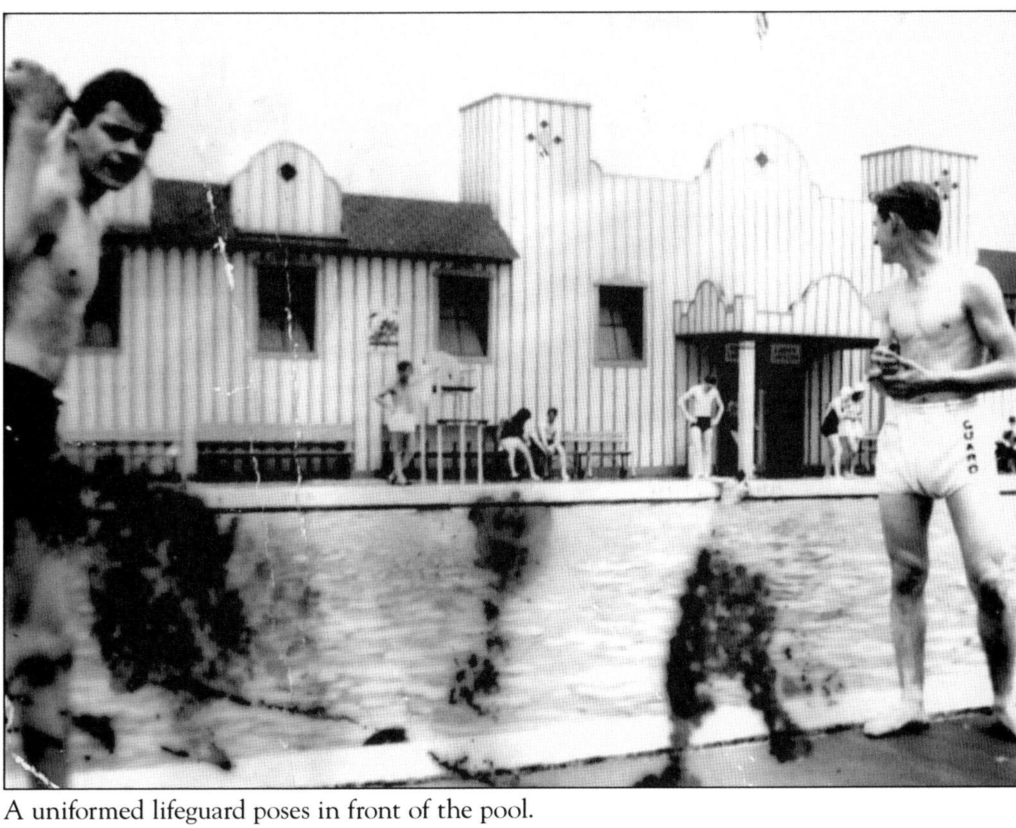

A uniformed lifeguard poses in front of the pool.

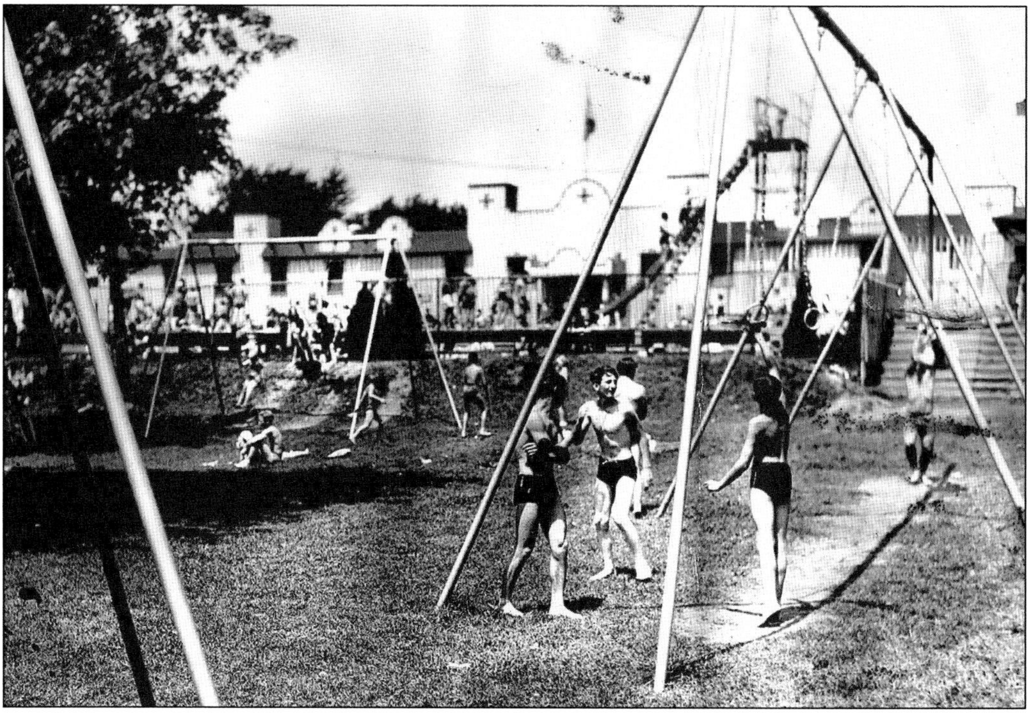

Besides swimming, Marble Hall offered swings, rings, slides, and picnic grounds.

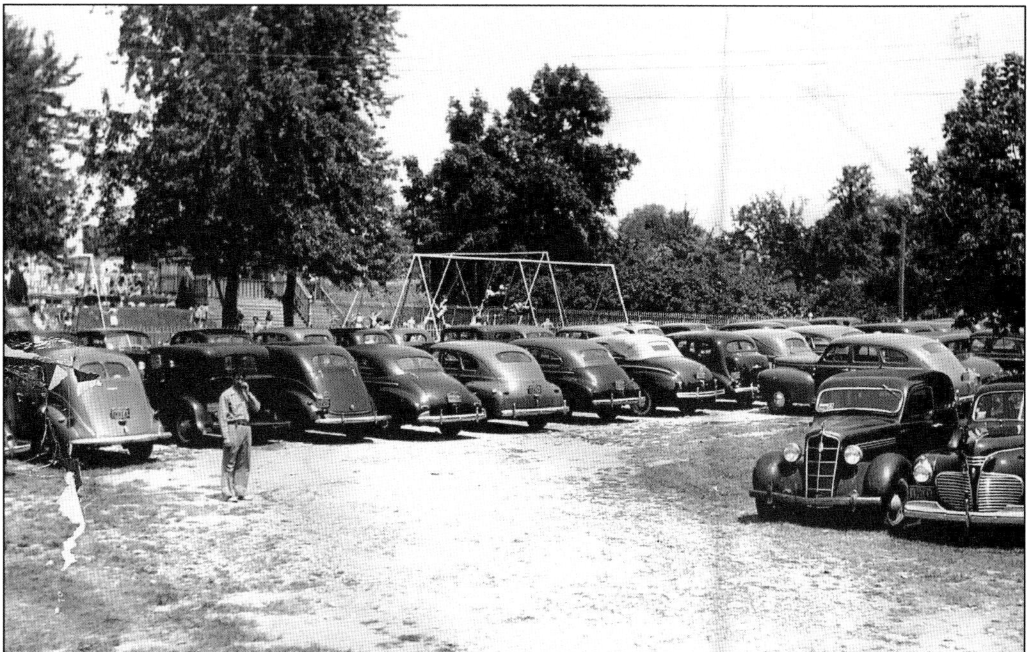

Even before World War II, parking lots sprang up everywhere to serve the growing car culture. By 1940, most people were driving to Marble Hall.

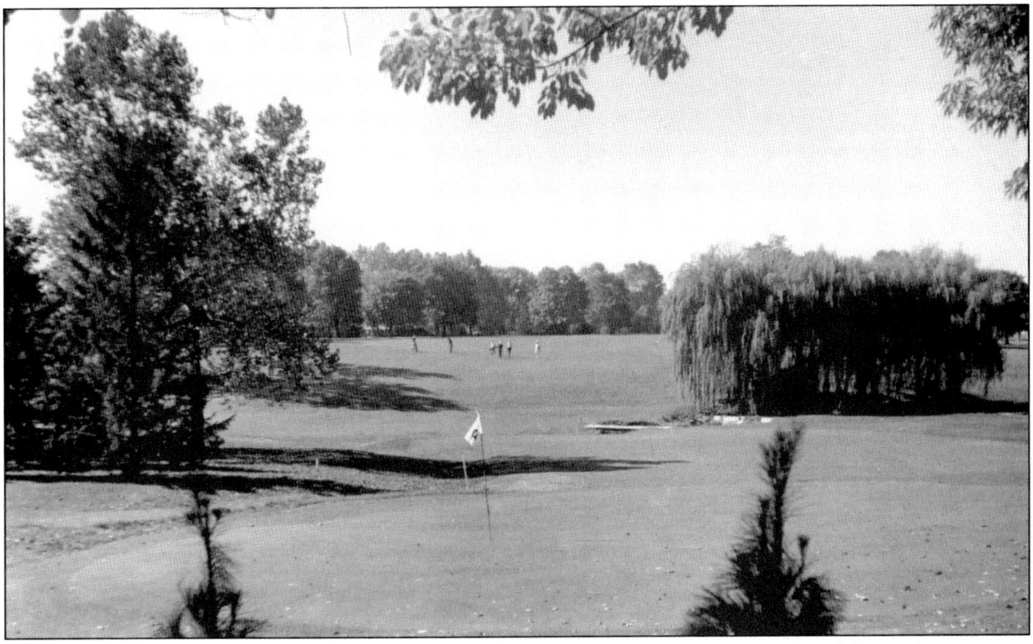

In 1920, the Philadelphia Cricket Club, which until then had been confined to its location in Chestnut Hill, purchased 375 acres of land just outside Flourtown and two years later opened an 18-hole golf course on the site. It was laid out by club member A.W. Tillinghast, one of the most accomplished golf-course designers in the first third of the 20th century. (Courtesy of the Chestnut Hill Historical Society.)

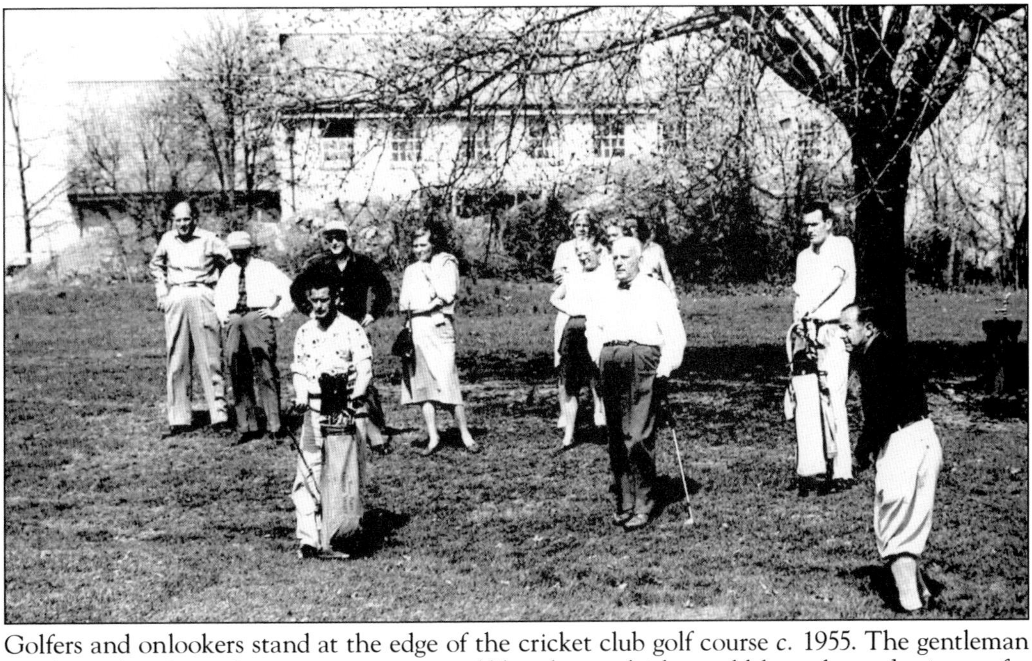

Golfers and onlookers stand at the edge of the cricket club golf course *c.* 1955. The gentleman on the right, Gene Sarazen, is wearing golf knickers, which would have been *de rigueur* for the links a generation earlier but had largely gone out of style by the 1950s. (Courtesy of the Chestnut Hill Historical Society.)

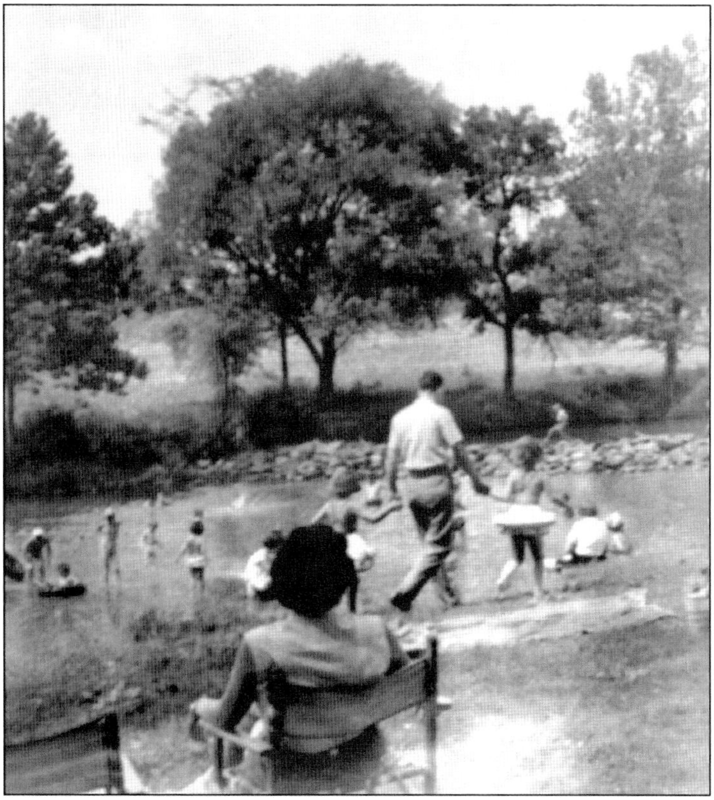

Fort Washington State Park was officially established in 1927 to commemorate the Revolutionary War encampments in the area 150 years before. It was also part of ongoing efforts to create a continuous band of parkland along the Wissahickon Creek from the end of Fairmount Park in Chestnut Hill to the village of Fort Washington. (Courtesy of the Department of Conservation and Natural Resources, Fort Washington State Park.)

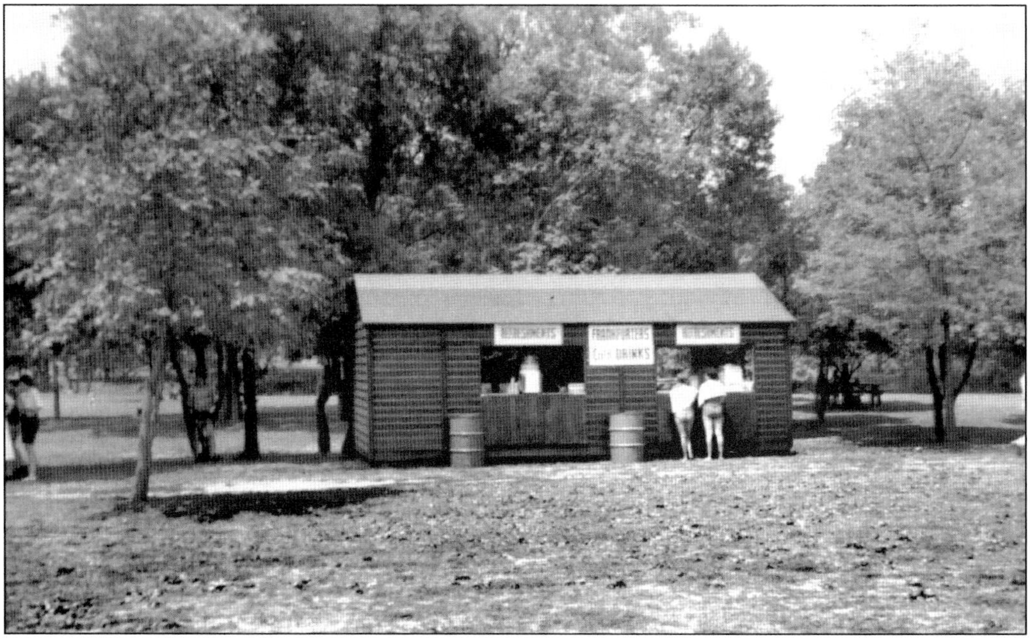

During the 1950s, modern improvements were made to Fort Washington State Park, including the construction of latrines and a snack bar with frankfurters and cold drinks. (Courtesy of the Department of Conservation and Natural Resources, Fort Washington State Park.)

The centerpiece in Fort Washington State Park, the speakers' platform, was dedicated in a 1936 ceremony. A plaque reads, "This speaker's platform is dedicated as a memorial to all who served our country." (Courtesy of the Department of Conservation and Natural Resources, Fort Washington State Park.)

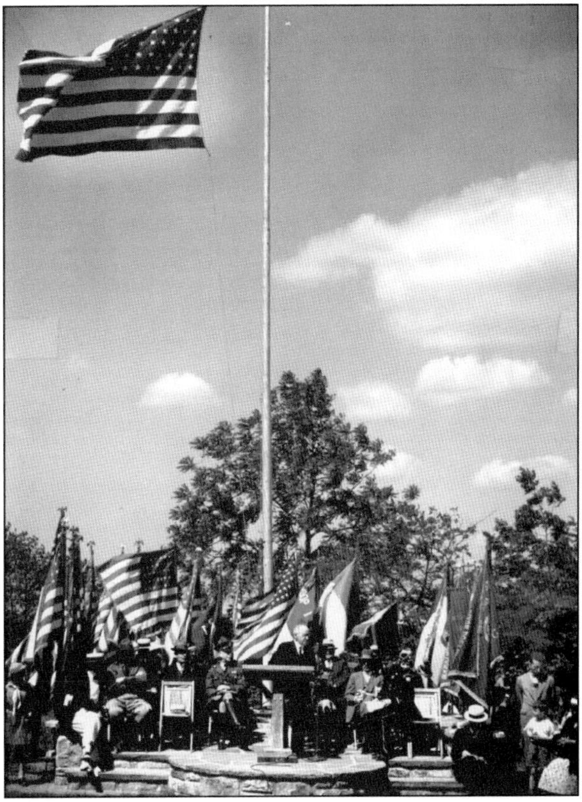

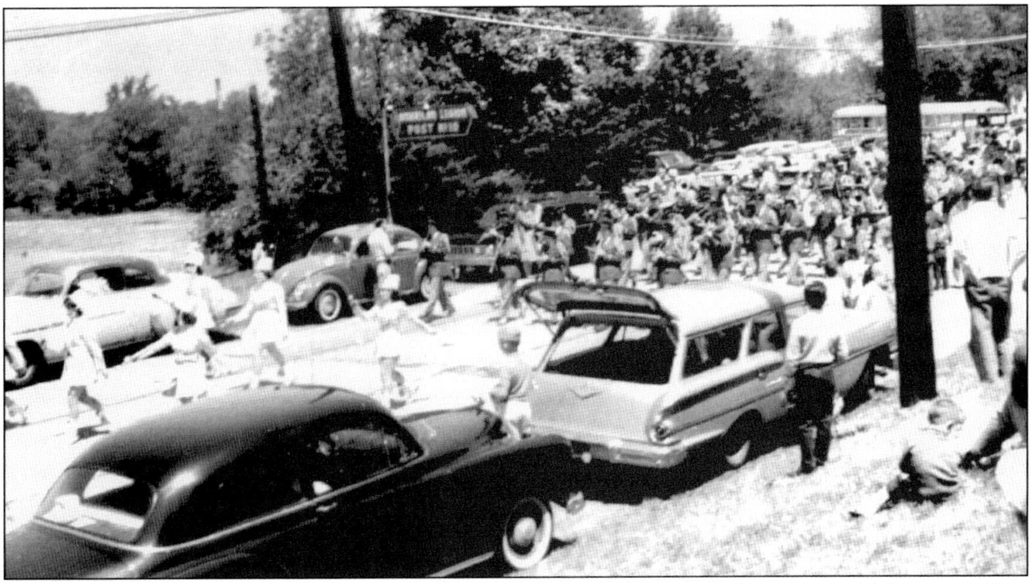

The American Legion Post No. 10 in Fort Washington sponsored an annual Memorial Day parade, featuring majorettes and marching bands from nearby schools. In the late 1950s, the parade route extended along Bethlehem Pike, past the Legion post and Fort Washington State Park. (Courtesy of the Department of Conservation and Natural Resources, Fort Washington State Park.)

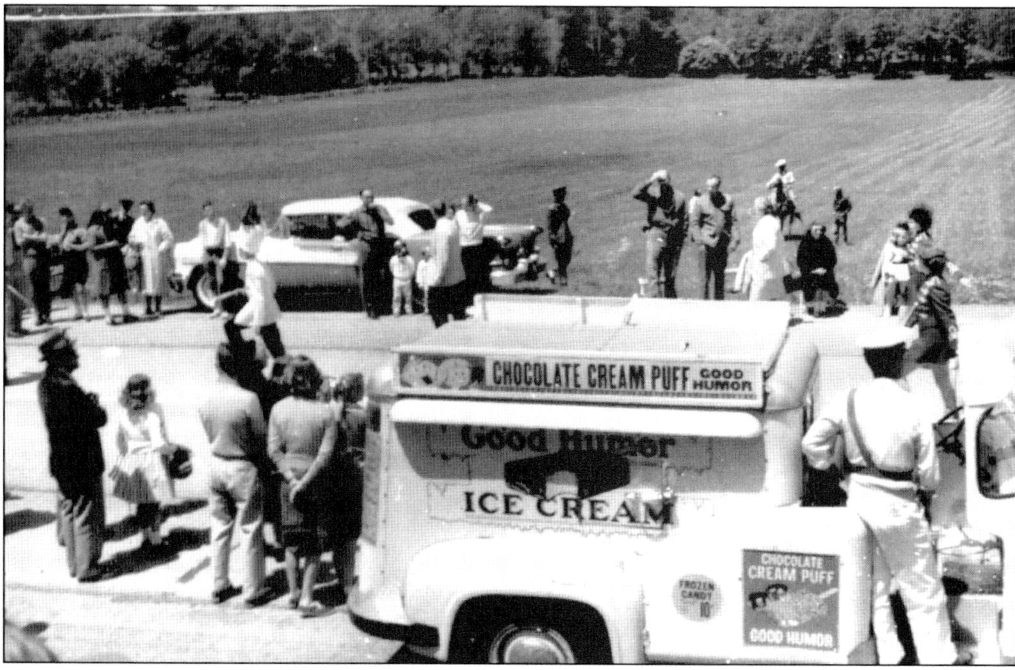

Ready to serve hungry parade watchers, the white-uniformed Good Humor man stands by his truck in the late 1950s. (Courtesy of the Department of Conservation and Natural Resources, Fort Washington State Park.)

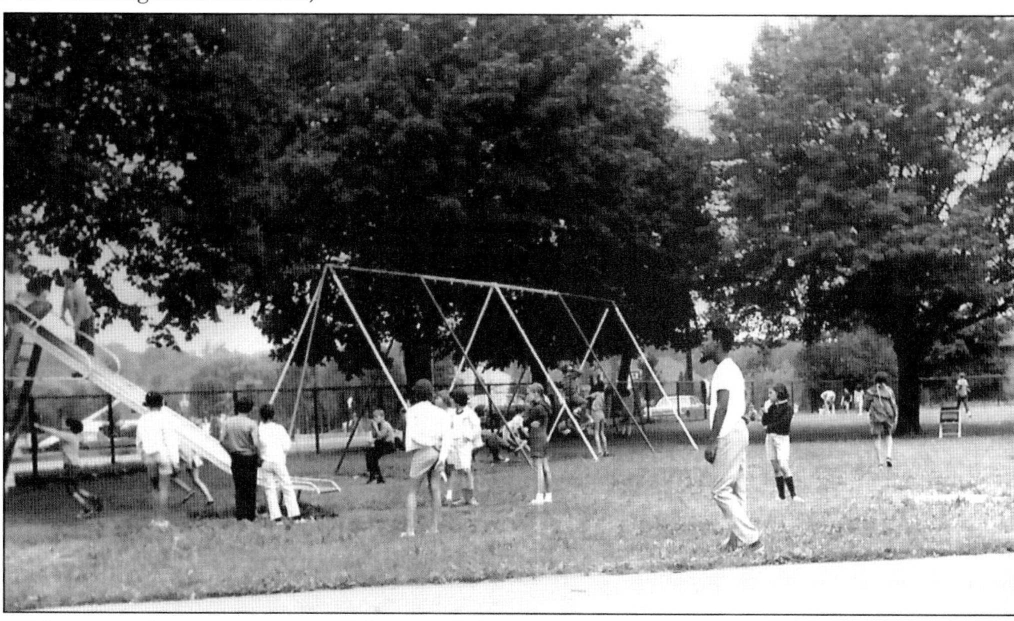

With a growing recognition of the need for community recreational space, Plymouth and Whitemarsh Townships established several parks. Plymouth Park, on Hallowell Road, was the first, built as part of the trolley-line construction in 1895. With the housing boom of the 1950s, many new parks appeared in Plymouth, including Colwell Park, as part of Farmview Village, and Palmer Park, developed along with Woodside Estates. (Courtesy of Plymouth Township Parks and Recreation.)

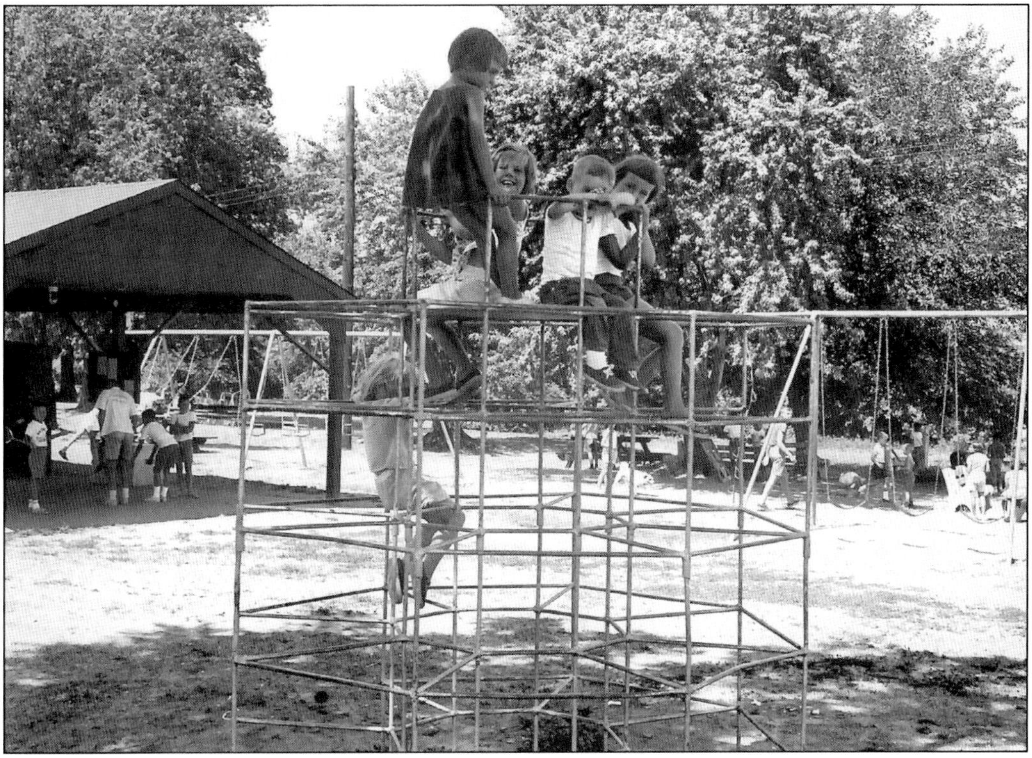

Whitemarsh Township features four public parks—Miles Park, Cedar Grove Park, Leeland Park, and Valley Green Park—as well as Fort Washington State Park.

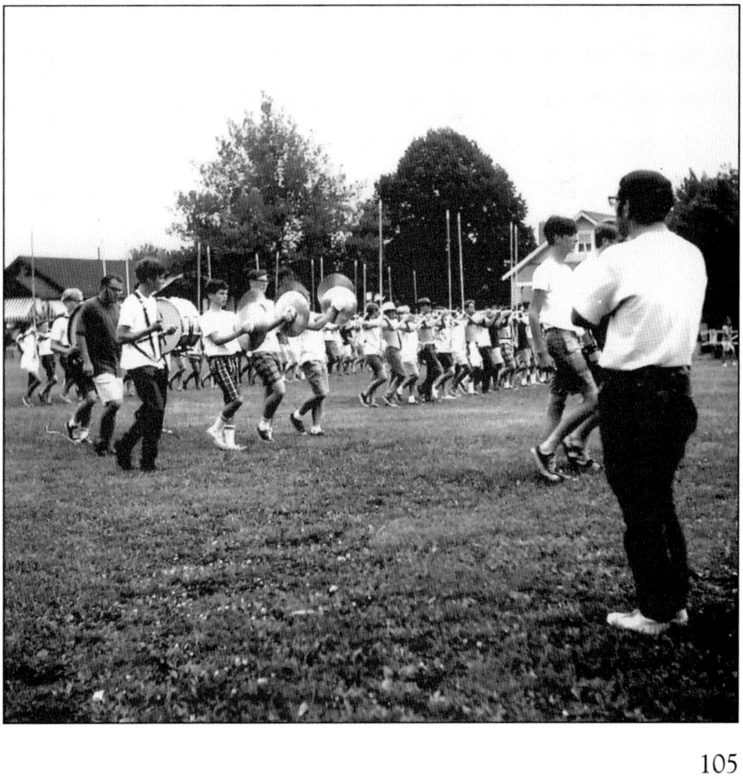

Residents used their public parks year round. In this undated photograph, the Plymouth Whitemarsh marching band is practicing. (Courtesy of Plymouth Township Parks and Recreation.)

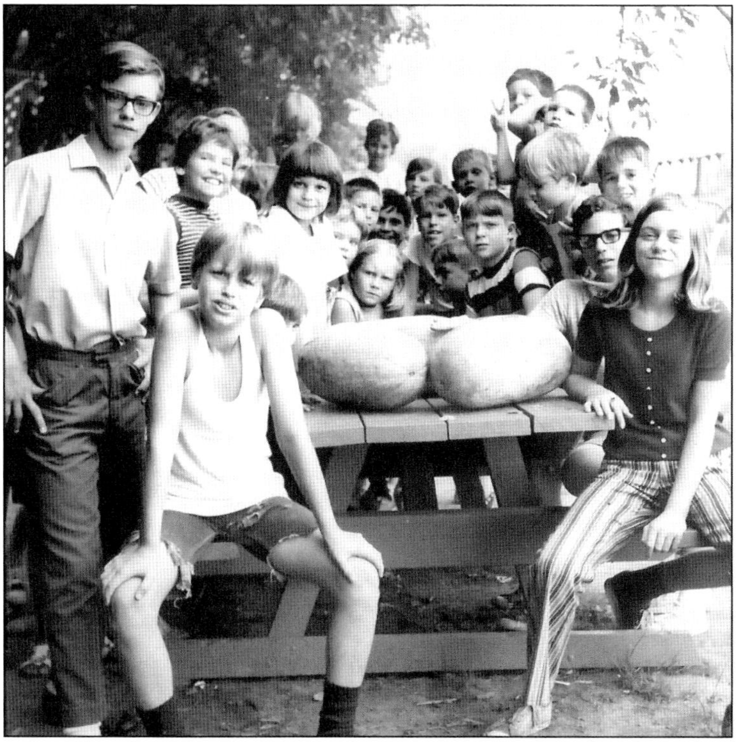

Watermelon parties have long been popular events for young people, sometimes held several times a summer. To the left, children in Plymouth Township's recreation program pose before a watermelon treat. Below, Whitemarsh kids compete in a no-hands watermelon-eating contest. Besides such eating races, parties often featured seed-collecting contests. (Courtesy of Plymouth Township Parks and Recreation, Whitemarsh Township Parks and Recreation.)

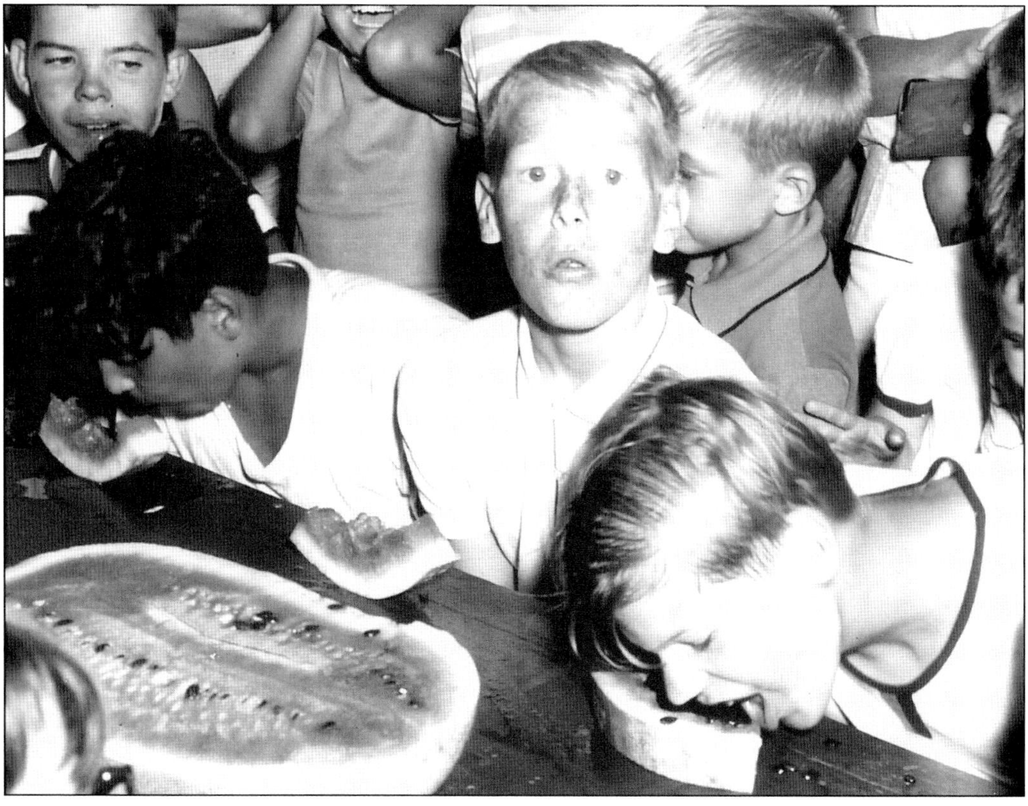

During the 1950s, the townships established youth basketball leagues, with junior teams drawn from area communities, including Barren Hill, Spring Mill, Harmonville, and Cold Point. The "Biddy Basketball" league chose team names such as the Bears, Cubs, Hawks, Colts, Eagles, Rams, Owls, and Tigers. Shown here is the 1956 Hawks team. (Courtesy of Whitemarsh Township Parks and Recreation.)

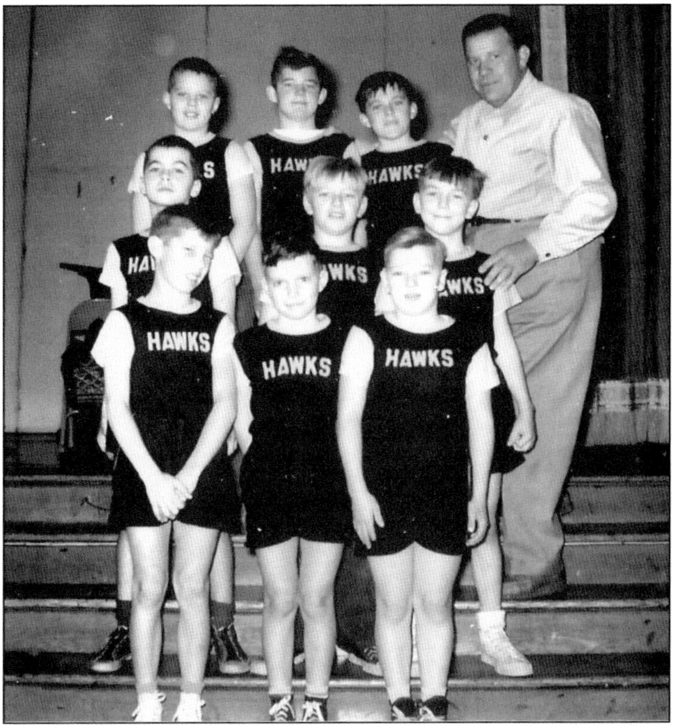

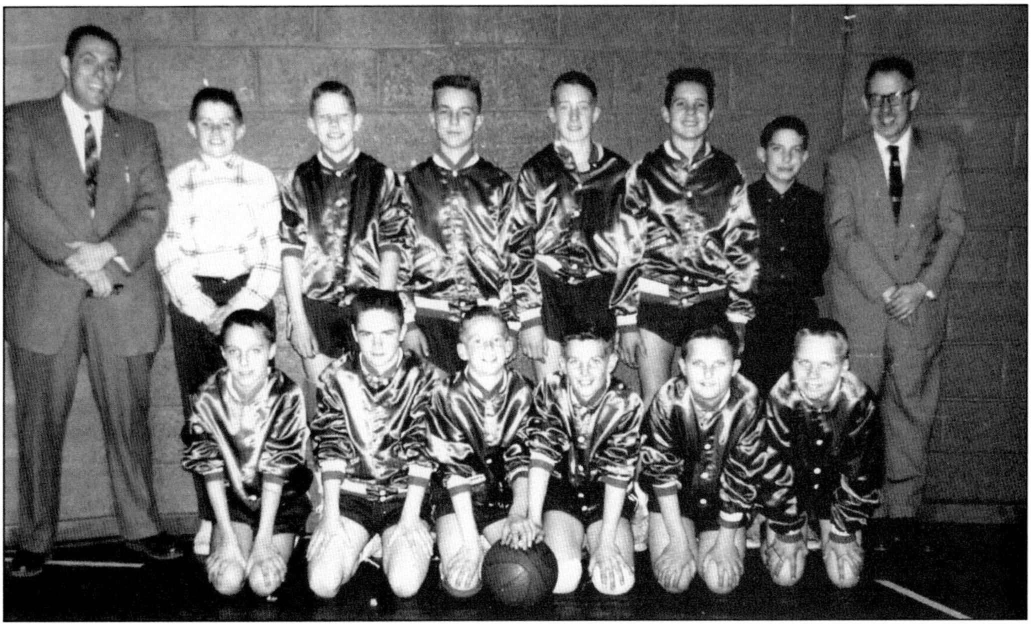

At the end of the season, all-star teams played against competitors from nearby communities. The 1959 Whitemarsh Township Biddy Basketball all-stars were the Philadelphia-Chester champions. Pictured, from left to right, are the following: (front row) Pete Burton, Joe Gontram, Mars Seiferth, Joe Jordan, Jim Ferrier, and Frank McNight; (back row) coach Charles Loyer, Bill Bogle, George Kiehl, Jim Moore, Fred Heitman, Ed Gansz, John Hanley, and coach Eric Schofield. (Courtesy of Whitemarsh Township Parks and Recreation.)

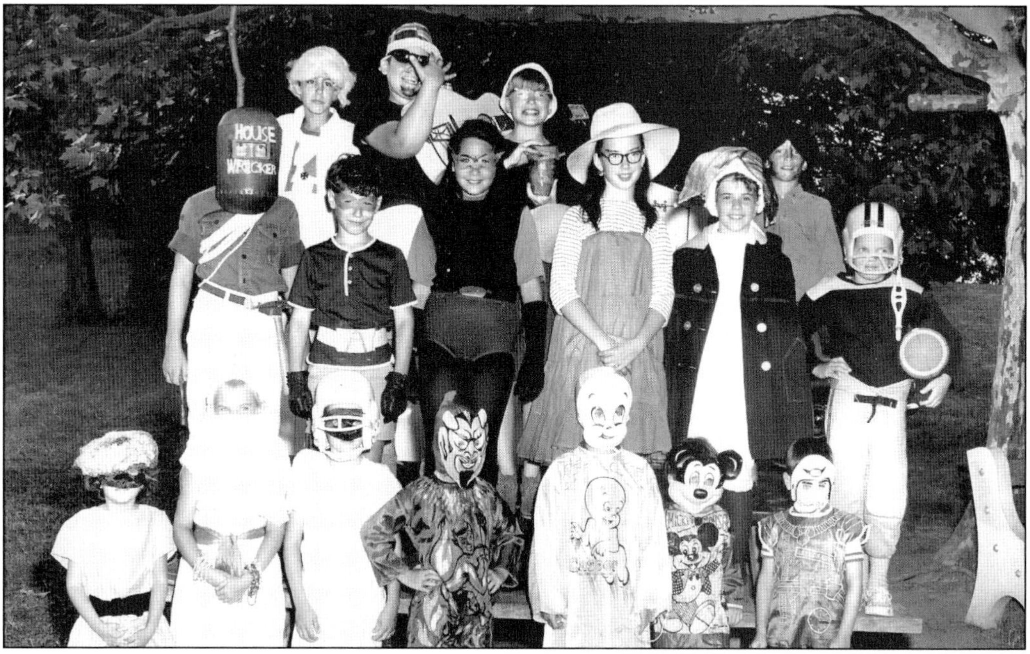

The first Whitemarsh Township Community Costume Halloween Party took place in 1950 at St. Peter's and featured a grand march with prizes, themed relay races, apple-eating contests, a scavenger hunt, and a jack-o'-lantern contest. This later photograph depicts a group showing off in their costumes. (Courtesy of Whitemarsh Township Parks and Recreation.)

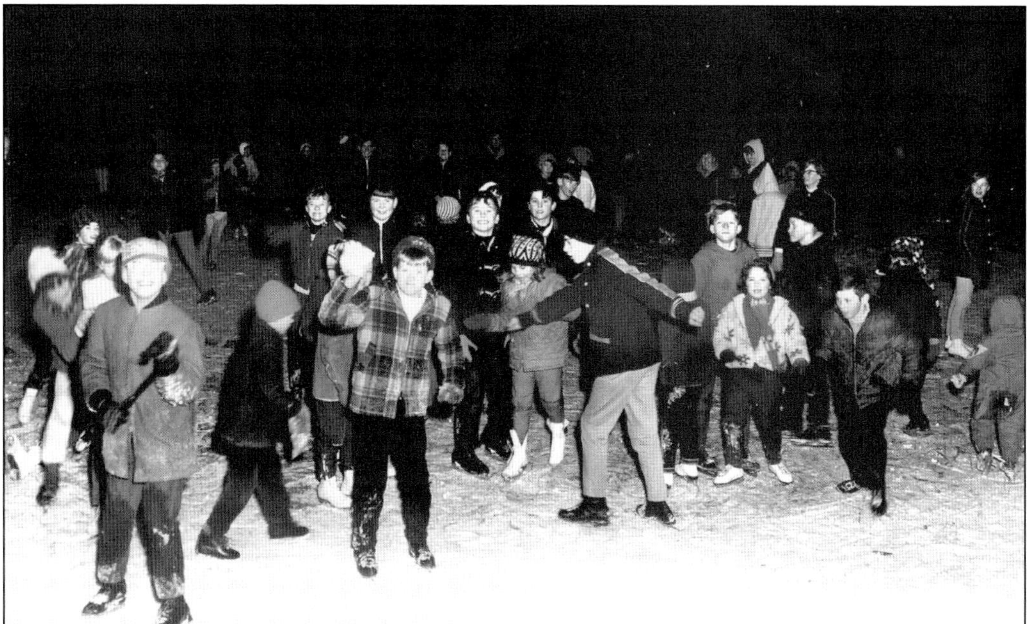

During the winter months, ice-skating was an enjoyable outdoor sport in both townships. In East Plymouth Valley, the Caracappa tract, part of an old farm, had a pond used for skating. In Whitemarsh, the basketball courts at Miles Park were flooded, and lights allowed for nighttime skating. (Courtesy of Whitemarsh Township Parks and Recreation.)

Archery was an enormously popular community sport throughout the 1950s and 1960s, when virtually every park featured an archery range. For safety reasons, it was gradually phased out and eliminated by the late 1970s. (Courtesy of Plymouth Township Parks and Recreation.)

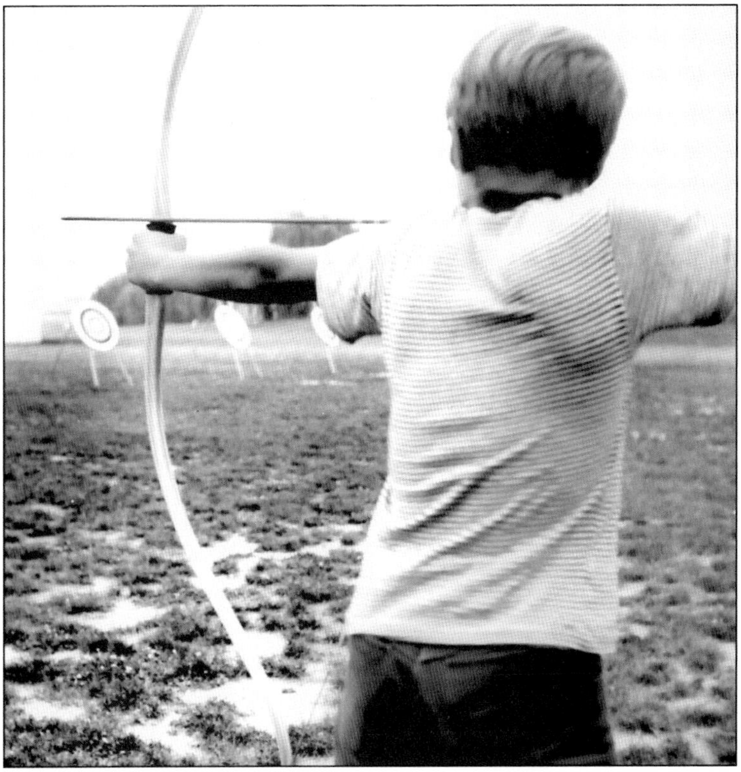

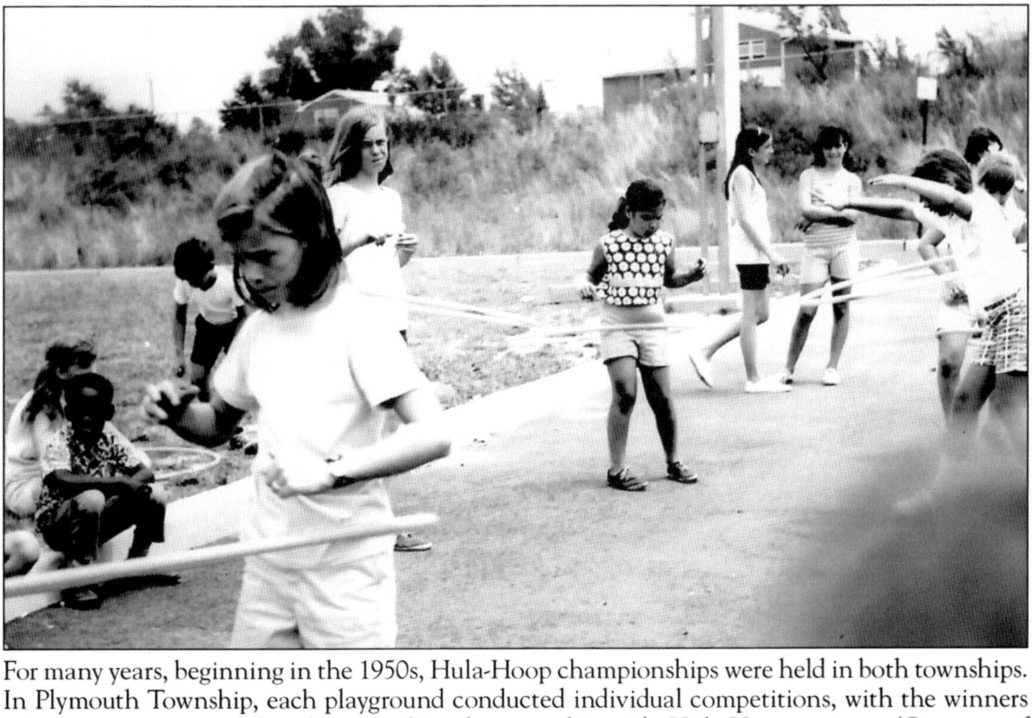

For many years, beginning in the 1950s, Hula-Hoop championships were held in both townships. In Plymouth Township, each playground conducted individual competitions, with the winners going on to represent the playground in the township-wide Hula-Hoop contest. (Courtesy of Plymouth Township Parks and Recreation.)

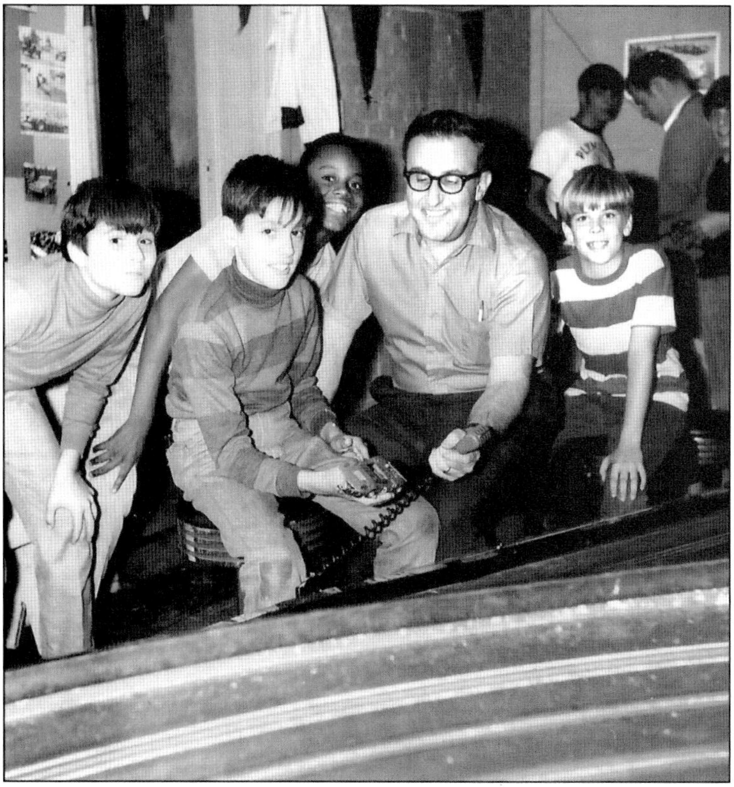

In 1969, a very successful slot-car club was established, charging a fee of $5 per season. Ed Curson, liaison to the Plymouth Recreation Board, operates a car on the eight-lane track with (from left to right) Bob Natelini, Ray Gilette, Jackie Roberson, and Dave Derby, a club founder. (Courtesy of Plymouth Township Parks and Recreation.)

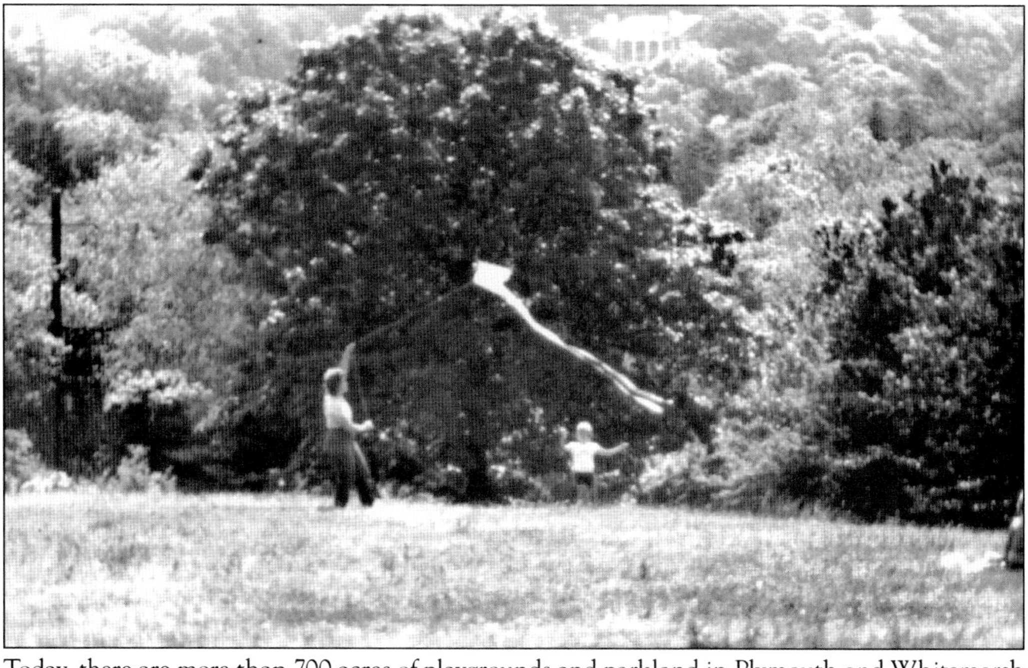

Today, there are more than 700 acres of playgrounds and parkland in Plymouth and Whitemarsh Townships that have been enjoyed in the past and will be enjoyed for years to come.

Six

To Serve and Protect

Over the years, hundreds of men and women have volunteered their time and energy or have taken jobs in the public service sector to make life safer and more comfortable for their fellow citizens. At the same time, these noble pursuits have given volunteers and employees a sense of solidarity and pride, as well as an outlet for fun and socializing.

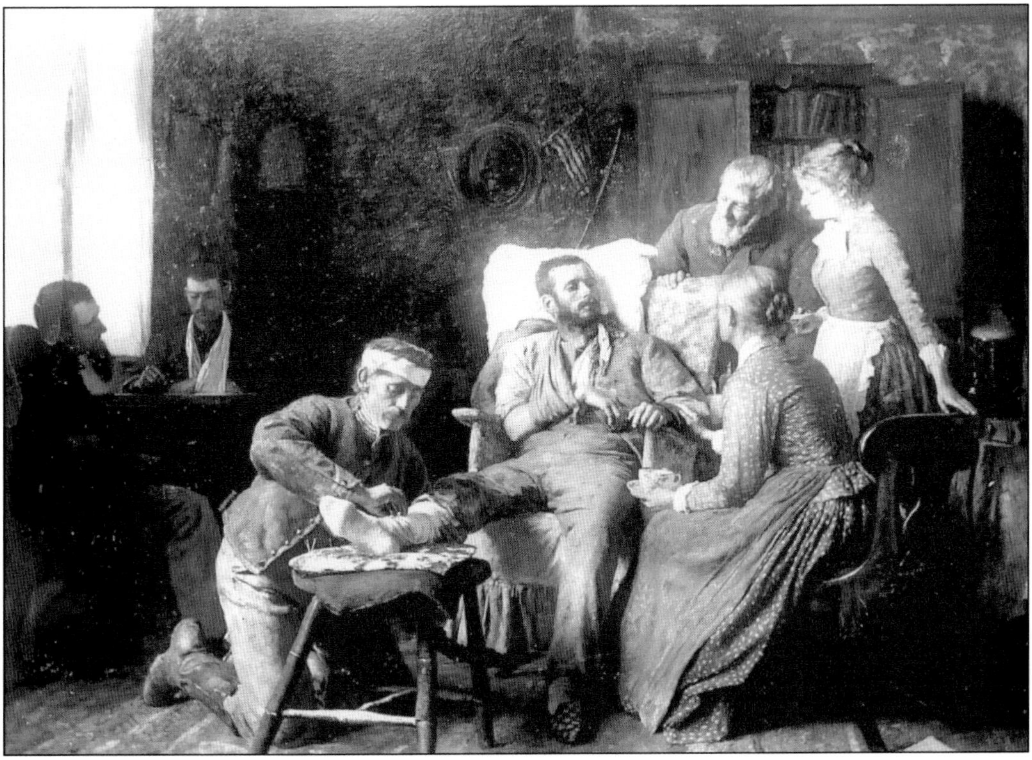

In the Hands of the Enemy (1889), Thomas Hovenden.

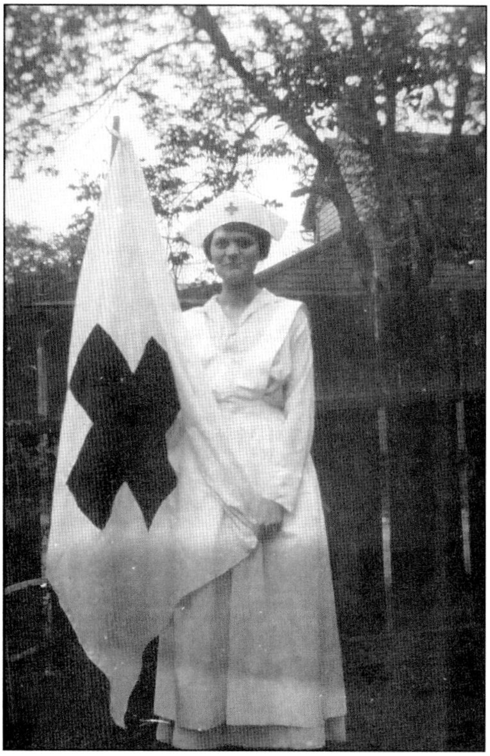

During World War I, young soldiers shipped overseas, leaving behind brides and girlfriends. Lonely and wanting to help their country, many women volunteered for organizations such as the Red Cross.

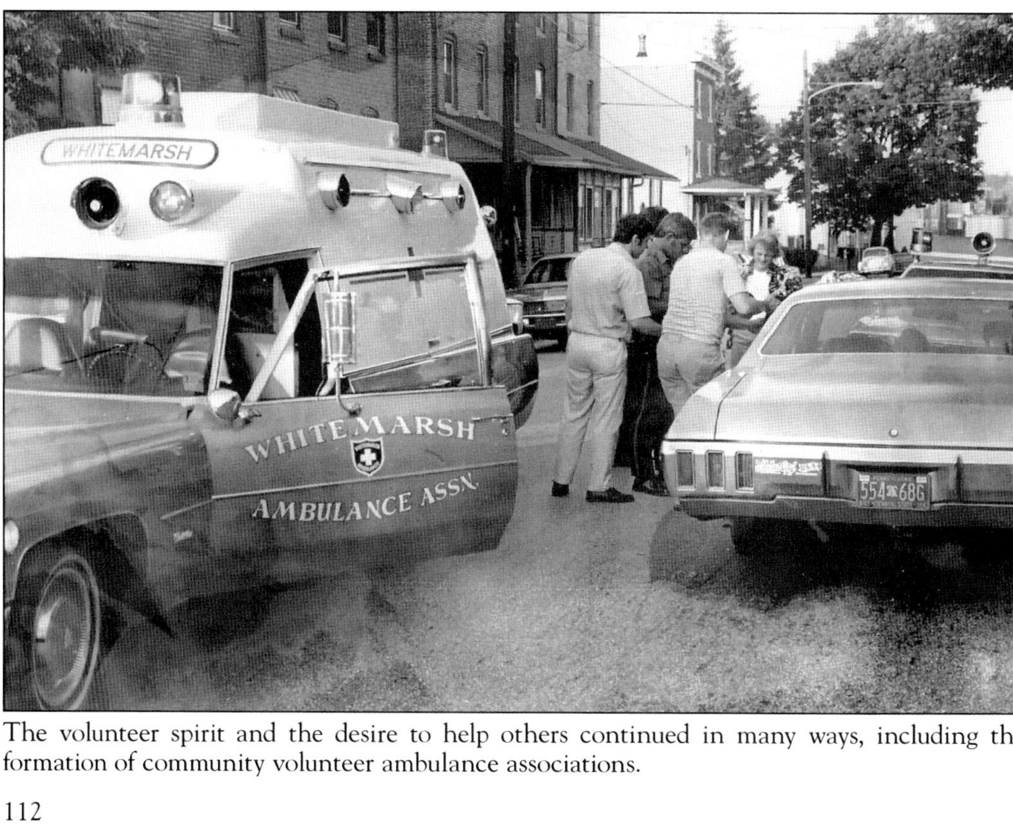

The volunteer spirit and the desire to help others continued in many ways, including the formation of community volunteer ambulance associations.

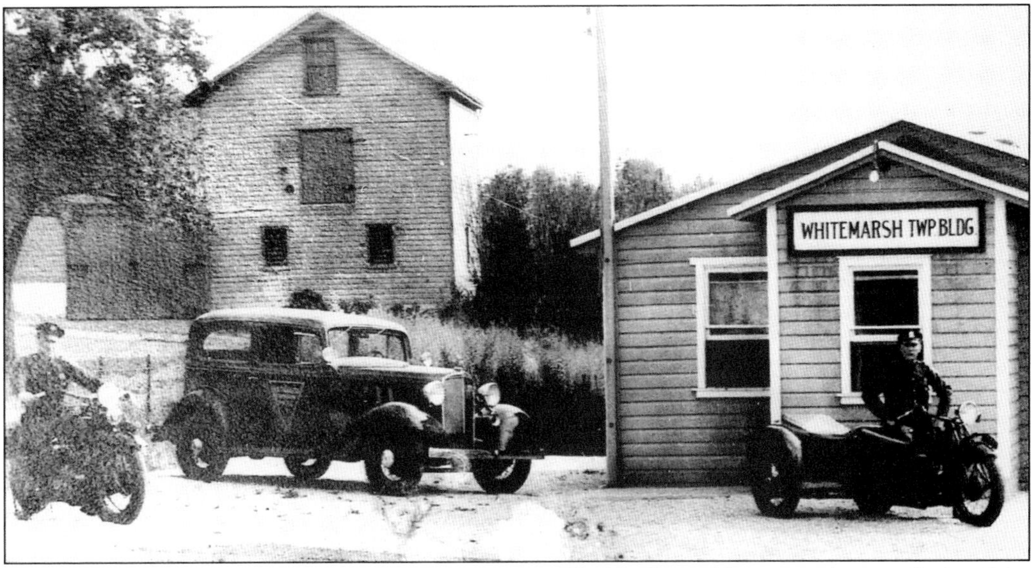

The first Whitemarsh Township building occupied half of an old scout cabin on Ridge Pike opposite Crescent Avenue. Local government offices were housed here until a larger building was constructed on Joshua Road in 1955. The police department was formed in 1930 with two officers as the result of a petition to Montgomery County by the Women's Club of Whitemarsh. At first, the department's equipment was limited to two motorcycles and a car. Plymouth Township followed two decades later, establishing a police force with a chief and three officers in 1951.

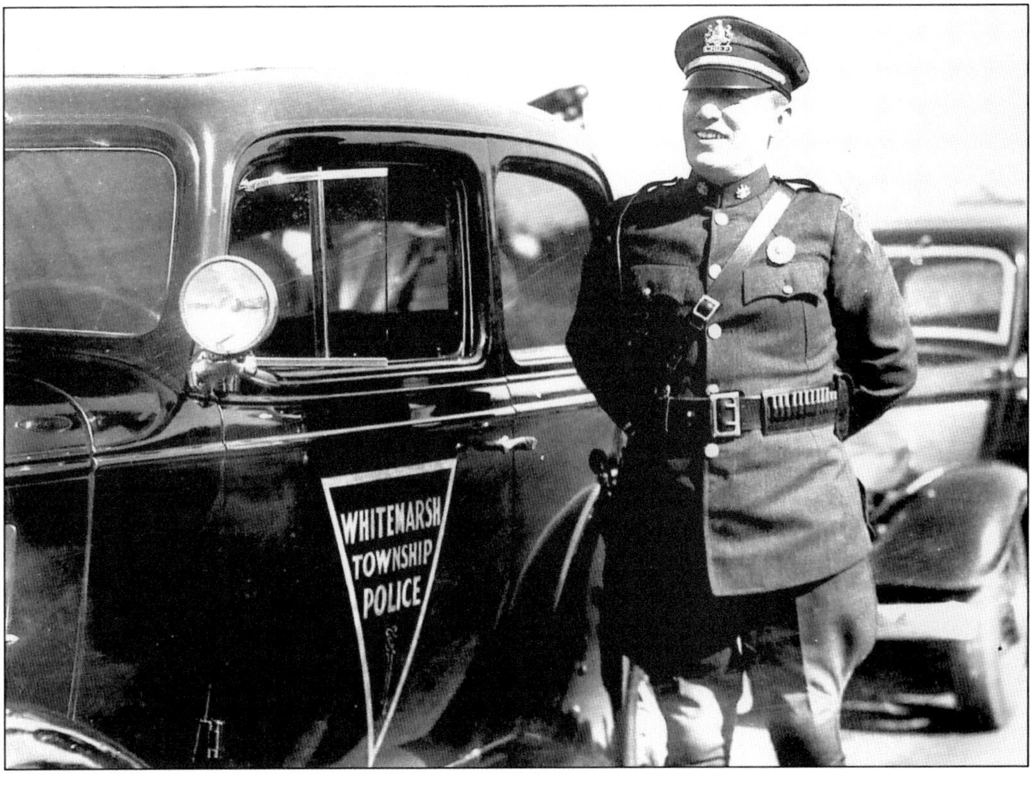

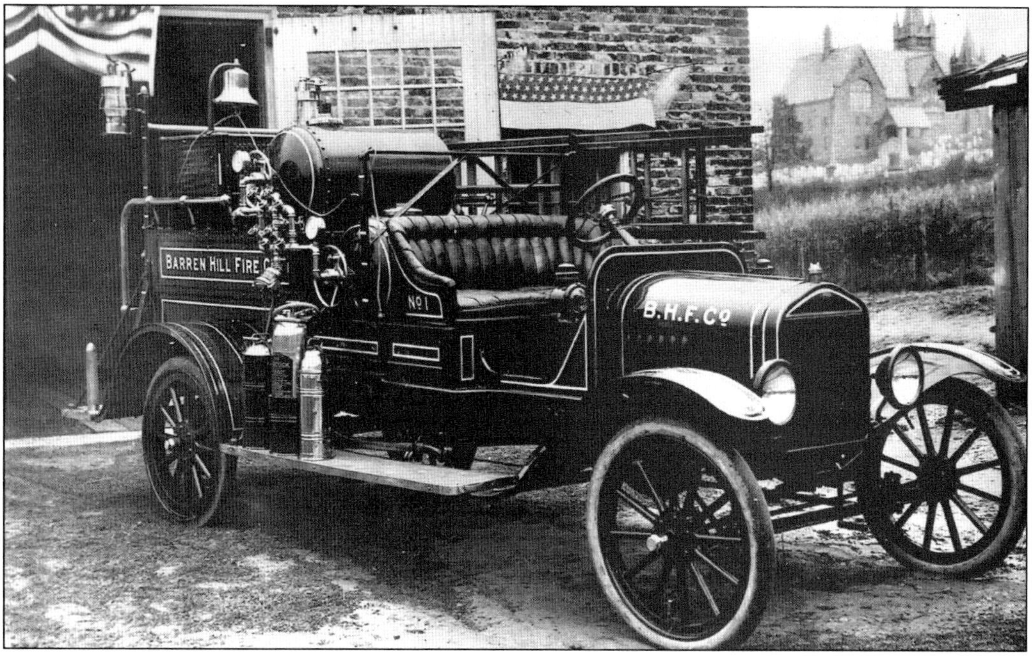

In 1915, after a disastrous fire in a barn behind the Whitemarsh Inn, citizens of Barren Hill formed a volunteer fire company. Plans were made for a modern firehouse on a plot of land on Germantown Pike. The new building for the Barren Hill Fire Company was completed in February 1925. The fire company later expanded with a new building on an adjacent lot. (Courtesy of the Lownes Family Funeral Home.)

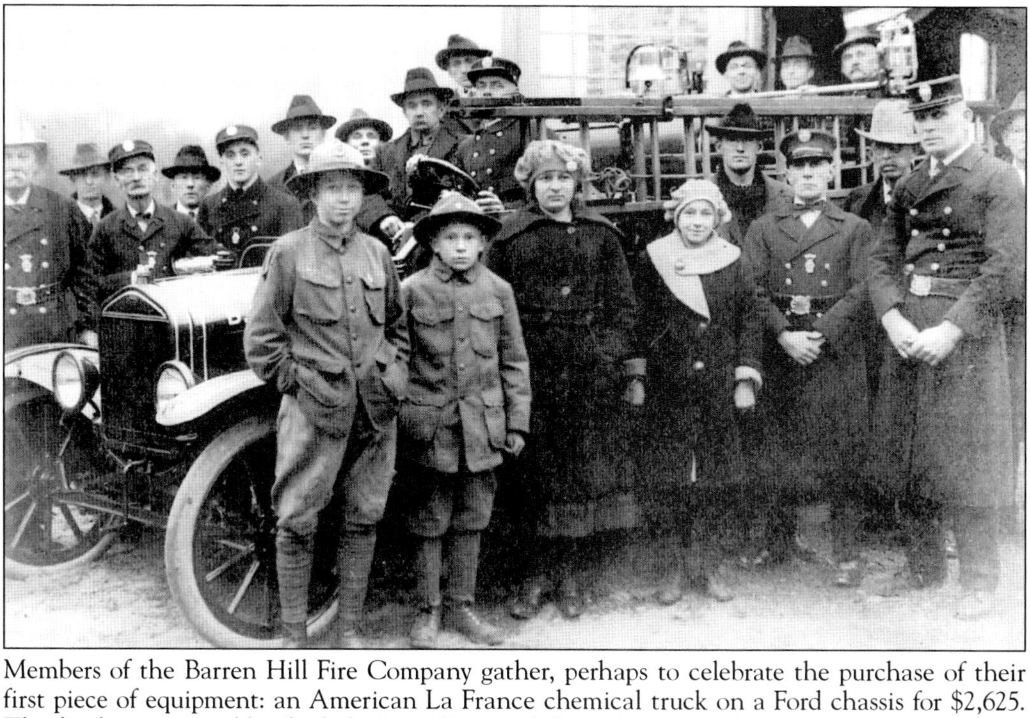

Members of the Barren Hill Fire Company gather, perhaps to celebrate the purchase of their first piece of equipment: an American La France chemical truck on a Ford chassis for $2,625. The funds were raised by the ladies' auxiliary and through various donations.

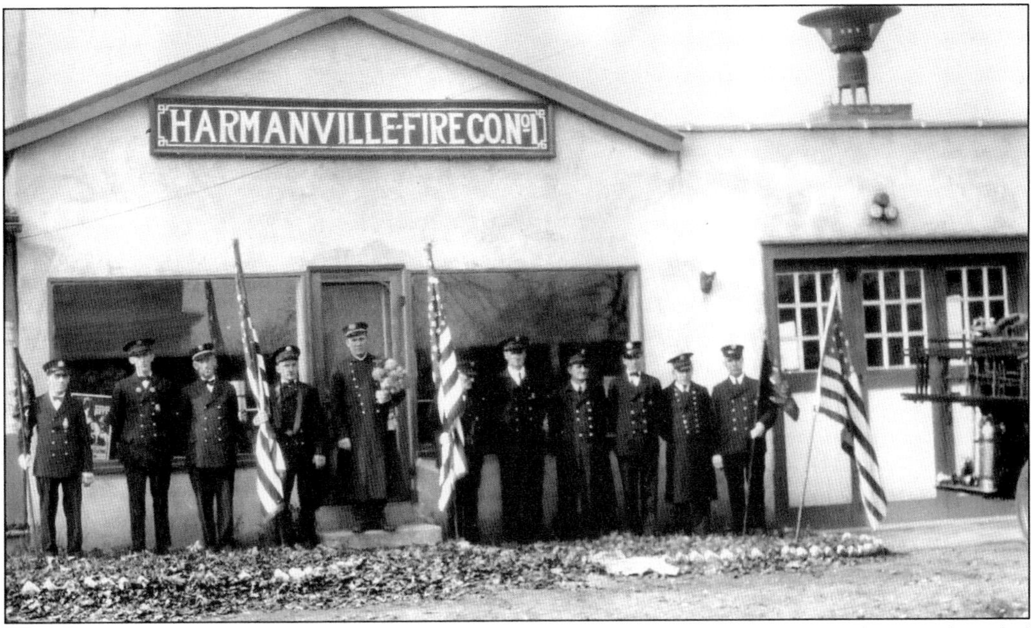

The Harmanville (later Harmonville) Fire Company, at Karrs Lane and Butler Pike, was founded in 1924 and supported financially by the Plymouth Township Board of Commissioners. The Harmonville company was the second in the area, the Plymouth Fire Company having been established in 1901. This photograph of Harmonville members was taken in 1930, during the leadership of Elias Slavin. (Courtesy of the Harmonville Fire Company.)

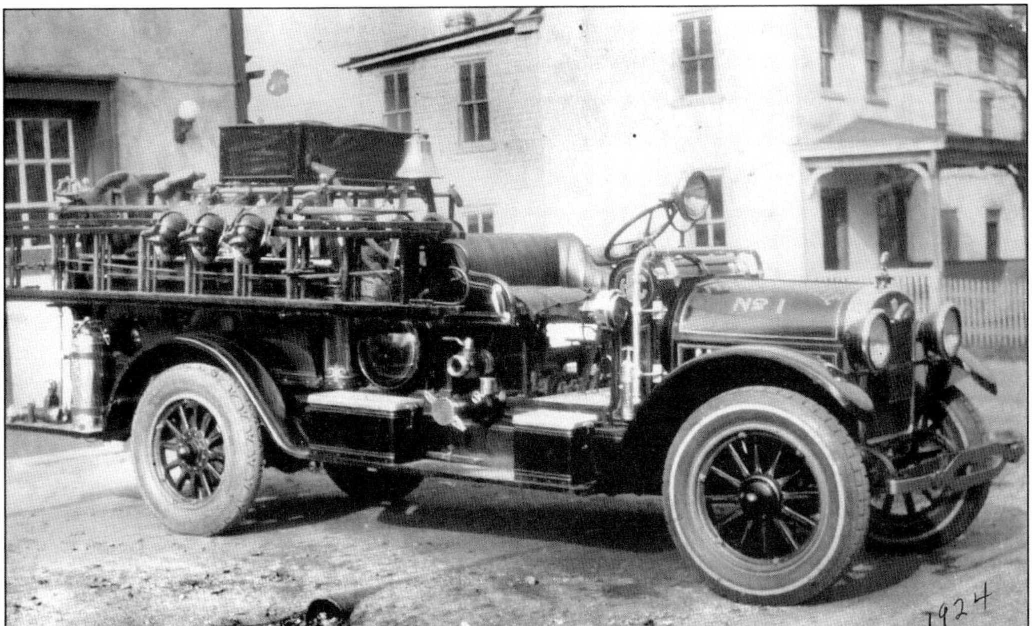

The first truck acquired by the Harmonville company was this 1924 Reo, a used model purchased from another organization. (Courtesy of the Harmonville Fire Company.)

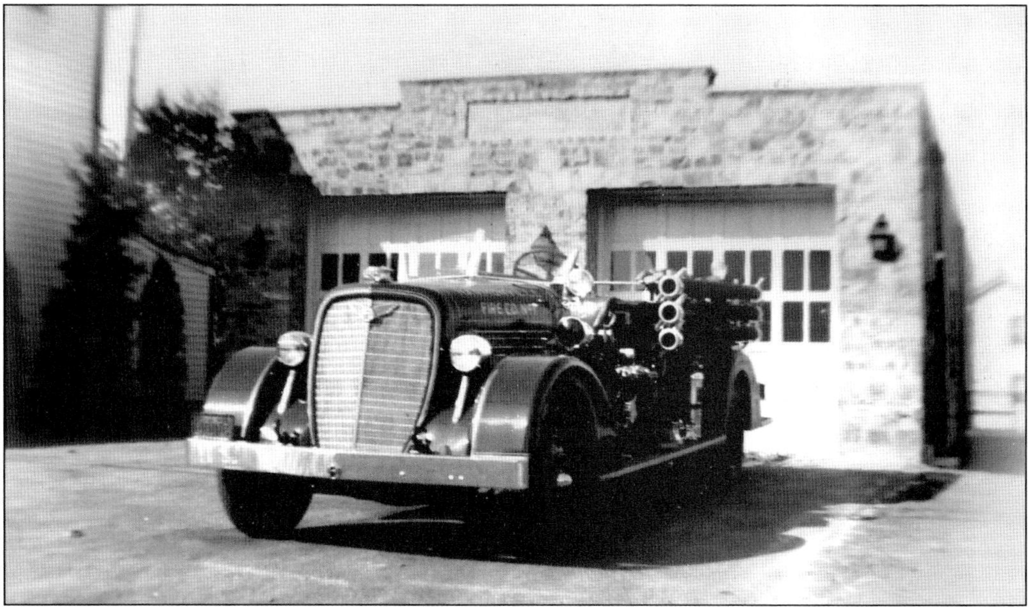

This two-bay garage held a new 1939 Hale fire truck, which is still owned by the Harmonville Fire Company and is awaiting restoration. The original garage was built in 1924, expanded to three bays in 1939, and enlarged again to accommodate the length of a new hook-and-ladder truck. The building still stands on Butler Pike and now houses offices. (Courtesy of the Harmonville Fire Company.)

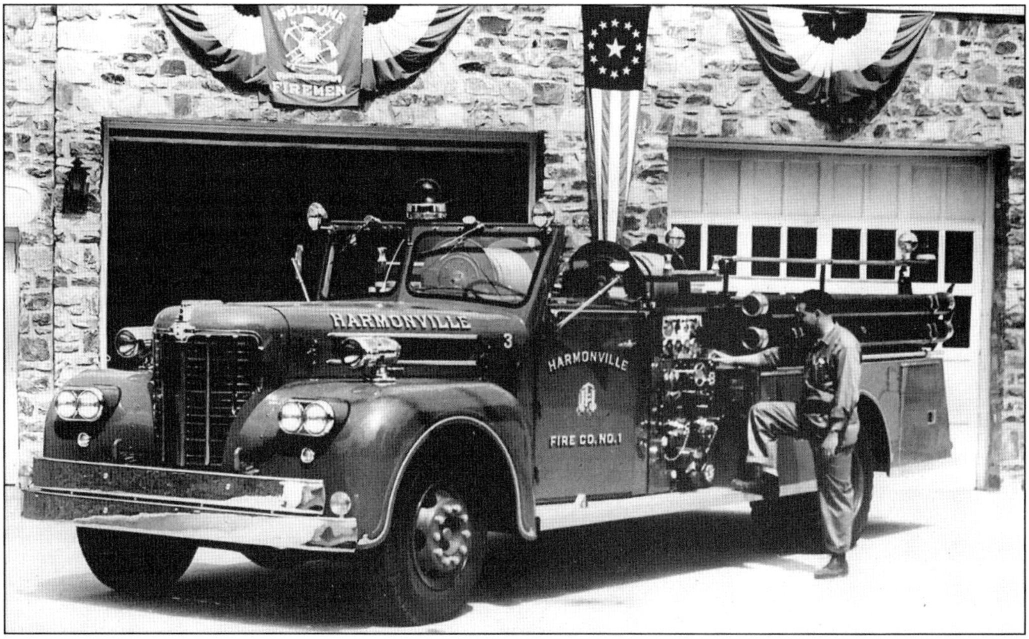

Joe Foster Sr. admires Harmonville's new 1959 Maxim truck, featuring a straight-six Waukesha engine and a Hale Pump capable of pumping 750 gallons of water per minute. Joe Foster was chief from March 1977 to December 1980, and his father, John Foster, was chief from January 1944 to December 1948. The flag bunting was part of the celebration for the new piece of equipment. (Courtesy of the Harmonville Fire Company.)

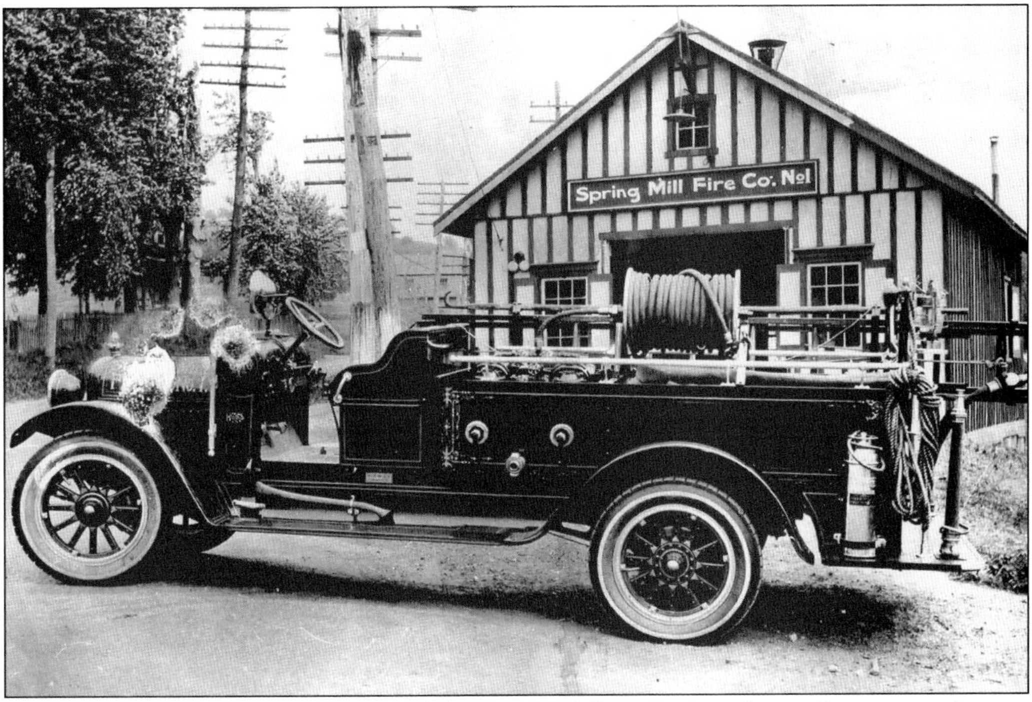

In September 1923, a dozen residents of the Spring Mill area met to discuss forming a volunteer fire company and filed for a charter two months later. The company purchased its first piece of equipment in 1924—a Hale Pump on a Reo Speed Wagon chassis, with a 12-foot ladder, at a cost of $2,500. The first firehouse was a small shop located at Barren Hill and Cedar Grove Roads. (Courtesy of the Spring Mill Fire Company.)

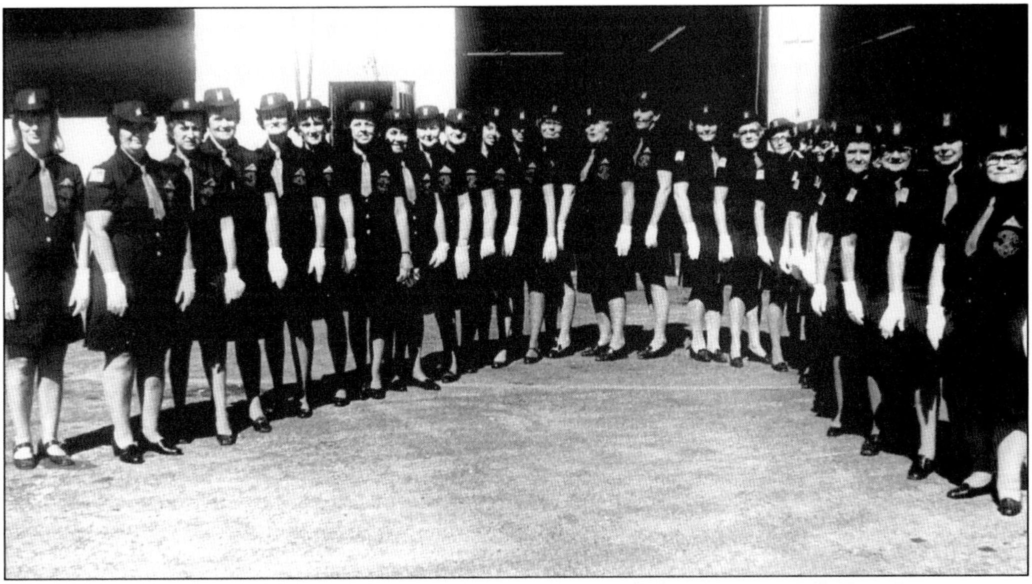

A ladies' auxiliary was organized in 1925 and supported the Spring Mill Fire Company in various ways. Perhaps in a gesture of appreciation, the annual banquet, formerly a stag affair, was opened in 1930 to the ladies' auxiliary and to the families of firemen. (Courtesy of the Spring Mill Fire Company.)

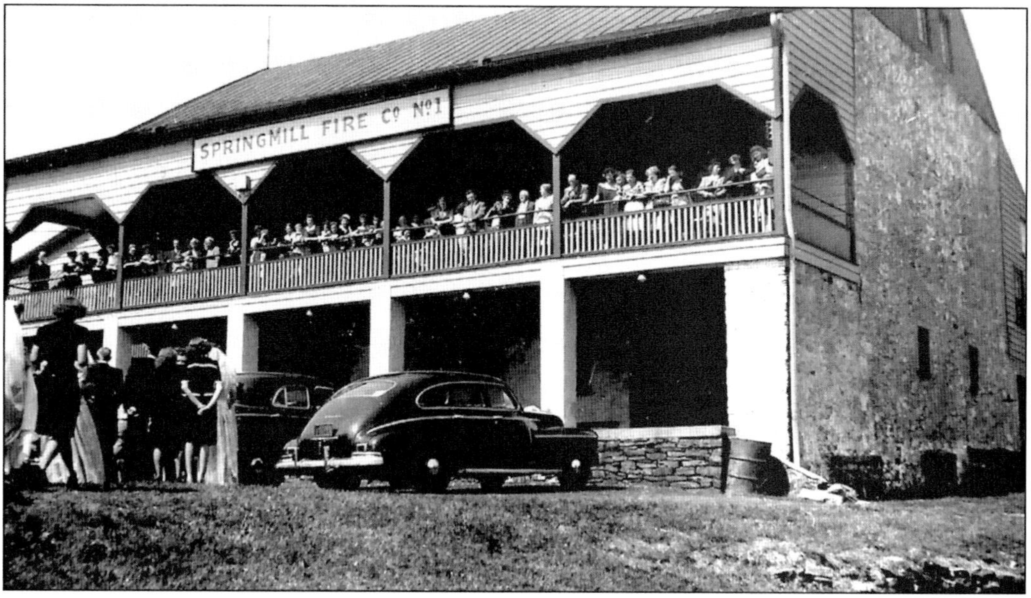

On July 24, 1928, the Spring Mill Fire Company agreed to purchase from the Philadelphia Electric Company the former Spring Mill Country Club property, with its 32 acres and historic buildings, for $37,000. Both as a country club and firehouse, the converted barn was a popular site for wedding receptions. (Courtesy of the Spring Mill Fire Company.)

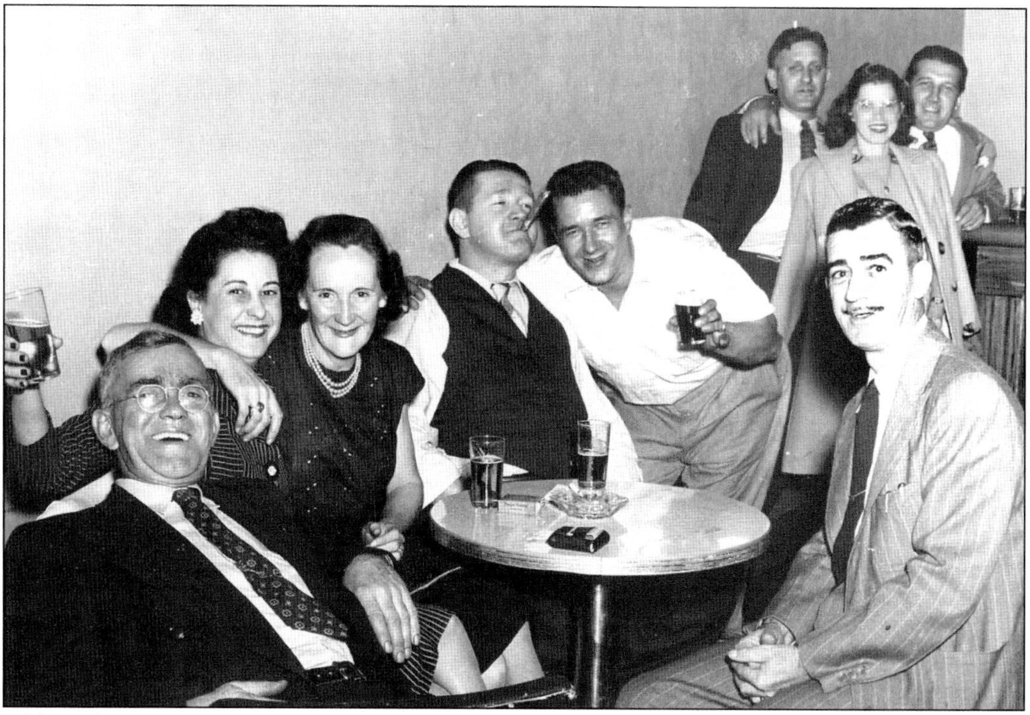

Although joining a fire company was a noble act of volunteerism, participation could greatly enrich a member's social life. Here, in what could be a scene from a 1940s movie, members and friends relax in the fire company lounge. (Courtesy of the Spring Mill Fire Company.)

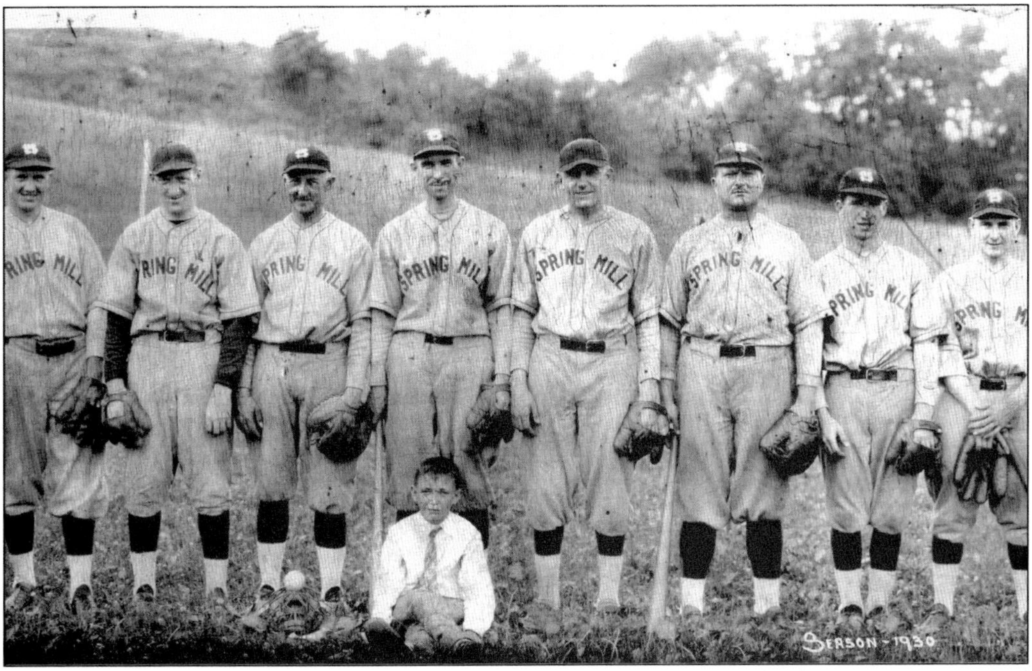

Prior to the fire company's purchase of the Spring Mill Country Club, the property was used on Sundays by the Philadelphia Athletics baseball team; professional sports were illegal on Sundays in Philadelphia because of the Quaker City's stringent blue laws. The fire company continued this baseball tradition with its own team, posing here in 1930. (Courtesy of the Spring Mill Fire Company.)

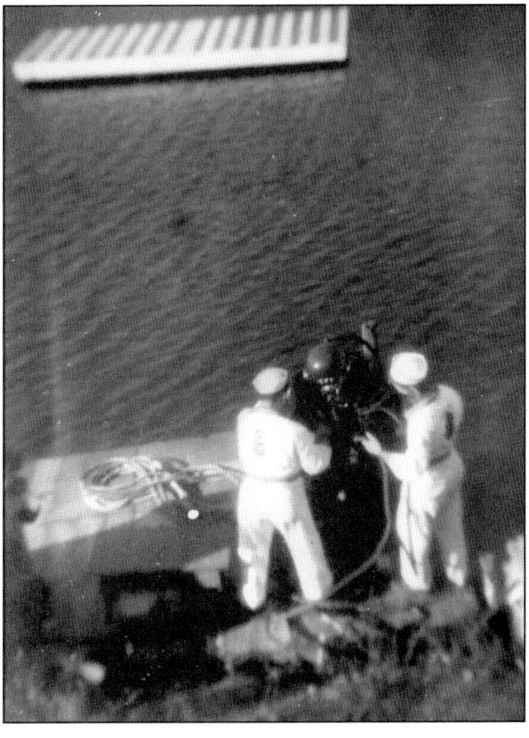

Expanding its services to include water rescue, the Spring Mill Fire Company trained members in scuba diving, often utilizing abandoned quarry holes that had filled with water. Here, members of the fire company practice underwater rescue in Potts' Quarry, which was located along Cedar Grove Road near Butler Pike. Potts' Quarry was also a popular swimming place, as indicated by the float visible to the upper left. (Courtesy of the Spring Mill Fire Company.)

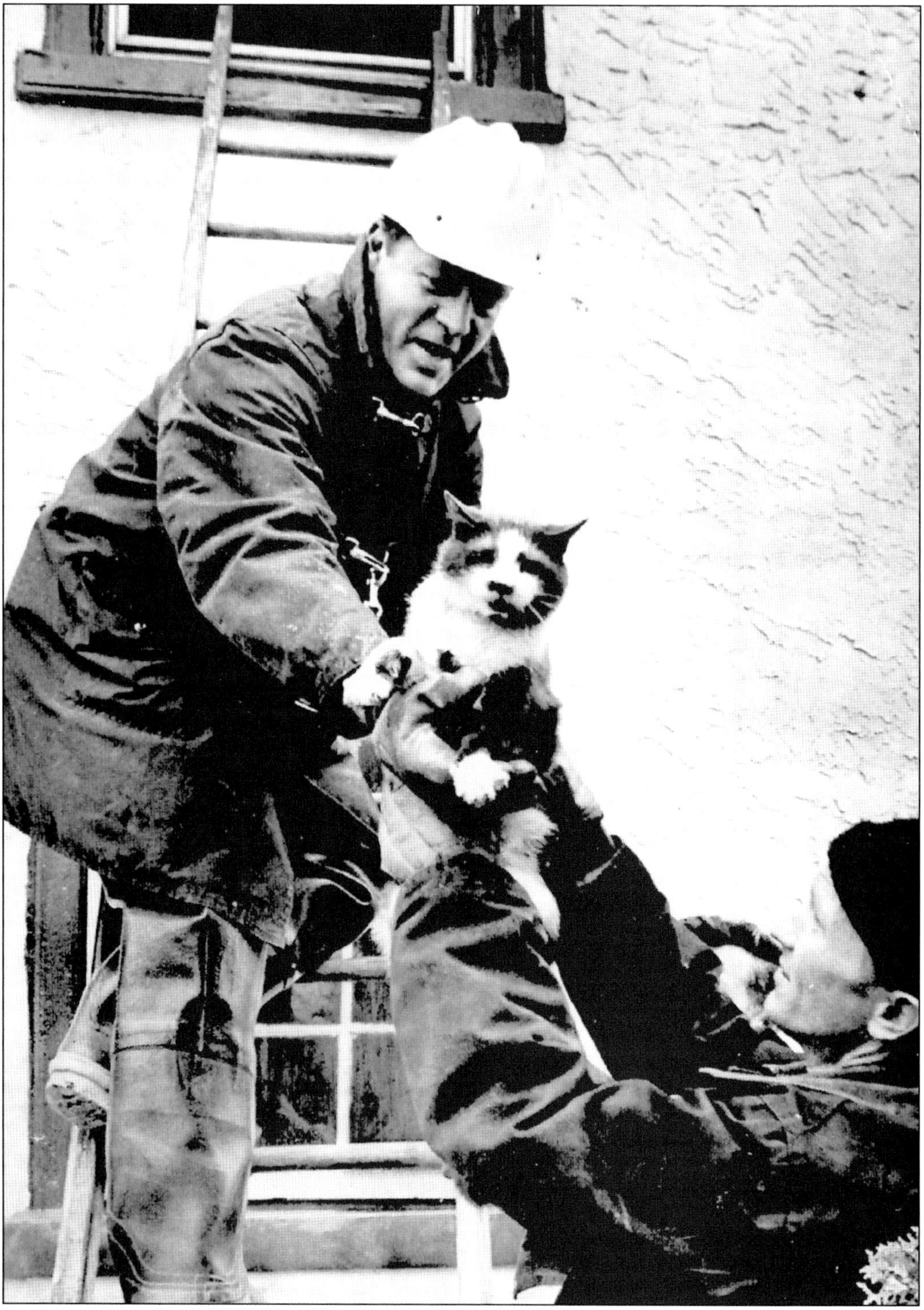

In Plymouth and Whitemarsh Townships, volunteer firefighters have always been ready to serve the community, whether battling a blaze or rescuing the family cat. (Courtesy of the Spring Mill Fire Company.)

Seven

POSTWAR INDUSTRY AND SUBURBAN DEVELOPMENT

Events after World War II put an end to the relative isolation of the two townships. The postwar suburban boom, made possible by increasing prosperity and generous veterans' benefits, coupled with better highway access into the area, brought thousands of new residents, along with many new businesses and industries, and a newly consolidated Plymouth Whitemarsh school district. The townships' old villages became so engulfed with housing and commercial development that it became increasingly difficult to recognize that they once had been the focal points of economic and social activity. At the same time, development and population growth threatened to overwhelm remaining open space.

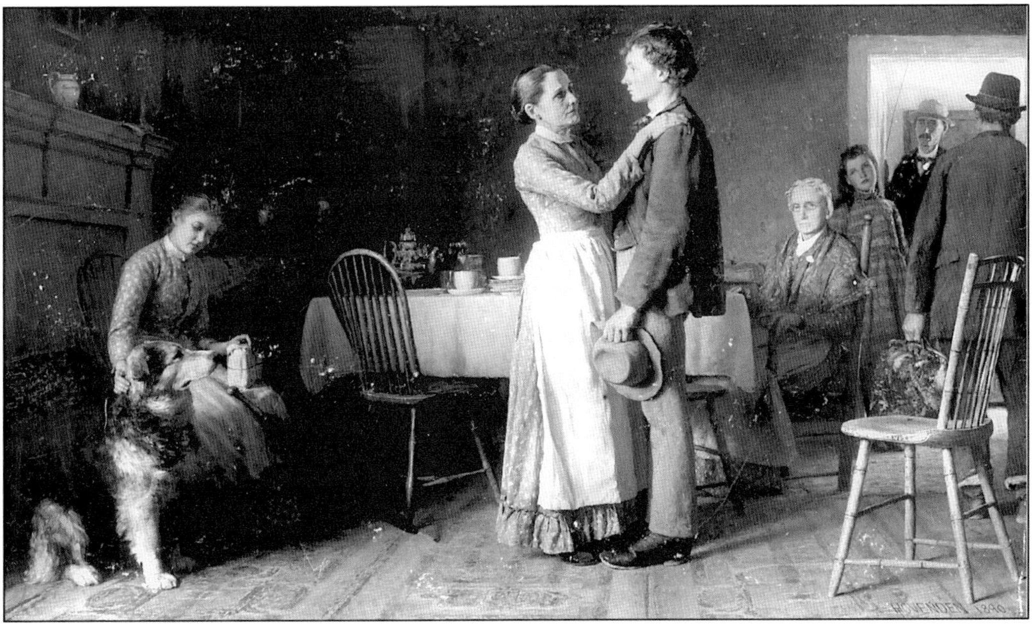

Thomas Hovenden's *Breaking Home Ties* (1890) depicts an emotional scene of a young man leaving life on the farm.

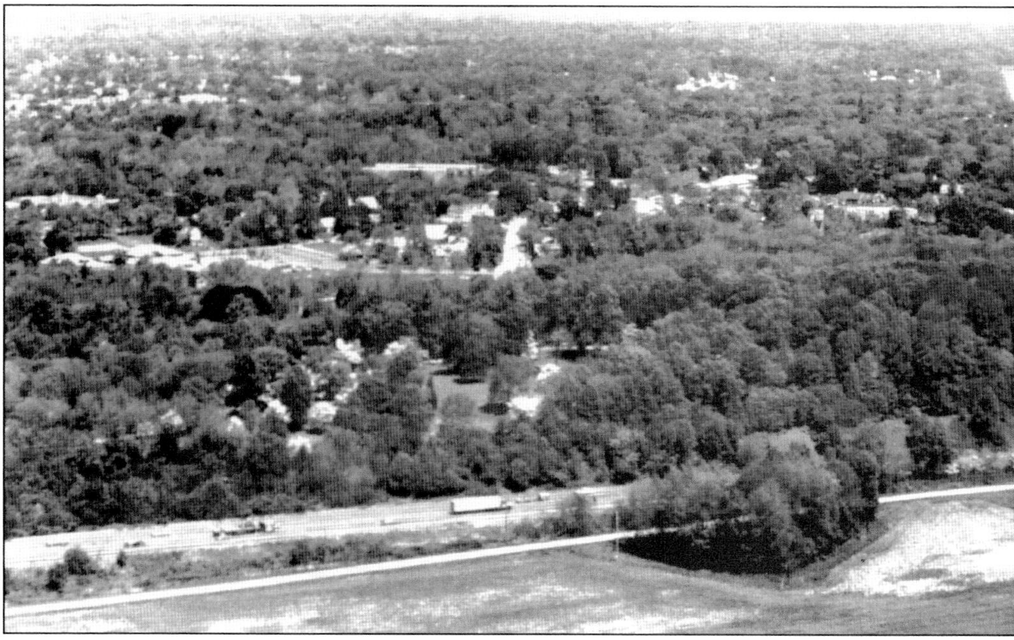

In 1956, the local communities became less isolated with the completion of the Pennsylvania Turnpike's Delaware River extension from King of Prussia to the New Jersey Turnpike and the completion of the Northeast Extension a year later. The opening of the Norristown exit of the turnpike, just above the Plymouth and Whitemarsh boundary line, launched a residential and commercial boom in both townships. (Courtesy of Fort Washington State Park.)

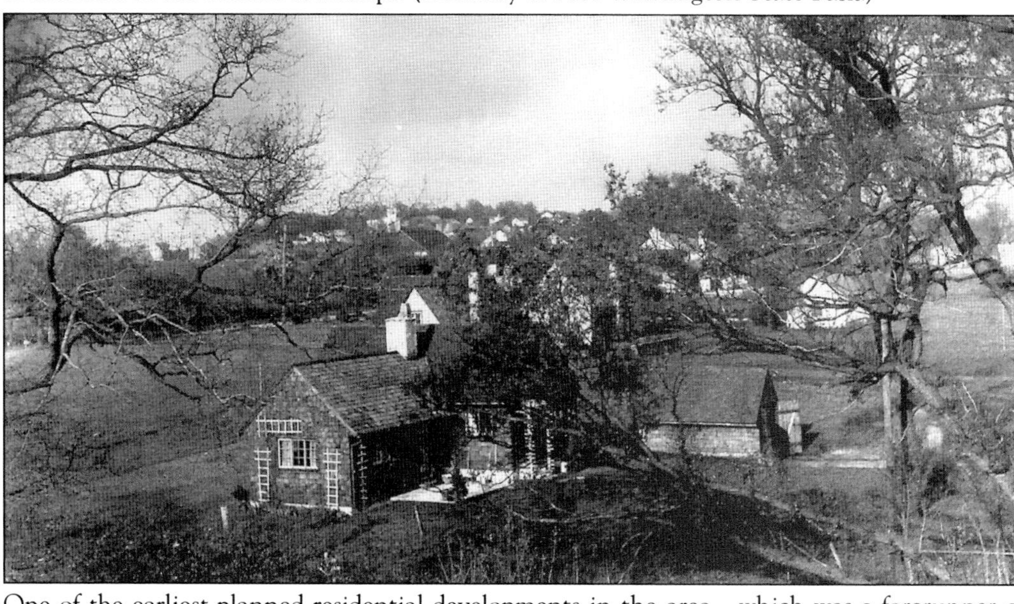

One of the earliest planned residential developments in the area—which was a forerunner of postwar suburban development—was the English Village, built on Plymouth Road near Cold Point. Nine houses, offset around a central driveway, were designed and built by architect Franklin R. Fow between 1919 and c. 1930. Fow's idea was to build attractive homes for newlyweds. Boundary fences were forbidden, as was hanging laundry on clotheslines. (Courtesy of Bill Lukens.)

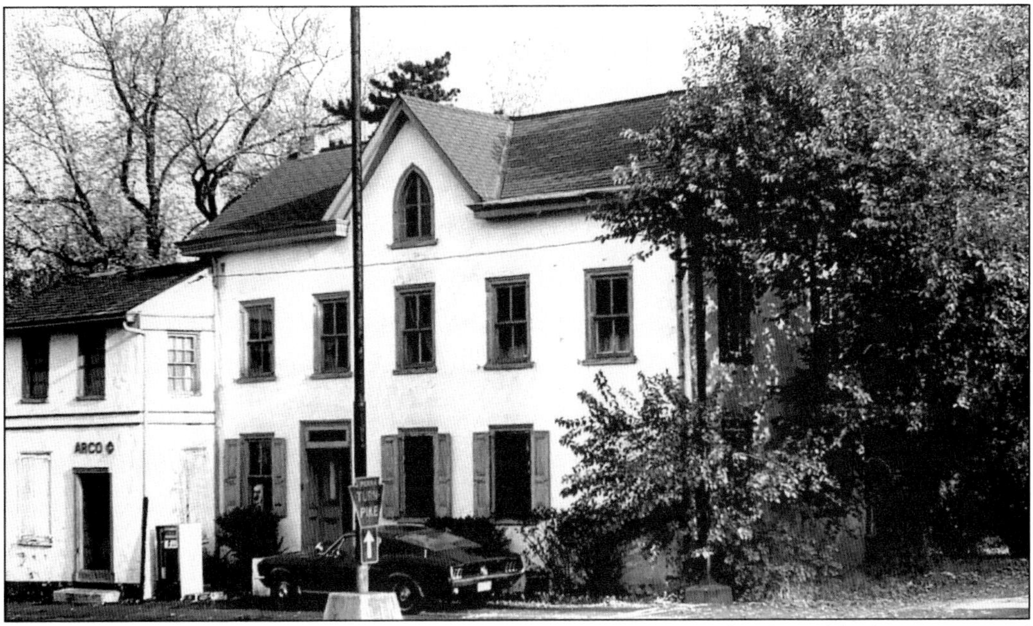

Easy access to the turnpike made properties on Germantown Pike desirable for commercial use. The Leedom House, at the northeast corner of Germantown and Butler Pikes, has been home to an unusual assortment of businesses over the years, including a gas station, offices, a golf driving range and pro shop, a restaurant named Le Bistro, and a snack bar.

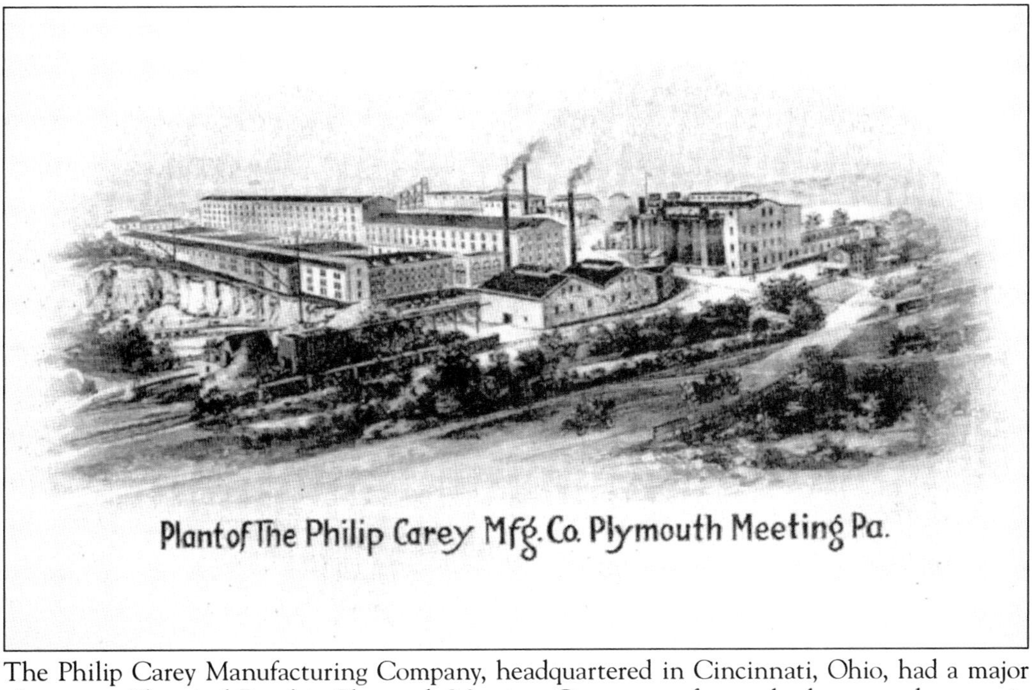

The Philip Carey Manufacturing Company, headquartered in Cincinnati, Ohio, had a major plant near Chemical Road in Plymouth Meeting. Carey manufactured asbestos and magnesia products, primarily pipe and boiler coverings.

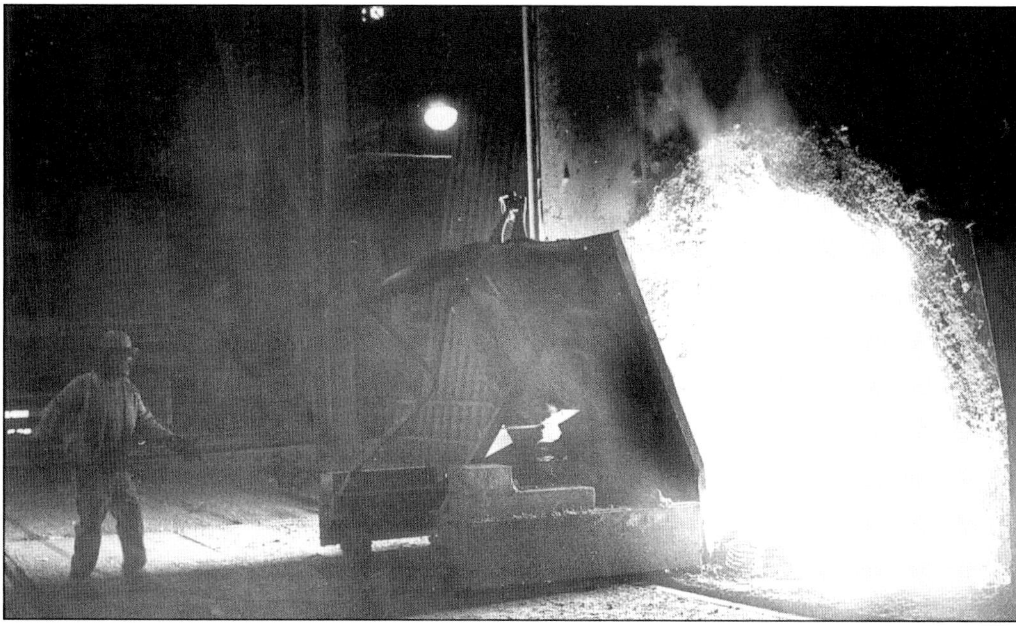

The Alan Wood Steel Company traces its history to the Hickorytown Forge, an iron-smelting company established in 1826 and owned by the Wood family. Alan Wood Steel opened in the early 1900s as a result of the consolidation of John Wood's iron mill in Conshohocken and his brother Alan Wood's iron plant in Plymouth. Rapid expansion was partly due to the plant's location near the railroad, and Alan Wood Steel soon became Plymouth Township's largest employer. For many reasons, including price competition from foreign producers, the company declared bankruptcy in 1977, shortly after these photographs were taken. (Courtesy of the Urban Archives, Temple University.)

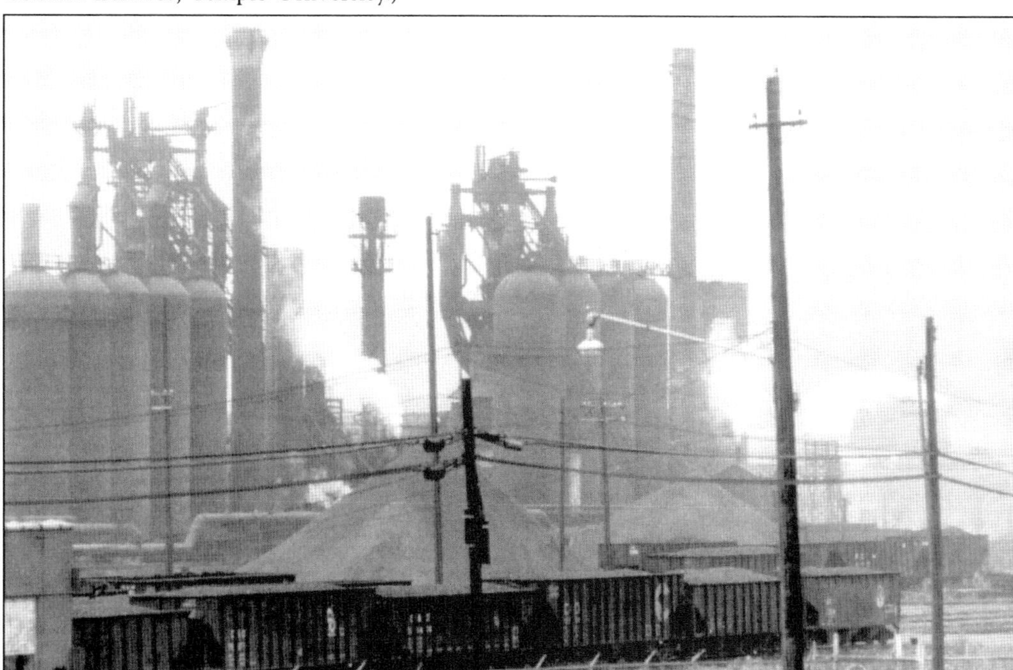

This aerial view of the Corson Lime Quarry, on Joshua Road and Stenton Avenue, shows the vast expansion of the company since the early days when limestone was loaded by hand into carts pulled by mules. The Corson Kiln, a superior device that greatly increased the amount of lime that could be processed, replaced the old hillside limekilns.

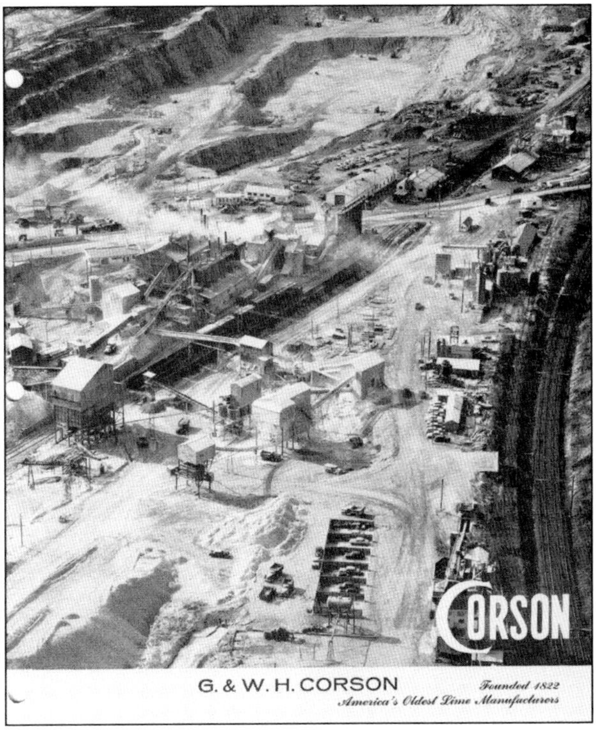

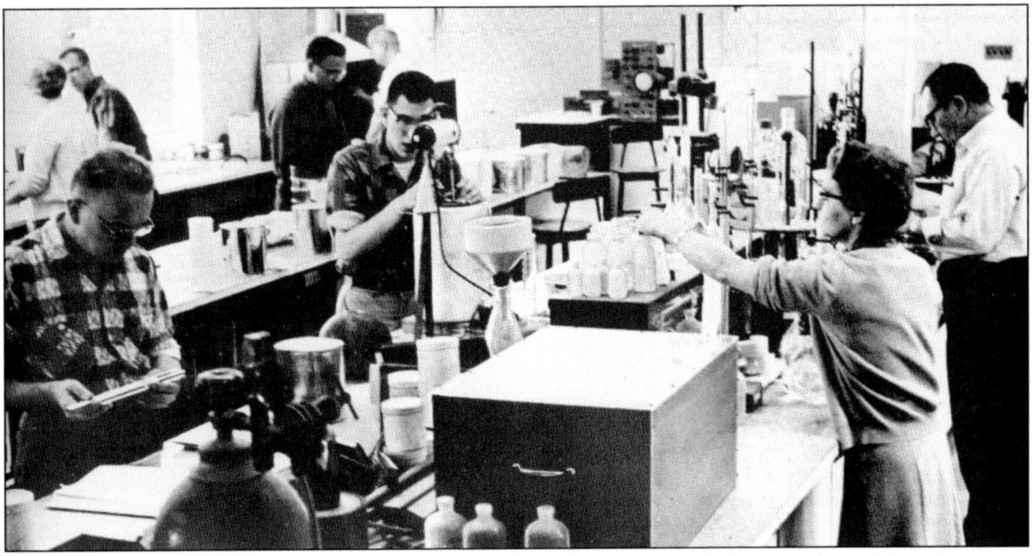

During the 1930s and 1940s, Corson invested heavily in successful research and development, which led to its trademark Miracle Lime, a hydrated, extra-strong and durable product. To improve their products, particularly the new Miracle Lime, Corson formed a research department in 1937. The department expanded rapidly, resulting in the development of many new items for the industry, as well as for the growing do-it-yourself market.

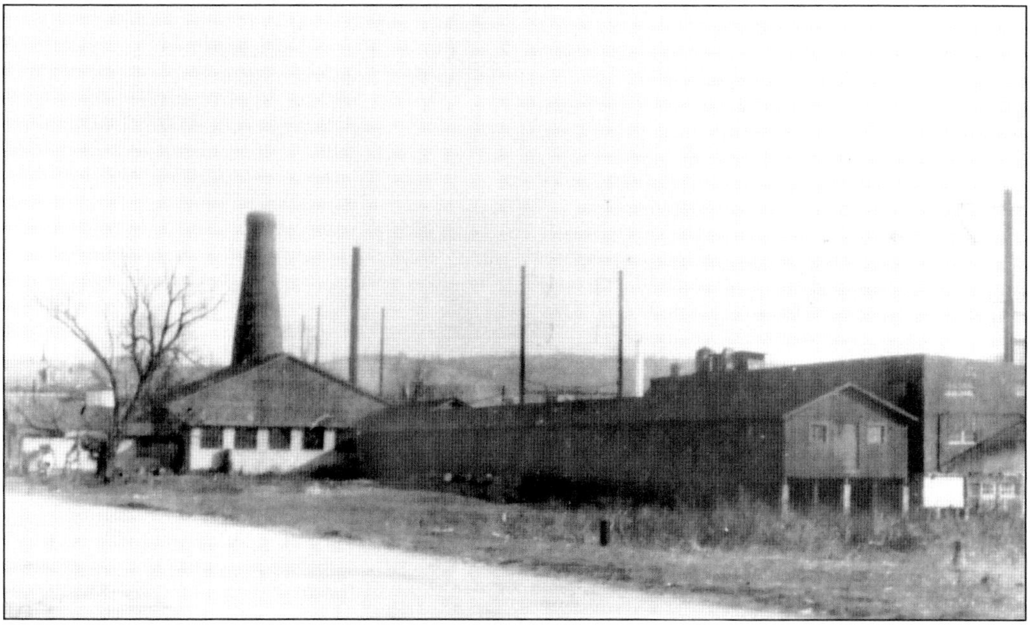

On November 11, 1978, the Quaker Oil Products Corporation began operations, manufacturing oil products for lubrication and the textile industry. Originally located in Conshohocken, the plant and offices were moved to Spring Mill in 1927. In 1931, the company reorganized and took on the broader name of Quaker Chemical Products Corporation. (Courtesy of the Quaker Chemical Products Corporation.)

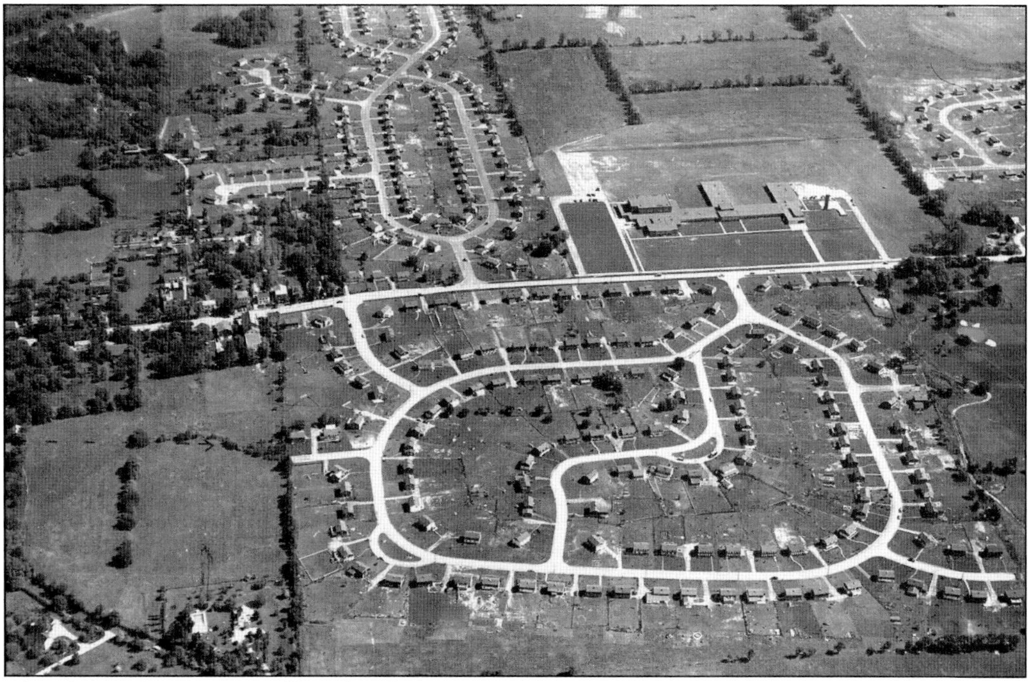

The Plymouth Meeting Village development, located just off Germantown Pike and across from the Plymouth Whitemarsh High School, was completed in 1951. With more than 100 homes, it was one of several new communities built for the post–World War II housing market.

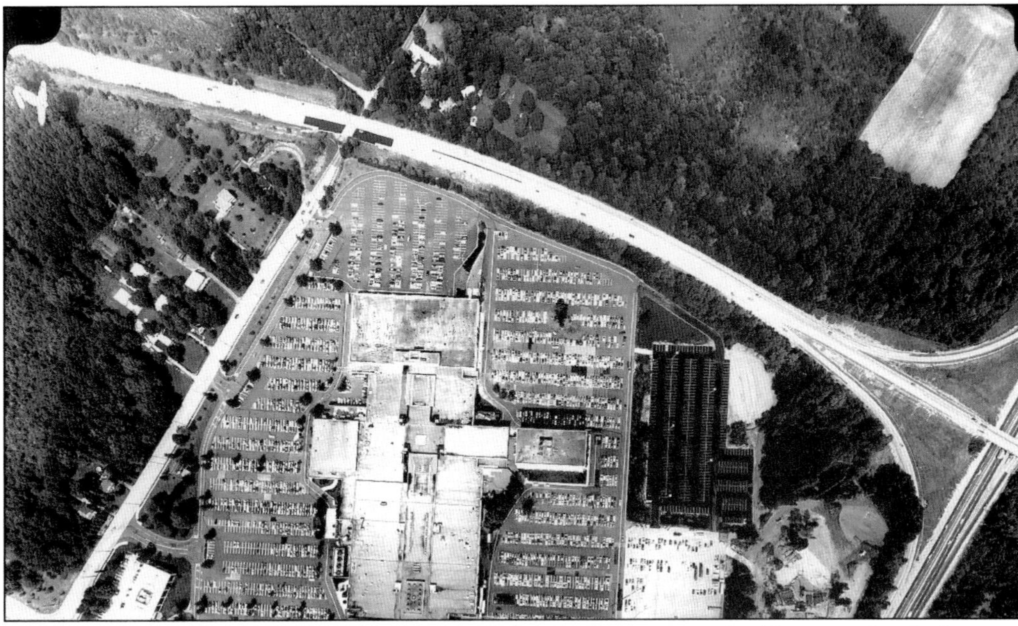

In the early 1960s, the Rouse Company submitted plans to build a two-level shopping mall, taking advantage of the area's housing boom and of the easy access to and from the Pennsylvania Turnpike. Designed by architect Victor Gruen, Plymouth Meeting Mall was built in 1965 and 1966 on 89 acres of farmland and a former Meehan Nursery. At the time, it was the largest enclosed mall east of the Mississippi River, and it became an attraction for both shoppers and tourists.

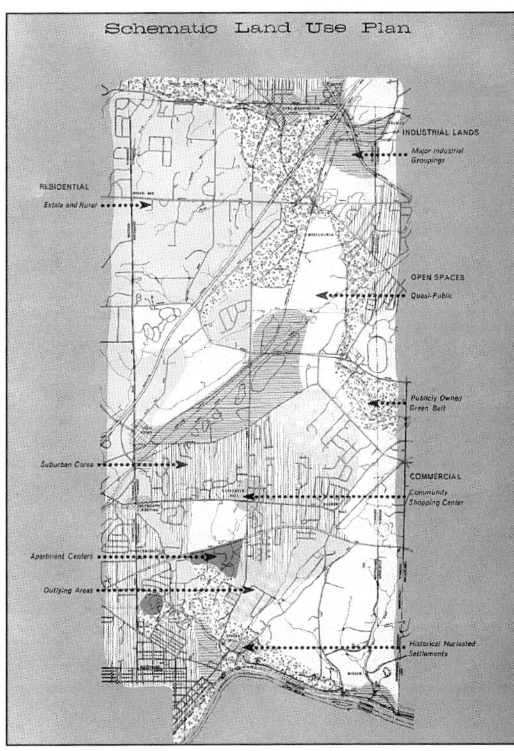

With the completion of the Blue Route (Interstate 476) in 1991, the Mid-County Interchange at Plymouth Meeting became the largest in Pennsylvania. This confluence of highways touched off another construction boom in the townships, which now threatens to overwhelm some of the most important areas of open space, worsen traffic congestion, and increase pollution. More than ever before, careful land-use planning is crucial to maintaining the quality of life in Plymouth and Whitemarsh Townships.

BIBLIOGRAPHY

The main sources consulted for this book are the materials archived at the Plymouth Meeting Historical Society, which is also the source of photographs not otherwise credited. The materials consulted are as follows:

Addison, Edward T., Jr. *The Village of Cold Point and Its Neighbors: A Land Title Study*. 1978.
Addison, Edward T., Jr. "A Brief History of the Spring Mill Complex." *The Bulletin of the Historical Society of Montgomery County*. 1992.
Bean, Theodore W., ed. *History of Montgomery County, Pennsylvania*. Philadelphia: Everts & Peck, 1884.
Corson, Hiram. *The Corson Family*. n.d.
Edward, Lee M. "Noble Domesticity: The Paintings of Thomas Hovenden." *The American Art Journal*. 1987.
Herring, Phyllis L. "The Highlands: A 20th Century Wuthering Heights or a Potential Showplace?" Philadelphia: *The Green Scene*. Pennsylvania Horticultural Society, 1976.
John Milner Architects. *Dickinson-Albertson House, Historic Structures Report*. 1993.
Roberts, Ellwood. *Plymouth Meeting: Its Establishment, and the Settlement of the Township*. Norristown, Pennsylvania: Roberts Publishing Company, 1900.
Terhune, Anne Gregory. "Thomas Hovenden: Images of Heritage and Hope." *Thomas Hovenden: American Painter of Hearth and Homeland*. Philadelphia: Woodmere Art Museum, 1995.
Toll, Jean Barth. *Montgomery County: The Second Hundred Years*. Edited by Michael J. Schwager. Montgomery County Federation of Historical Societies, 1983.
Yeakle, William R. "The Old Burial-Ground Near Erdenheim." *The Bulletin of the Historical Society of Montgomery County*. c. 1936.